MAKING MUSIC IN MUSIC CITY

MAKING MUSIC IN MUSIC CITY

Conversations with Nashville Music Industry Professionals

JOHN MARKERT

With a Historical Introduction by Don Cusic

CHARLES K. WOLFE MUSIC SERIES

Ted Olson, *Series Editor*

THE UNIVERSITY OF TENNESSEE PRESS

Knoxville

THE CHARLES K. WOLFE MUSIC SERIES was launched in honor of the late Charles K. Wolfe (1943–2006), whose pioneering work in the study of American vernacular music brought a deepened understanding of a wide range of American music to a worldwide audience. In recognition of Dr. Wolfe's approach to music scholarship, the series will include books that investigate genres of folk and popular music as broadly as possible.

First Edition.

LIBRARY OF CONGRESS CATALOGING-IN-PUBLICATION DATA
Names: Markert, John, 1945– author.
Title: Making music in Music City : conversations with Nashville music industry professionals / John Markert ; with a historical introduction by Don Cusic.
Description: First edition. | Knoxville : The University of Tennessee Press, 2021. | Series: Charles K. Wolfe music series | Includes bibliographical references and index. | Summary: "John Markert conducted more than one hundred interviews with music industry professionals (producers, publishers, songwriters, and management) who work in Nashville's music industry. The book naturally pivots around the country music industry but also discusses Nashville's role in other forms of modern music such as rock, rap, and Christian. Markert analyzes just what it takes to make music in Nashville, shedding light on how the industry continues to propel Music City, both regionally and nationally, while allowing its key players to speak for themselves"—Provided by publisher.
Identifiers: LCCN 2020055811 (print) | LCCN 2020055812 (ebook) | ISBN 9781621906445 (hardcover) | ISBN 9781621906452 (pdf)
Subjects: LCSH: Music trade—Tennessee—Nashville.
Classification: LCC ML3790 .M3504 2021 (print) | LCC ML 3790 (ebook) | DDC 781.64209768/55—dc23
LC record available at https://lccn.loc.gov/2020055811
LC ebook record available at https://lccn.loc.gov/2020055812

To the memories of

DOROTHY MAE "DOT" YEAGER MARKERT
(June 17, 1919–April 23, 1960)
Favorite Artist: Patsy Cline
Favorite Song: "The Tennessee Waltz"
(Song by Pattie Page; lyrics and music
by Redd Stewart and Pee Wee King)

ELIZABETH ANN "BETTS" BAYLESS JENKINS
(May 1, 1931–October 13, 1981)
Favorite Artist: The Beatles
Favorite Song: "I Can See Clearly Now"
(Song and lyrics by Johnny Nash)

Contents

Preface

It is somewhat surprising that the potpourri of occupations within the music industry has escaped analysis. Music has certainly been examined. One common approach, both popularly and scholarly, is to critique the content of music lyrics. Among the miscellany of lyrical analyses are those studies that examine how lyrics revolving around drugs and alcohol may encourage or discourage listeners to use-abuse drugs;[1] the misogynistic message in rap music has been intensely scrutinized and criticized for promoting sexist behavior.[2] Music in advertising,[3] video games,[4] television,[5] and film[6] are just four areas where music lyrics have been scrutinized. Meanwhile, the complexities of getting a song before the public have largely escaped analysis.

The music industry is comprised of a multitude of support personnel. One tends to forget this with all the attention that revolves around the artist on stage.[7] Behind the artist in the limelight, however, are a host of others who help shape the artist's music. This obviously includes executives at record labels, but it also includes such behind-the-scenes contributors as the songwriter, music publisher, the artist's manager, and studio musicians, as well as the stage personnel who help make the artist's performance "work." Of all these myriad occupations within the music industry, only two have received attention. One set of studies examines executives at the major labels; another draws attention to hit songs penned by songwriters.

The major labels have justifiably garnered a fair amount of attention. Warner Brothers, Columbia, and EMI, among others, have been dissected,[8] and record luminaries, such as Clive Davis, have penned autobiographies.[9] These types of analyses tend to revolve around the artists who were involved with the labels, such as Frank Sinatra, Barbra Streisand, and Bob Dylan.[10] The same holds for those independents, such as Sun Records and FAME Studio, whose label executives made a name for themselves by discovering new, cutting-edge artists.[11] These analyses, as instructive as they are from a who's-who standpoint, provide little information about how the whole system of production works. This study examines the pivotal role of the multitude of independent labels and the significant impact they have on making music. In doing so, often unrecognized distribution and promotional activities that are critical in getting a record before the public are assessed.

After label executives, the only other people in the music business who have received their fair share of attention are the songwriters. A substantial body of work in this area includes autobiographies by famous artist-songwriters, such as Merle Haggard, Johnny Cash, Waylon Jennings, and Charlie Daniels. These stories tell us more about the artist than the songwriter. Even autobiographies by noted songwriters, such as Bobby Braddock, swirl more around famous artists the songwriter knew or wrote for, like George Jones, than the process of songwriting.[12] There is also a fair number of works that critique the making of a hit song.[13] These analyses don't often acknowledge the long trek in a songwriter's career path that ultimately resulted in his or her hit song (or the fact that one can be a successful songwriter without a Number 1 hit); they also often don't acknowledge the increasingly important co-writing dimension of contemporary songwriting. This study focuses on the career path of seasoned songwriters: how they gravitated to their career and the process of staying on the cutting edge. It also assesses those young songwriters with hit song aspirations who, with a few exceptions, are still struggling to make a name for themselves, and how they go about establishing themselves in their new profession.

Music publishers and other support personnel involved in making music tend to escape critical attention. The contribution of the sound engineer, for instance, is largely limited to esoteric publications, such as *Sound on Sound* (*SOS*) and *Mix Magazine*. These professional publications delve into the minutia of recording, but the technical jargon[14] generally used does not give the uninitiated a firm understanding of the sound engineer's critical role in helping shape the sound that the listener hears. The role of the sound engineer, like so many other support personnel, is undergoing dramatic change at the outset of the new millennium. This book sheds light not only on the complexities of the industry and the occupational changes taking place, but also on the critical role played by those who are not in the limelight in shaping the music that ultimately reaches the public.

Chapter 1 begins this study of the music business after a brief introduction delineating the critical role Nashville has long played in creating music. Chapter 1 focuses on the songwriter, since, to quote the adage of the Nashville Songwriter Association International (NSAI), "It all begins with a song." Their point is well taken because an artist must have a song to sing. This sounds a bit simplistic, mainly because the public typically assumes the artists write their own songs. Historically, artists relied on professional songwriters to supply them with songs. This has changed only recently with the ascent of artists known as singer-songwriters, but even then, artists often reach beyond their limits by seeking good songs that fit their repertoire but were penned by others. Indeed, at the heart of what makes Music City the country music capital of the world is the fact that songwriters flock to Nashville because, to paraphrase one songwriter, "Nashville is where the action is."

One can write songs anywhere, but one is not considered a serious songwriter, and certainly not a serious country songwriter, unless one is writing in Nashville. This chapter articulates the changes that have taken place in penning lyrics. The different styles of songwriters are enunciated by dichotomizing younger (under 40) songwriters who have more recently relocated to Nashville from seasoned (40 and over) songwriters who have worked in the business for twenty-some years or more. The chapter challenges the creative myth of "inspired" geniuses by underscoring the work ethic that is necessary to climb to the head of the songwriting community: seldom do musical lyrics jump into one's head while sitting on the front porch strumming a guitar and drinking sweet tea. In an area where talent abounds, most songwriters are quick to appreciate that their hard work is often augmented by a healthy dose of luck. The chapter concludes by looking at the role Professional Rights Organizations (PROs) play in helping their songwriting members, as well as how they monitor songs played so that songwriters and publishers are fairly compensated for their works.

Songwriters generally need someone to help them get their songs to an artist or producer. Chapter 2 examines the strategic role of the music publisher. Other cities may rival Nashville for its musical venues, but none surpasses Nashville for music publishing: Nashville generated $1.1 billion in revenue from music publishing in 2017 with New York coming in just slightly behind at $1 billion while Los Angeles came in a distant third with only 725.8 million.[15] Music publishing is a major factor in making Nashville Music City. The music publisher, compared to other publishers, like those in the book industry, are more than gatekeepers who simply screen lyrics and pass those they feel "work" onto an artist or label head. Nashville publishers actively work with songwriters to help them hone their songs. All the seasoned songwriters in this study had publishing contracts and most of the younger ones who didn't have a publishing contract would give their eyeteeth for one. A publishing contract is valuable to songwriters because it can provide them with a draw: a basic stipend that provides them with an income so they can devote their time to their craft and not scurry around looking for a way to pay their bills. A draw is recouped by a publisher when one of their songwriter's songs charts; if a song is never recorded, the publisher is out whatever draw they were contractually obligated to pay.

Music publishers tend to have a very sharp ear: they can be out tens of thousands of dollars if they "misread" a songwriter's potential. Their ear is sharpened by twenty-some years in the business: one just doesn't open a publishing house without industry contacts, and industry contacts are honed over time. Chapter 2 delineates and explores the crucial roles of the music publisher in advocating for their songwriters and their in-house plugger in pitching or plugging the songs to an artist or producer. One doesn't just go in and play a song to a prospective artist or label executive: there is a real strategy involved in finding talented songwriters and in pitching songs. A key component of this study is to enumerate the critical role of the publisher and his or her plugger, positions which are often unrecognized by those outside the music profession.

Chapter 3 naturally follows the next step along the career path: how to get the song produced. There are only three major labels (though all have myriad subsidiaries) but there are another 60-plus record producers listed in *Music Row Magazine*, a local trade publication. Increasingly today, labels are expanding into artist management and record production to compensate for the decline in record sales. This chapter examines the contemporary state of record production; specifically, ways small independents attempt to get their artists placed on streaming sites, such as Spotify, and how their small labels serve as viable outlets for the multiplicity of artists the major labels either never touch or pass over until the artist garners some internet attention.

It also touches on how studio work has dramatically changed in the digital age. Most industry professionals consider studio work critical in developing a quality recording, and the studio still reigns supreme in cutting the final version of an album. The digital age has allowed those closed out from this expensive process to release their music by utilizing their computers to build tracks. Some even argue that work done by solo musicians at their computer rivals the sound produced in a studio. This may be debatable, but the digital age does allow small labels to cost-effectively release records that might otherwise be passed over by the majors. The chapter concludes by examining the pivotal role radio plays in getting music to the public and how people in promotion still, in the best old-school tradition, travel around the country knocking on radio station doors in an effort to get their artists' songs played.

Chapter 4 looks at the role played by others in the industry who support the artists once a record has been released. One of these is the artist manager, who handles the artists and helps shape their career path. Managers in all industries require a certain amount of people skills, but artist managers—and others who work with creative people in allied fields—may be unique because their roles pivot on their ability to "handle" their sometimes volatile and often sensitive clients.

Another player who helps the artist garner a following is the talent agent, also interchangeably referred to as a booking agent because their role is to book shows for the talent to perform. Like many things in the business, this looks relatively simple to outsiders: pick up the phone, call someone and book a performance date—if February 3rd is not available, all one has to do is slot an appearance on February 6th. Booking, however, is an art unto itself, and the function of this portion of the chapter is to examine the complexities of booking an artist and how the right booking dates in the right venue may be critical in helping build an artist's momentum or maintaining their presence. Once the show is booked, the artist performs, but he or she doesn't just walk onto a platform and sing—at least not today. There are a lot of bells and whistles that go into making the stage set work. Fans who attend a concert don't fully appreciate all the hard work that goes into enhancing the artist's performance on stage. Chapter 4 concludes by examining the complexities of staging a show, another vastly overlooked dynamic essential to creating an enjoyable musical experience.

A concluding chapter offers final analysis. The focus of this chapter is to put all the dynamics into play by showing how all the disparate fields come together to create music.

Making music is as fulfilling as ever to those involved in their respective fields, and it remains so even if making music continues to grow more multifaceted. The world is increasingly complex; it is not surprising that making music is too. This book is intended to enunciate just how interconnected and complicated the music business is.

Methodology

This book takes as its starting point *Gig: Americans Talk About Their Jobs* (2001),[16] which is broken into industry sectors where individuals employed in the designated sector talk about their jobs: a waitress, pretzel vendor, and food stylist are among those who detail what they do in the food industry, while a high school basketball coach, sports agent, and bookie are among those who discuss their jobs in the sports industry. *Gig* follows the format of Studs Terkel's landmark 1972 book, *Working*. Both are written in the first person. This critique is written largely—though not exclusively—in third person, allowing the comments of the various interviewees to be interwoven with one another, creating a composite picture of their contribution in their area of expertise. The approach also allows the incorporation of extant studies into the interviews to shed light on the occupation of those in the field.

Like most studies that examine dynamics within the industry, this study is based on in-depth interviews with key music professionals. Many of those interviewed work in Nashville, referred to alternately as "Music City," "Music City USA," or "The Country Music Capital of the U.S.A," a term serendipitously tossed off in 1950 by disc jockey David Cobb of station WSM.[17] The term Music City stuck, however, in no small part because, writes John Lomax III, "members of the then-fledgling industry tirelessly worked to lodge the slogan in the public consciousness."[18]

The term Music City has been widely applied to Nashville's country music tradition. This skews interviews largely, but not exclusively, to the country genre—rap, rock, and Christian also garner their fair share of attention. Regardless of the musical genre the person interviewed worked in, their input can often be generalized to those in other musical fields, and the similarities and differences between allied musical genres are often enumerated by those interviewed.

Each chapter focuses on three to five central figures who are considered key informants in their respective fields and whose insights reflect some of the two dozen or so individuals interviewed in many of the areas studied. These key informants quickly become apparent because they are often cited at length. The bulk of the interviews took place in 2016 and 2017 and all touched on 1) the role the subjects play in the musical pantheon, 2) changes that have taken place during their sometimes lengthy careers and 3) what they see in the offing within their respective areas. Call-back, clarifying interviews took place during 2018 and 2019. Follow-up interviews typically addressed 1) areas that were hazy or unclear in the earlier interview or 2) questions necessary to clear up confusing or conflicting information.

In addition to offering insights into their respective fields of specialization, a large portion of the interviewees also shared insight into fields in which they formerly worked or had considerable knowledge. For example, most seasoned songwriters can shed light not just on the music publisher they are presently associated with but also on other music publishers at different points in time: Mark Irwin was associated with Ten Ten Music Group shortly after his arrival in Nashville, then EMI, then BMG, then Red Vinyl, before he struck up a relationship with his current publisher, Olé. In a similar vein, both Bobby Rymer and John Ozier, who are in music publishing, cut their teeth as A&R personnel at labels, while Barry Coburn spent fourteen years as a concert promoter before starting Ten Ten Music and Tony Harrell spent nearly a quarter century as a studio (keyboard) musician before gravitating to publishing.[19]

In most cases these individuals are identified in the body of the text (see also Appendix A). In some cases their remarks are not attributed in the body of the text, their remarks simply being referred to as "one young songwriter said" or "a studio musician remarked." This avoids the need to constantly clarify the origin of each passing comment. It also allows this analysis to include off-the-record comments. There were times when one or more of the interviewees (core or otherwise) did not want to be identified for a critical comment made. Since critical comments are essential to any detailed analysis of dynamics taking place within the field, circumventing specifics is a means to include an interviewee's comments without putting them on the spot. All interviews were taped to ensure accuracy and all interviewees were informed that off-the-record comments would be included in the analysis but unattributed. The majority of interviews were conducted in the person's office, while a few were either conducted at the person's home or at a small coffee shop just off Music Row. Follow-up clarifying interviews, sometimes lengthy, were often conducted by telephone. A snowball sample was used to select individuals working in the music industry.[20] In all, slightly over 100 (N=110) interviews were personally conducted; this size can be tripled if one allows the interviewees to make comments about additional fields in which they had previous experience or intimate contact with others.[21] The sample size is comparable to other studies that appraise the contribution of individuals in the cultural arena.[22]

Interviews were a mixture of closed and open-ended questions, which is also traditional in studies that revolve around career decision-making. The closed portion ensured critical demographic data was included: first interest in music, education, age when career path started, first job in the industry, and so forth. The open-ended format allowed the interviewee to expound about their jobs with the interviewer at times probing into aspects that were brought up but not enumerated upon; e.g., "You said you did such and such. Why did you decide on that course of action rather than . . . ?" Personal interviews were augmented by scholarly studies of the music business, as well as public domain interviews with those in their respective fields.

Acknowledgments

There are many people to thank for their participation in this study. There are all those in the music industry who warmly gave input about what they or their company were doing. The time they allocated me from their extraordinarily busy schedules is greatly appreciated. I also want to recognize the contribution made by Lois Cunningham whose friendship went way beyond the meager compensation provided for helping me with the burdensome transcriptions. I also want to thank Thomas Wells at the University of Tennessee Press who saw some promise in this modest endeavor and who encouraged me to work through the critiques made by reviewers.

Coronavirus Postscript

The bulk of the interviews were conducted between 2016 and 2017, with much of the writing taking place during 2018 and 2019. The world of music changed radically in 2020. Many of those in the music business, like many in other artistic enterprises, have been dramatically affected both personally and financially by the coronavirus. It is my hope that in the not-too-distant future we might all be able to return to the scenarios depicted in this book where musicians get to perform before a crowd that appreciates live music.

MAKING MUSIC IN
MUSIC CITY

Historical Introduction

It's not really a Nashville *sound* but rather Nashville *sounds* that make it known all over the world as Music City U.S.A. Nashville is the "Capital of Country Music" but it is much more than that. In Nashville there are musicians, songwriters, producers, executives and others involved in pop, rock, jazz, rap, classical, gospel and contemporary Christian music.

The city's focus on music didn't happen overnight. Nashville has a long history as a city identified by music, a musical history that dates back over 150 years.

Nashville and music have been publicly linked since the Fisk Jubilee Singers began touring during the 1870s. During the 1920s a number of radio stations began broadcasting in Nashville; the most powerful of these were WSM and WLAC. Nashville was a dance band town from the 1920s through the 1940s, and there were a number of excellent local big bands led by both white and black band leaders.

In November 1925, the Grand Ole Opry began on Saturday nights on WSM, although it was not called the *Grand Ole Opry* until 1927. This was the first public link between Nashville and country music. However, at the end of World War II in 1945, there was still not a single recording studio or record label in Nashville. (The first recording for a major label came in 1944 when Eddy Arnold recorded four songs in WSM's studios).

In 1946, Nashville had its first recording studio when three WSM engineers formed Castle Recording Studio in the Tulane Hotel. That same year Nashville's first record label, Bullet, began issuing its first releases. They released a wide variety of music, from rhythm and blues, white gospel, black gospel, and country to pop records. The first million seller from Nashville was a pop song, "Near You," by the Francis Craig Orchestra on Bullet Records. That record was number one on the pop chart in *Billboard* for 17 weeks.

In 1944, *Billboard* published its first folk music chart based on jukebox play; Ernest Tubb was the only Nashville-based artist to appear on that chart. Tubb continued to be a major country artist, and his sales success and the success of

Castle Studio recording Bullet's records and other small label acts led Tubb to request that he record in Nashville.

Since Tubb was a major seller for Decca, the label agreed to record him and Red Foley at the Castle Studio in August 1947. That was a tipping point for Nashville becoming a major recording center. Another tipping point came in 1946 when Red Foley left WLS's *National Barn Dance* in Chicago—the major competitor to the *Grand Ole Opry*—and joined the Opry. That led the sponsor of *National Barn Dance*, Alka Seltzer, to drop its sponsorship and thus the Barn Dance's regular Saturday night network spot on NBC. The Opry had been on the NBC network since 1939.

In October 1942, Fred Rose and Roy Acuff formed Acuff-Rose Publishing, the first major publishing company for country songs in Nashville. In 1946, they signed Hank Williams. Also in 1946, Hill and Range Publishers opened an office in Nashville, followed by Cedarwood and Tree Publishers.

After the August 1947 recording session at the Castle Studio, Decca continued to record its country acts in Nashville, which led to other labels recording at Castle. Nashville had a strong pool of musicians, many from the WSM orchestra, as well as bands connected to singers. (Red Foley's band was the first "A Team" of Nashville musicians.) The musicians' union was strong and, after Pee Wee King's group was allowed to join the union in 1937, the Nashville musicians' union allowed country and other non-reading musicians to join.

RCA Victor had been the lone holdout in holding recording sessions in Nashville because it had a union agreement to only use its engineers for recording. However, in 1950 Steve Sholes, head of RCA Victor's country division, began recording in Nashville, bringing one of their union engineers in for the sessions. In late 1954, RCA Victor opened the TRAFCO Recording Studio in the same building that housed the Methodist Television, Radio and Film Commission.

Owen Bradley, a big band leader at WSM, became the point man for Paul Cohen, head of Decca's country division, organizing sessions and taking the role of session leader. Bradley built several studios in Nashville before he and his brother, Harold, opened Bradley's Film and Recording Studios on 16th Avenue South, the first music-related business on what became known as Music Row. The Bradleys built a Quonset hut behind the house they had bought, and that became the studio where recording sessions were held.

Nashville studios also benefitted when their major competitor for country music recordings, Jim Beck's studio in Dallas, closed after Beck died in 1956.

In 1950, two songs published by Acuff-Rose reached number one on the pop chart. Red Foley's "Chattanoogie Shoe Shine Boy" became a number one record on both the pop and country charts in *Billboard*, and Patti Page's recording of "Tennessee Waltz" became a number one pop hit for 13 weeks. Those songs opened the doors for New York record producers to look to Nashville for songs, and a number of pop acts, including Frankie Laine, Rosemary Clooney and Jo Stafford, had pop hits with Nashville songs, leading the city to become known as a "songwriter's town" or "Tin Pan South."

The 1950s were a time of strong growth in Nashville as a recording center with country and pop hits recorded there. Led by producers Owen Bradley (Decca), Chet Atkins (RCA Victor), Don Law (Columbia) and Ken Nelson (Capitol), along with Anita Kerr, an uncredited producer as well as an arranger and vocal group leader, Nashville became a busy recording center for major labels.

In January 1956, Elvis Presley recorded "Heartbreak Hotel" at the TRAFCO Studio in Nashville, his first hit for RCA Victor, which reached the country, R&B and Hot 100 charts. That ushered in the rock 'n' roll era, and rock 'n' roll hits recorded in Nashville include "Gone" by Ferlin Huskey, "Young Love" by Sonny James, "A White Sport Coat (And a Pink Carnation)" by Marty Robbins, "Be-Bop-a-Lula" by Gene Vincent, "Rocking Around the Christmas Tree" by Brenda Lee and "Jingle Bell Rock" by Bobby Helm.

That led to a "crisis" in country music because records by those artists as well as those by early rockabilly pioneers like Jerry Lee Lewis, Carl Perkins, and the Everly Brothers were listed on the country charts as well as on the Hot 100 chart, crowding out singers with a more traditional country sound. That led to a decrease in bookings for country artists whose sales could not compete with the rock 'n' rollers.

Nashville producers, led by Owen Bradley and Chet Atkins, developed the "Nashville Sound" to counter the effects of rock 'n' roll. The "Nashville Sound" encompassed several things: (1) the sound of fiddles and the steel guitar was replaced by the piano and violins on recordings; (2) a core group of session musicians—five or six on a recording session using "head" arrangements instead of sheet music—who recorded three or four songs during a three-hour session; (3) a change in the "look" of country singers, from rhinestone outfits to sports coats, suits or tuxedoes; (4) the fact that making records this way and on this scale was profitable; and (5) a handy marketing term that linked Nashville and country music as a smooth-sounding alternative to the sounds of rock 'n' roll. The new sound appealed to middle-class Americans, and Jim Reeves and Eddy Arnold were leaders in introducing this new sound to American record buyers.

Those factors led to the formation of the Country Music Association (CMA) in 1958, which viewed rock 'n' roll as a threat to country music.

Nashville executives lobbied *Billboard* and other trade magazines to take the early rockabillies off the country charts. The CMA was an outgrowth of the Country and Western Disc Jockey Convention, which served as a gathering for country radio programmers and show promoters. Country music is the only musical genre with its own trade organization, and the organization serves as a "chamber of commerce" for country music.

The CMA focused its early efforts on convincing advertising agencies to purchase time on country radio stations. This led to more radio stations programming country music during a time when stations became "formatted," programming only one type of music. The CMA's efforts were helped by an FCC ruling that station owners, who simulcast their stations on both AM and FM, had to program their AM and FM stations separately. The new FM stations first thrived with "underground" radio, programming alternative rock recordings. As FM programmers increasingly moved over to pop/rock programming because of the better sound and the growth of hi-fi receivers and record players, a void was left on AM, and country music moved into those slots. As country music proved to be popular, it too moved over to the FM dial and the AM stations declined.

By the end of the 1960s, Nashville was a magnet for those wanting to be involved in the national recording industry, which became centered in New York, Los Angeles, and Nashville. There was a strong business infrastructure in Nashville: numerous studios were built; a pool of talented, accomplished musicians who were fast and good and who received union wages for their work; a strong pool of songwriters; performing rights organizations BMI, ASCAP and SESAC that collected money for publishers and songwriters from radio and TV airplay; booking agencies; managers, attorneys and others who worked in the recording industry. By the mid-1960s, every major record label had an office in Nashville, and most major publishing companies did as well.

Nashville became attractive to rock performers as well after Bob Dylan recorded all or part of five albums in Nashville. This led other pop/rock acts, such as Joan Baez, Neil Young, the Byrds and others to record in Nashville.

Country music found it difficult to break into TV, but in 1969 there were important shows on network TV. *Hee Haw, The Johnny Cash Show* and the *Glen Campbell Goodtime Hour* all featured country music. That same year, the CMA Awards Show was broadcast live for the first time. It had first been held in 1967, broadcast only on radio; then in 1968, as a delayed broadcast, airing after the awards were presented. The CMA Awards Show is now one of the most-watched awards shows on television, drawing consistently high ratings.

Nashville as a tourist destination for country music fans came with the opening of the Country Music Hall of Fame in 1967. It was aided further with the creation of Fan Fair, an alternative to the annual disc jockey convention, which had become problematic because so many fans came to what was intended to be a business gathering and showcase of talent for country radio programmers and country show promoters who booked country acts.

The first Fan Fair was held in 1972 and it grew each year, the only annual gathering for fans of a genre of music. The year before, the Country Radio Seminar began, which became an annual gathering for radio DJs and programmers which laid the foundation for country radio to become more "professional."

During the mid-1970s the "outlaw movement" began, led by Waylon Jennings and Willie Nelson, which attracted fans from the rock world with its more rock-oriented sound. Their album, *The Outlaws,* became the first million-selling album by a country act.

In 1983, The Nashville Network (TNN) and Country Music Television (CMT) went on the air and provided daily TV shows that ranged from videos to game shows to an evening talk show hosted by Ralph Emery. This brought country music into American homes each evening and further popularized country performers and songs.

During the early 1990s, SoundScan technology led to a more accurate reporting of country music sales. That's a technology linked to bar codes; when you scan a SoundScan bar code the computer records what album was bought. Prior to SoundScan, people underestimated the sales of country records, but with accurate reporting of sales, retailers could quickly see what was selling, and they increased their stock in those albums. Garth Brooks was a major beneficiary of SoundScan; he could not have been as big without SoundScan showing retailers how fast his albums were selling.

The year 2000 was the top year for sales of recordings; it was also the year that Napster was introduced and the recording industry was plagued by fans getting music free from illegal downloads. This led to a number of layoffs in the music industry. The decline continued until 2015, when the recording industry began receiving income from "streaming." A victim of this change was record stores, which went out of business. Today, there are only "specialty" stores that sell physical records and CDs and the musicians and fans have lost a great hangout for music where they could meet other music lovers and find out about new releases.

Streaming changed the business structure of recorded music income. People listened to hit singles instead of albums, and country acts had to engage in social media. Songwriters could no longer make a good living from album cuts; labels lost revenue because, instead of receiving about nine dollars for the sale of an album, they only received 67 cents for a download from iTunes; artists lost money from royalties.

Prior to streaming there were three major revenue streams in the music industry that can be summarized as "the three P's": Personals, Performances and Purchases. Personals came from artists performing shows live. Performances were monies collected by the performance rights organizations for songwriters and publishers from terrestrial radio and TV airplay. Purchases were consumers purchasing recordings; that money went to record companies, artists, songwriters and publishers. Performers still receive money from personals, there is declining income from terrestrial radio and TV airplay, and albums are now often merchandise sold at live shows. The old model still works—but not like it used to.

Marketing involved an artist releasing an album every 12 to 18 months that contained three to four singles for radio airplay. Between the record and the consumer was a "media layer" which consisted of print, radio and TV. Artists engaged with the media layer for exposure, and record labels sought those outlets to entice retailers to stock the albums. In between were radio promotion men and women who regularly called the radio stations that reported to the trade magazines for chart positions. Salesmen regularly called retailers to stock the latest recording.

It was a well-oiled machine in which publishers decided which songwriters to sign, record labels decided which artists to sign and promote, radio stations decided which records listeners could hear, and retailers decided which records to make available for consumer purchases. Store space was limited; older albums and songs were often not available.

That ended with social media and streaming. The country artist who led the way for social media engagement was Taylor Swift who, as a young artist, was actively engaged with social media. Social media also put the burden on artists to develop fans one-on-one. Streaming meant that anyone could listen to anything anytime they wanted. Technology meant that anyone could record a digital single or album cheaply on software in their own bedroom and upload it to social media and the streaming services where anyone could find it.

The recording industry has changed a great deal since 2000 while, at the same time, remaining timeless. It is still a matter of getting a song before the public so people will hear it, like it, buy it and then "buy" the artist by attending concerts and shows. Those who place their bets on being in the music industry know that it is a high-risk, high-payoff industry, but young dreamers ignore the risks. They are rewarded with being in a creative community unlike any other in the

United States. Back in small hometowns, not many play music or write songs professionally and there is a lack of support—musical as well as emotional—for those who chase musical dreams. In Nashville, there's a whole community who speaks the same language and chases the same dreams, inspired by those who make it and inspiring others to give it a shot.

Nashville has grown but it is still a city of dreamers who follow their hearts chasing musical dreams. It is a place that is a magnet for musicians, songwriters and others who want to be involved in the music industry. It ain't easy but the business of music has a structure that allows for opportunities to succeed. The "creative" side of the music industry is often at odds with the "business" side, which can seem cold, but the art cannot succeed on its own; it requires marketing, promotion and doing the things that business does to make it commercially successful. Nashville is a town where success in music sits at the corner of art and business. It is a town of entrepreneurs and individualists but also a town of teams. No one who succeeds does it alone; it takes a village to make a star.

Still, it is a business that begins with a song and an individual with a dream married to desire and grit. The changes brought by technology now allow independent country music artists and songwriters to decide on their own what to record and what to release. The country recording industry has lost its control on which artists to sign, promote and make available. Social media can distribute a song to the world, but distribution isn't marketing, and it takes savvy marketing for a song or artist to find a home. It is troubled times for major record labels and publishing companies, but they still have the power that only big business can provide.

On the other hand, it has meant that long-forgotten recordings are now available to hear and artists who dream of country music stardom have a way, outside the established norms, to make their dreams come true.

Making it in the music business is hard but it is a fun business. It is a business of bringing fun and joy to the world. That's why it's called "playing" music! There's an old saying that came from the studios: "You're only three minutes away from the Riviera." That meant that three minutes of song magic can send an artist and songwriter around the world. That magic has happened in the past and is still happening today.

Don Cusic
Belmont University

1 SONGBIRDS

It is appropriate to begin this study of the music industry by first looking at those who create the songs since "it all begins with a song," the motto of the Nashville Songwriting Association International (NSAI). When NSAI was formed in 1967, the group was fighting to simply get the songwriter's name on the record. It took four years to achieve this modest goal. Songwriter acknowledgement on labels remains problematic, however, for at least three reasons: 1) the artist and song are announced to the radio audience, but not the songwriter; 2) those who purchase the record may never read the line notes that give the name of the songwriter; and 3) complicating matters in today's digital era is that most streaming services do not give songwriting credit.[1] These factors all contribute to the public's failure to appreciate the critical role songwriters play in making music. Even more surprising is the lack of awareness among some of those in the industry regarding the songwriter's role. Steven Tyler, for example, the Demon of Screamin' front man for Aerosmith, was flummoxed to learn after moving to Nashville in 2014 that professionals wrote songs and then handed them off for others to sing. After a visit to the Bluebird, one of a host of Nashville music venues that feature songwriters, Tyler realized, as have many other professional musicians who have come to Nashville, the quality of the songs being performed by "a bunch of kids sitting around a table."[2]

Songwriting is at the heart of what makes Nashville Music City. Austin justifiably rivals Nashville with country bands; indeed, Austin may actually surpass Nashville in the number of country music venues around town.[3] But if one wants to be a songwriter, and certainly a country songwriter, Nashville is where one has to be. In his book on how to advance as a songwriter,

Grammy-winning songwriter Kelley Lovelace quite succinctly summarizes this imperative in his chapter head, "Must Be Present to Win."[4] Benji Harris, for example, one of the three young country artist-songwriters in this study who has roots in Texas, typifies the reason these individuals decided to come to Nashville:

> Dallas is a huge metropolis and there were tons of gigs to play. I was doing well, making solid money, but it was all cover stuff:[5] playing in restaurants and clubs. You could make really big money doing the party scene in Dallas, as well as the corporate scene. But I wanted to go another route. There is a ceiling in Dallas. And I wanted to try doing it on a national level and being really involved in the writing. In Dallas, you only get to play other people's stuff.

The reason to be in Nashville in order to move forward in one's career is because the social environment in Nashville is so conducive to songwriters. It was the driving reason why all songwriters interviewed in this study, none of whom are native to the area, decided to move to Nashville.

Situating Creativity

There are two interrelated historical notions on creativity: the inspirational view and the romantic view.[6] The former holds that artists are freethinking individuals who are inspired because they are mad geniuses, or, at the very least, a little "strange."[7] This view harkens to hereditary factors shaping one's artistic predilection. The romantic notion postulates that artists suffer some romantic agony to bring forth their creative compositions. Both views have been widely challenged in contemporary academic literature, but continue to find favor among the public. The lingering popular notion of these theories suggest, insofar as music is concerned, that songwriters sit around idly ruminating about their troubled lives while strumming their guitars or tinkering with keys on the piano until they suddenly have a moment of divine inspiration and dash off "the song" that instantly makes them millionaires. This widespread belief may influence the public's attitude toward reimbursing songwriters since it suggests they don't work all that hard at creating their products. This chapter challenges the popular perception and seeks to detail the hard work that goes into the creation of a song; it seeks further to outline some of the social exigencies that affect the creative process.

The social environment as a stimulus to creativity has gained ascendency in recent years. Social factors have always been a part of milieu studies. The cultural milieu acknowledges that the environment in which artists intermingle is a kind of middle ground that helps shape their artistic sensibilities, though it does not intimate that it directly affects the ultimate artistic outcome. For instance, the Lost Generation of the 1920s—Hemingway, Fitzgerald, Pound, Eliot—"hung out" with one another on the Left Bank of the Seine (*La rive gauche*). Likewise, the Beat poets of the 1950s who mingled with their compatriots in New York's Greenwich Village and in San Francisco's famed Haight-Ashbury District were replaced in these same environs a generation later by the folk musician community. By being around others who share one's artistic temperament, they influence one another, but more by osmosis than by direct collusion; that is, they are exposed to the works of their contemporaries and this helps them "assess" their own work in relation to others in their artistic community. The social ecological influence, as milieu studies have always implicitly done, more explicitly acknowledges that some cities or regions of the country may benefit more than others from a highly creative atmosphere and, therefore, have an advantage over other, less creative places.[8] Indeed, Menger writes that artistic communities, in particular, "show a very high level of spatial concentration in a few locations or even in one dominant city in each country."[9] Nashville may be called Music City, and a wide range of music has filtered out of the city over the decades, but it is renowned around the globe for its country music legacy. In short, saying you are a songwriter in Nashville gives you more creditability than saying you are a songwriter in Milwaukee; and saying you are a country songwriter in Nashville gives you more authentication than saying you are a country songwriter in New York or Los Angeles. The social environment directly affects the final artistic product and, therefore, goes well beyond milieu studies.

A major contribution of the current recognition of social factors that takes it beyond traditional milieu studies is the emphasis on the effect of extrinsic factors in shaping the artistic product. Musically, these extrinsic motives can influence the decision to become an artist, a songwriter, or an artist-songwriter, the latter of which, for reasons that will subsequently be explored, is becoming more critical in a songwriter's career trajectory. It also affects the style of songwriting one selects, be it country, pop, crossover country-pop, or even country rap, which is the career path former Atlanta native Colt Ford carved out in Nashville.[10] Included in extrinsic factors are strategies to get one's songs recognized, and today that increasingly means exploiting social media and establishing a musical presence on any of the various internet platforms, as well as the increasing cost-efficient use of electronic media to produce a demo. It also explains the selection of Nashville over other cities for songwriters to ply their trade, since just being in Nashville is quasi-legitimization that one is serious about their chosen profession. In this sense, Nashville provides outlets for songwriters to test their songs among their peers and obtain feedback that can directly affect the development of lyrics and melody, and prominently today, more so than in the past, that means connecting with another writer to co-write songs. Co-writing can dramatically impact the lyrics or melody of a song and thereby greatly enhance the potential of having one's song recorded, even if it cuts into one's royalties. "I used to write my own stuff," Ken Mathiesen said. "But [Nashville] is a co-writers' town. . . . Sometimes I can have a bad day and the other guy is on fire. The next time it might be the other way around. . . . Besides," he quipped, expressing a common sentiment among songwriters toward the co-writing experience, "50 percent of something is better than 100 percent of nothing."

THE MUSICAL MUSE AND THE NASHVILLE CONNECTION

The participants in this study were divided almost equally between young songwriters (under 40) and seasoned songwriters (40 and over). Those over forty typically had been songwriters for twenty years or more. The youngest songwriter in the study was 16; the oldest 63 in 2017 when the majority of interviews were conducted. The only exception to this age division is Ken Mathiesen, who was 61 (2017) and moved to Nashville to pursue songwriting in 2014. He is the only older person in the study who cannot be considered an older, "seasoned" musician. Albeit, Mathiesen is a songwriter who takes his profession seriously, often co-writing with budding young songwriters at NSAI, where he is kind of a father figure. Mathiesen falls outside the norm, however, because he is retired and doesn't rely on writing songs to make a living, as all the others in this study do. Since age is a factor in one's evaluation of their profession, in those cases where a person's name is given but their age is not contextually clear, I've parenthetically followed the name with the designation "Y" for young or "S" for seasoned: e.g., John Berry (S), Jaida Dreyer (Y). The distinction is an important one because they speak from distinct perspectives: most young songwriters are just starting out, even if they have a publishing contract, while the seasoned ones not only typically have an existing publishing contract but have been with a number of different publishing firms over the years.

As is the case throughout this critique of the industry, some people have requested anonymity, in which case they are simply mentioned as "one (seasoned) songwriter said. . . ." In other cases, the participant is known but the sensitivity of the topic requires discretion and the person is not identified, so a similar stratagem is employed. The author's sample of songwriters is augmented by numerous public domain interviews with songwriters.[11] When the person that is discussed or quoted was a participant in this study, no further reference is necessary: e.g., "Marc Beeson (S) said. . . ." Similarly, when a number of songwriters within an age group (Y vs. S) are mentioned, they are not all identified: e.g., "Jordan Minton (Y) said . . . , while another young songwriter also mentioned. . . ." Three or four people with the same perspective (here and elsewhere) are often quoted to underscore the perspective is widely shared by others in the group (e.g., songwriters, publishers, managers). In those cases where I rely on secondary information, the source is provided.

The gender division was slightly uneven: two-thirds male, one-third female. This tends to reflect dynamics within country music, which is similarly disproportionately male.[12] There was no significant difference separating younger from seasoned female songwriters, which suggests the number of female songwriters is not something attributable to changing social factors and is not a new phenomenon, despite some recent observations that female country artists are beginning to challenge the historical "bro-dominated" music scene.[13] All participants were actively pursuing their songwriting career at the time of the interview except a few who have gone on to other careers in the industry: one is now a producer, another started a music publishing company. With only a few exceptions, the songwriters, whether younger or seasoned, discovered their musical muse at a fairly early age:[14] Benji Harris's (Y) said his father "had a guitar in his closet and I was obsessed with it when I was little . . . I thought it was so cool that you could make different sounds. I took an old chord book into my room and taught myself how to play chords." It was enough of a start to lead him to enter and win an eighth-grade talent contest. Jordan Minton (Y) started when he "was a kid; I played guitar and when I was in high school someone asked me to take the lead at chapel Saturday night." Adam Wood (Y) picked up the muse when his "dad gave me a guitar when I was thirteen; I learned three-quarter time and immediately wrote a song." Thornton Clines (S), the only songwriter in this study who has an advanced degree in music, was encouraged by his parents when he was reciting nursery rhymes at age three and began taking piano lessons at five years of age. Even Ken Mathiesen, who didn't start his professional songwriting career until he was 58, always played around with music. "When I was in second grade, I got a dollar a week allowance and would go to the record store and buy a 45. Every Monday the top 40 came out. At the time, the chart had the lyrics to the number one song and I would hand-writer the lyrics on a piece of paper," so, he says with a chuckle, "I was writing number one lyrics at age ten."

Most, whether seasoned or young songwriters, have a college education, though only a few who attended college majored in music. Only a handful did not have a college education. One young and one seasoned songwriter were not academically orientated so there was little interest in attending college. Another aspiring songwriter is still in high school though she plans to attend Belmont University because of its music program and proximity to Music Row. While a number of younger songwriters (15 percent) in this study attended Belmont University, Belmont graduates are widely represented among the staff at music publishing companies or record labels. Belmont graduates are more prominent than those from nearby Middle Tennessee State University (MTSU) in Murfreesboro—which has long had a strong music program—largely because Belmont is located in Nashville and is proximate to Music Row. Belmont also has strong ties to the music industry thanks to a number of well-known artists (Brad Paisley, Trisha Yearwood, and Steven Curtis Chapman) who attended the university and strong moral and financial support from Mike Curb of Curb Records.

Many (60-plus percent) came from musical families, even if their family's music experience was not professional. Amy Gerhartz (Y) was the only one in her family to pursue music as a career, even though her grandmother was a church organist and her father played fifteen instruments. Calista Garcia's (Y) mother, an attorney, took music as a minor in college and sang in choirs. Byron Hill (S) was one of those in this study who was a mediocre student in high school, so there was no expectation that he would attend college; his "turning point" came at sixteen when his father, a music aficionado, sat down with him one day and said, "'Listen to this song, really listen to it.' It was an amazing moment. It made me realize how lyrics and feelings make a good song." These musical backgrounds may be why the families were uncritical of their offsprings' decision to pursue music as a career. Nevertheless, most families encouraged their children to finish college so that if their career aspirations didn't work out, they'd have something to fall back on. This suggests a degree of skepticism of their child's career choice, even if they often morally, and sometimes financially, supported their offspring. Not having a college education can be just as important: it was for Marc Beeson (S) because "not going to college kind of benefited me in the long run because I didn't have a skill I could go back to. With no bridges to go back to, I had no choice but to keep going forward."

Not all families were supportive. Marc Beeson's (S) father reflects a popular perception that such a career choice was a dead end since it was "just partying and fun." It "didn't go over well" with Drew Kennedy's (Y) family either, since he had been accepted upon graduating from college into a number of respectable law schools, and, by his own admission, wasn't a particularly good songwriter. Still, Kennedy's logic follows the trail of many: "I didn't know any better [at that age], and besides, I just loved songwriting so much. I figured I can be a young man and try to do this and if it doesn't work out I can be an older man and go to law school. But I cannot do it the other way around."

For most, Nashville was the place to be. Marc Beeson (S) went to L.A. because, not being a country music fan, he didn't realize (late-1970s) that there was "a place where people just wrote songs." It did not work out because, even though there were some great songwriters in L.A. at the time [Jackson Browne, Don Henley], "the window had closed." So he came to Nashville in 1990 and has done very well. A few, however, were torn between Austin and Nashville, since both have strong country music reputations. Jaida Dreyer (Y) selected Nashville over Austin because Nashville is a songwriter's town, and she had no aspirations to be an artist. Drew Kennedy (Y) initially chose Austin and spent more than ten years pursuing a successful artist-songwriting career, often spending a grueling 200-plus days on the road. He decided a few years ago, if he truly wanted to develop as a songwriter and not just a Texas troubadour who, though successful in Texas, was largely bounded by Texas, that he needed to venture to Nashville to accentuate the songwriting side of the artist-songwriter dichotomy.

Roughly one-fourth of the songwriters in this study did not directly pursue their musical career after graduating from college. John Miller (Y), for example, who had played clubs in and around Gainesville while attending the University of Florida, spent a number of years in sales before deciding it was not something he wanted to spend his life doing. His moment of truth came when he was being seriously considered for an executive position and he realized that if he accepted the promotion, the die would be cast and there would be limited opportunity to return to his musical aspirations. Others in this category had small sidesteps. Amy Gerhartz (Y), who majored in music theatre at Florida State, took a job in Virginia after graduating, then moved to New York City where she sold commercial real estate while playing cover music in clubs before moving to Atlanta to perform. In 2015, Gerhartz moved to Nashville to pursue her artist-songwriting career full-time.

Like Gerhartz, if perhaps a little more directly, another fourth of those who participated in this study followed the artist career more so than the songwriting side, though many also wrote at least some of the songs they performed. Drew Kennedy (Y) is one of these, as is John Berry (S), both of whom had to decide to "fish or cut bait." Both are excellent examples of individuals who knew they were at turning points in their life.

John Berry started playing acoustic guitar for a restaurant group on Mondays and Tuesdays in Atlanta, then moved to Athens, Georgia, where he played regularly around town from 1986 to 1992. He was making good money, married, and had a nice house on a spread that would eventually encompass 150 acres. Driving home one night from one of his shows he heard an old Joe Diffie song on the radio, "Ships That Don't Come In,"[15] when he realized that, while he felt he was on top of the world, he was, in reality, just a big fish in a small pond. The song prompted him to reconsider his future and, after some discussion with his supportive wife, "give it a go in Nashville." They booked a few shows at Douglas Corner, a well-known local club that has launched a few careers,[16] and decided to "go for broke," figuring that if he didn't make it, he'd at least tried. He sent out some two hundred invitations to industry professionals and had a sparse turnout. But as luck, or God—which many songwriters mention in acknowledging their good fortune—would have it,[17] one of the people in the audience was from Capitol Records, and he introduced Berry to Jimmy Bowen at Capitol, who signed him to a deal.

He stayed at Capitol until management changes led, as they inevitably do, to artist-songwriter changes. He soon signed with Lyric Records (1999) as an artist-songwriter. It was shortly after that that they sold their home in Georgia and moved to Nashville to be closer to the label. He did his first Christmas show shortly thereafter and twenty-plus years later he is still doing that bread-and-butter twenty-some-day Christmas tour from late-November to mid-December. In between, he's written scores of songs, including "Don't Think I Ain't Country Because I Don't Drive a Big Truck," which was inspired while he was driving his old Dodge Durango down Interstate 65 and some "big ol' guy in a big ol' pickup truck" sped past him. Similar stories dot many other artist-songwriters' experiences.

Few struck pay dirt upon arrival in Nashville. Most who moved to Nashville specifically to pursue their songwriting careers had minor sidesteps. Benita Hill (S) is an excellent example of someone whose career aspirations were temporarily derailed. Hill accentuated the artist side but also strongly incorporated songwriting into her career aspirations: "I thought, 'Well, the Beatles write their own music, James Taylor writes his own music.' I was in love with Dolly Parton, too, and she wrote her own songs and had a great singing career. So, I thought I could do that, too." She was in college in Murray, Kentucky, and started to make and send cassettes of her songs to publishers in L.A., New York, and Nashville in the late 1970s-early 1980s. "I actually got a little attention from a publisher in Nashville, who had J. J. Cale at the time. And Owen Bradley, who was running MCA [formerly Decca], was going to cut a couple of my songs with a new girl he was developing. I thought I had made it. I was going to go to Nashville."

It didn't pan out because the woman who was going to cut Hill's songs at MCA was let go. But Hill was connected to the publisher who was handling J. J. Cale and joined Cale's group on the road as a back-up singer. It was her first road gig, and, in the best networking tradition, that gig let to another: one with Conway Twitty, who was doing some casino shows in Reno and Las Vegas. "It paid $700 a week. Seven hundred dollars a week in 1980 was amazing." She got to pitch some of her songs to Twitty, "who was very supportive" even if none were incorporated into his musical oeuvre. After Twittty, she spent two years on the road with the Allman Brothers. After that tour, she had a few small publishing deals and then things fell apart for a few years.

In the early 1990s, Hill began piddling around again and cut an independent album that got a little attention. A friend in the business told her that Allen Reynolds, who was Garth Brooks's producer, needed someone in the office to answer the phones and such. She welcomed the extra income and she started working three days a week. "I was starstruck, but I asked Allen if I could pitch [Garth] a few songs. Because I was a writer [with some credentials], he said, 'Sure!'" Garth liked the song but it didn't go anywhere; nevertheless, he encouraged her to pitch others and "let's see what happens; I really like your work." In the meantime, Brooks listened to the songs on her self-produced album and decided to record the first song on it, which rather surprised Hill because "Take the Keys to My Heart" was more jazzy than country, but she felt Brooks could tweak it into a Texas swing song.[18] Then came her first real hit, "Two Piña Coladas," which Brooks was hesitant about but was persuaded to cut by his producer. This roundabout progression from arrival to hit typifies the laborious songwriter route to "stardom."

Hill got her first publishing deal shortly after coming off the road with the Allman Brothers, which would have been within the traditional five to seven years that most songwriters and publishers mentioned is the time it takes to establish one's Nashville connections. "Two Piña Coladas" came five to seven years after that. A number one hit is every songwriter's aspiration, and "Two Piña Coladas" put the money in the bank that would allow Hill to buy the house she presently lives in. It is worth enunciating, for those who adhere to the "easy money" route, that it took ten-plus somewhat bumpy years for her to get to that point. One young songwriter in this study managed to sign a publishing deal within three years of arriving; another young songwriter did even better, garnering a publishing contract within eight months of moving to Nashville and a few years later had a number one hit. Most of the other young songwriters in this study, typically having lived in Music City between two and five years, were still trying to land a publishing deal. Conversely, most of the seasoned writers have publishing deals and had some number ones, the exception being Jennifer Schott (S), a songwriting veteran of nearly twenty years who has never had a number one song. However, Schott has been in a long-standing contract with her current publisher and has produced numerous hits, underscoring the fact that one can succeed in the music business even if they don't get that coveted number one hit.

NETWORKING

The years Benita Hill spent building a social network earned her gigs as a backup singer and opened a few publishing doors. Though he was connected enough to pick one of the premier showcases in the city in which to perform, John Berry (S) didn't really know a lot of people when he took a shot at being discovered at Douglas Corner. He has since established a strong network after some twenty years in the city; he knew people he was able to call on when he did his 2017 television songwriting show at that very same venue, *Songs and Stories with John Berry*. Among the artist-songwriter intimates who were on the show in its first season were Billy Ray Cyrus, Delbert McClinton, Suzy Bogguss, and Craig Morgan, to name just four of the twelve guests who appeared on stage to tell their stories between songs. Other new songwriters to the city have had to work a little harder at establishing their connections: 80 percent of the songwriters in this study knew no more than one or two people (at best) when they figuratively "got off the bus."

Unlike John Berry, many who come to Nashville don't have a strong musical performance background and have to hone their craft: one of the recurring themes of songwriters reflecting on their initial arrival is how "blown away" they were at the local songwriting scene and how much they'd need to learn. In order to make progress in a new town with few contacts, they attempted to connect with others in the business on the off chance that this person will know that person who might open a door. The goal of the newly arrived artist-songwriter is to connect with an experienced writer. The problem, of course, is that many veteran songwriters have a well-established network of peers with whom they co-write. Still, many of these seasoned songwriters, at least today, keep the door open to working with young, aspiring songwriters because it keeps them young and on the cutting edge. The artist-songwriter network remains a vital stepping stone to success in Nashville.

Networking is key to succeeding in many areas, of course. It is a form of social capital. Social capital is very "simple and straightforward," Nan Lin argues: "it is investment in social relations with expected returns. . . . Individuals engage in interactions and networking in order to produce profits."[19] Lin outlines a number of ways social capital benefits those in the network. For one thing, network affiliation facilitates the flow of information that provides knowledge about opportunities and choices otherwise not available to those outside the network. It also exerts influence on those in the network; for example, "putting in a good word" carries a certain weight. Networking locations are an important part of the networking matrix because just "being there" (e.g., Nashville) can facilitate access to better resources.

Ken Mathiesen (S) put it nicely: "Nobody is going to come knocking on your door and say 'Hey, you got some songs?' You have to find the way. You also can't go knocking on just anyone's door. You have to have connections, no matter what kind. You can even know the person who cleans Martina McBride's house. It's *all* about connections."

The benefits of being connected in Nashville might best be examined by looking at one young artist-songwriter who spends more time outside of the Nashville network.

Amy Gerhartz (Y) has been pursuing her music career for ten years after a brief foray in New York selling real estate upon completing college. She gave that up for a musical career and moved to Atlanta, where she focused on the artist side and played clubs for a number of years. In 2015, she moved to Nashville to accentuate the songwriting side of her career and immediately connected with NSAI to lay the groundwork with fellow songwriters with whom to co-write. Her co-writing network is rather thin, however, because most of the time Gerhartz is on the road pursuing the artist side of her career. She is doing this for the same reason many initially follow the artist path over the songwriter one: she needs to pay her bills and put food on the table. Her primary means of generating an income is by playing house shows. A house show is usually a live performance for a private party in someone's house. Most house shows have a floor of twenty guests,[20] which generate a solid income, and this is often augmented by those at the party buying the artist's merchandise (T-shirts, CDs). Gerhartz has to make all these arrangements on her own and she often crisscrosses the country to fulfill engagements. She spends a lot of time in her car, but while she gets a lot of songwriting ideas while driving, "the road is not conducive to songwriting."

Gerhartz says she has 10,000 fans but realistically lowers this to "300-500 *loyal* fans." The bottom line for Gerhartz as a songwriter is that, despite performing her own material at house shows, she spends too much time away from Nashville and knows this affects her ability to move forward as a songwriter. Gerhartz hopes to raise her loyal fan base to 1,000 over the next few years, which, she feels, would generate the steady income that would allow her to develop as a songwriter. This is important because women artists are judged by their physical appearance more than men and, at age 35 (2017), Gerhartz feels she has only a few years left on the road. As a songwriter, she wouldn't have these same concerns since "no one judges you on your appearance as a songwriter."[21]

The ability to network is one of Nashville's greatest musical strengths, positively remarked on by practically everyone in this study regardless of their position, including Gerhartz, who recognizes she is not in Nashville enough to establish a strong co-writing network. The Nashville connection has been a hallmark of the city dating back to at least the 1950s and 1960s when Owen Bradley, Chet Atkins, and Roy Acuff ruled the roost. It remained strong through the 1990s heyday because activities continued to be geographically confined to Music Row, where everybody knew everyone. Even with the tremendous growth that has taken place in Nashville since the start of the new millennium,[22] not to mention the disbursement of musical activities beyond "The Row,"[23] Nashville is still a place for musicians simply because it is so easy to connect with other musicians.[24] Nashville is big, but big is a relative term. Nashville proper (Davidson County) has a population of 700,000 in comparison to music rivals New York City and Los Angeles County, which have populations of 8.5 million and 9.8 million respectively. Nashville's "bigness" is still comparatively small and, despite the recent influx (post-2010) of young professionals to the area,[25] the city continues to maintain its small town southern "hi, y'all" roots. It has actually gotten smaller musically: in the 1980s and heyday 1990s, there were, by all accounts, some 1,000-plus songwriters making a living in Nashville; today that number is around 300.[26] Though Nashville has grown as a city, the smaller songwriting community makes networking not only easier but also more critical in advancing one's career.

Many young arrivals quickly learn by word of mouth about NSAI; that is, if they are not waylaid getting off the bus by a shyster promising them a record deal for a few thousand up-front dollars.[27] The "international" in Nashville Songwriters Association International (NSAI) is a bit misleading, despite the fact that the organization's 150 chapters reach well beyond Nashville. Nevertheless, NSAI is a local phenomenon because 50 percent of its 5,000 members are based in Nashville.[28] Some 100-plus new arrivals go through NSAI every week.[29] NSAI embraces these newcomers with a potpourri of activities to acquaint the budding songwriters with ways to ply their trade, including regular weekly/monthly sessions where professionals in the field critique the songs of would-be songwriters.

At the very least, it makes newcomers feel welcome: "It made me not feel like such an alien," says Adam Wood (Y), since everyone else in his family are professional educators (teachers, principals) and he "went rogue" in his career path. Wood found NSAI was "very valuable in helping me meet people; I got some guidance and was finding myself with people that were like minded." This is, unquestionably, NSAI's greatest strength: connecting would-be songwriters with other aspirants. Every young songwriter interviewed in this study applauded NSAI for connecting them to others with whom they have established a co-writing relationship. Michelle Pereira's experience with NSAI is typical of younger songwriters: "I have been in Nashville [since early 2016], but for the last year my focus has been on the songwriting part of it. It is just phenomenal the people I have gotten to write with. The things that just come to me through NSAI and just being in Nashville."

Pereira had a degree in music engineering, and when she arrived she worked in a recording studio. That's when she decided "I wanted to be the person doing the session instead of just recording it. It was like a light bulb went off in my head.... I wanted to be part of creating the songs." Her recording background has helped her connect with other young songwriters because she can assist them in building tracks. It also has the potential of opening other doors because she met a few publishers "who liked the idea that I can help with the records, because it keeps their cost down."

> You know, being in Nashville, you want to establish yourself and you want to network. I have done that. That's where NSAI comes in. They provide numerous opportunities to us to focus on our writing and get it out there. They have what they call Thursday night workshops. In those workshops you can interact with other songwriters. Once a month they have a publisher and about sixty writers going through songs. We literally line up at the door. It is first come first served. It is a lengthy process, but I have been lucky enough to have two of my songs taken by publishers, though I never heard anything from those publishers. To me it is at least confirming to myself that I am on the right track. I must be doing something right, because they saw something in those two songs. It's affirmation that you are doing something right.

Those Thursday nights also connect her to others standing around waiting to get heard: "It is where I met most of my friends. You are talking to people just like yourself." When she finds a connection with someone, they might meet to co-write. NSAI has a number of co-writer working rooms, and Pereira works with other NSAI songwriters daily. Pereira's heavy co-writing days at NSAI are partly the result of her Canadian visa not allowing her to work, not even part-time. Still, Pereira, like everyone in this study, knows the importance of building a network. In Pereira's case, she's been "helping out" at a small publishing firm and she and the publisher have been talking about a publishing contract.[30]

The majority of young writers do not have the luxury of writing full-time because they have to work.[31] They tend to favor occupations with flexible hours that allow them to hone their craft at writers' rounds and other showcases around town. Besides being a means to making a living while still keeping one's time free to pursue their career, there is always the chance these jobs will lead to "a break." These positions can lead to serendipitous networking; that is, in their non-musical job the budding artist-songwriter can meet potential contacts.

The traditional form of networking is getting to know people in the business who will open doors. Serendipitous networking does happen, however. Byron Hill (S) went to eat at a local restaurant and met then-unknown Kathy Mattea, who was working there as a waitress at the time, and subsequently co-produced her first two albums. The city is rife with these kinds of stories: artist-songwriters who were waiting on tables and gave their song or EP to a publisher or producer and were called back shortly thereafter for an interview. This happens, but it is rare in the extreme. However, some doors were serendipitously opened for a few people in this study. John Miller (Y) is an early riser and drives Lyft from four to ten in the morning so he can do noon writers' rounds or be at NSAI to co-write in the afternoon. Twice he picked up the same person and the second time, having learned from the earlier ride that the man is an independent producer, pitched the man a song that he was working on, singing the first verse and chorus. The man said, "Let's write it!" The song, "How Do You Know," was set to be released shortly after our interview.

Mark Irwin (S) also connected in a fortuitous way. Shortly after arrival he started working at the Bluebird, which was then a small local artist-songwriter hangout. Every night, Irwin broke down the sound system and set up the tables for lunch the following day. "People would say, this guy is looking for songs, or this group is looking for writers. It is where I met my first publisher, Barry Coburn from Ten Ten," which was a newly formed publishing group that subsequently signed Alan Jackson, with whom Irwin co-wrote a chart-topping song.[32] Coburn couldn't provide a draw, which is a stipend paid monthly in advance of any royalties. That meant, with no income stream from his publisher, Irwin had to continue his night job,[33] but his five-year relationship with Ten Ten would lead to opportunities with Red Vinyl Music, which produced Tim McGraw.

Young or seasoned, whatever the time period, traditional networking is crucial in landing a deal. A songwriter doesn't just walk into a publishing house or a label and announce their presence; over the transom submissions, like Benita Hill's, are rarely examined today without someone providing some form of introduction. A popular way today to gain entry into the music business in Nashville is through an internship. This hasn't always been the case. Liz Hengber (S) took a full-time job as a secretary for six months after arriving in Nashville and wrote in her book, *The Do's Dont'sof Music Row*, "this kind of job is a *TRAP*." She left it to take the more traditional job as a waitress because it freed up her time to pursue her writing and after five long years she got her first publishing job.[34] I can only assume that Hengber's job was unrelated to the music business because Jennifer Schott (S) felt "fortunate to get a job [on Music Row] with a publishing company even if she only answered the phone and typed lyrics." Schott was there three years, during which time she got to network with a string of other writers and spend time honing her craft at night, "writing songs and meeting [other music] people." She signed her first publishing contract in 2000. Byron Hill (S) also felt lucky to get a job even tangentially related to the business. He started cataloguing songs for a publisher: "Back then it was reel to reel and every reel had about four songs on it. You had to catalogue the tapes so you'd know where to get the specific tapes that were needed so that song could be pitched. . . . Very grunt-level stuff.[35] Those kinds of jobs go to interns today."

For young artist-songwriters today, internships are a mainstay of gaining entry. Internships are typically legitimated by local college music programs, though the number of those attending the two dominant music schools in the Nashville area far surpasses the number of internships available, especially in a shrinking market. Even then, the foot-in-the-door technique does not necessarily give the decision makers exposure to the employee's talent: if you are hired to catalogue songs, that is pretty much all you do. Music networking, then, is more likely to be accomplished via more traditional mechanisms, and the primary way that is accomplished in Nashville is to showcase one's work at any of the writers' rounds that regularly take place throughout the city. This places a premium today on not just being a songwriter, but being an artist-songwriter.

WRITERS' ROUNDS

Most major cities have places where local musicians ply their trade. The club scene in Nashville is relatively sparse outside the touristy downtown honky tonks. Nevertheless, there is a potpourri of venues for songwriters to ply their trade in Nashville today. These venues give both budding and seasoned songwriters the opportunity to present new material and receive feedback: writers' rounds typically showcase four to five artists who each take a turn singing one of their songs, then the spotlight loops back to the first artist-songwriter and the process begins again. The Bluebird is one of the more recognizable places because it was one of the first (1982 - present) to enunciate the songwriting dimension of the artist-songwriter duality,[36] but similar songwriter venues dot the city.[37] They are typically situated in bars but can also be found at retail sites around town—anywhere the establishment can put a microphone and a stool. A writers' round is a cost-efficient way for the establishment to provide music to draw in customers. And at most "legitimate" writers' rounds (which exclude retail establishments that showcase a musician or musical group), a substantial part of the audience are people in the music business. Jordan Minton, who didn't know a soul when he arrived in Nashville in 2013 but was the first writer signed to Keith Urban's new publishing group in 2016, quips: "I was very surprised at the collaborative attitude here. I went to a writer round the other night and I knew 75 percent of the people there. And I don't hang around a lot with them. But you just get to know them. This is the biggest small town anywhere. I think it is one of the best things about Nashville."

This is not to suggest that producers regularly attend writers' rounds. This does, of course, occur, and stories abound of someone from a label who is in the audience and discovers the next Garth Brooks, which is, indeed, how Lynn Shults at Capitol discovered Garth Brooks at the Bluebird in 1988.[38]

Everyone appearing in the rounds is conscious that there may be that special someone in the audience who can fast-track their career. A more reasonable expectation is that someone in the audience either represents a music publisher, which is fairly common, or might mention to someone else in the business that they were impressed when they heard so-and-so at one of the rounds they recently attended—being a "big small town," to paraphrase Jordan Minton (Y), means the word tends to spread rather rapidly. Jaida Dreyer (Y) is a good case in point. Dreyer hit her first number one in 2016 at Sony with "Home Alone Tonight." She was signed to Sony after their senior vice-president of creative heard her perform at a small local venue. He didn't just happen to be there, however; he knew of the Luke Bryan song she wrote and wanted to hear her perform some of her stuff in person.

Nashville is very keen on personal contacts and it remains the best way for a young artist-songwriter to come to a publisher's or producer's attention. Indeed, it appears almost axiomatic that younger writers spend an inordinate amount of time attending and performing at numerous writers' nights every week, but as they start making connections their rounds start to decline and, while they still attend, they start becoming more discriminating about where they appear. Once a publishing contract is signed, their participatory attendance at rounds declines proportionately to the length of their association with a publisher, in no small part because they have an established network. All the seasoned writers had specific people with whom they regularly co-wrote, so they could be more selective in which rounds, and how many, they would play, but this is just as true with young songwriters who have been here long enough to make co-writing connections. Writers' rounds are particularly important for young songwriters because they hold the potential of connecting with a peer songwriter for future co-writing. While they don't often pay much, writers' rounds do give young artists the opportunity to showcase their work. Depending on the setup, any one person on stage might have the chance to showcase three to four songs during any one set. Performers typically don't get to go back on stage once their round is completed because the following round goes to the next group of artist-songwriters.

Writers' rounds are beneficial, even if there is no one in the audience who might have a contract in their back pocket, because it gives the performer a chance to try out their material and get feedback, not just from other members on stage, but also from friends in the audience. Seasoned writers are often involved in some of these writer events. Generally, they participate with other seasoned artist-songwriters, but they also occasionally do rounds with neophyte artist-songwriters. However, it is more common for seasoned songwriters to attend rounds to keep abreast of developments in the industry: who the up-and-comers might be, but also new musical sounds that young artists might be incorporating into their work. More often than not, however, writers'rounds are dominated by aspirant artist-songwriters performing for other aspirant artist-songwriters, with a sprinkling of representatives from publishing groups.

Everyone in this study participates in writers' rounds, though some are critical of them. One criticism, since the rounds are so frequent, is how much time they take up—on any one night in Nashville there is a one-night venue of the week (e.g., on Monday night, "X" club might have a writers' night; on Tuesday night "Y" club has one); quite a few venues have rounds that run seven nights a week. This heavy schedule can be quite exhausting. Michelle Pereira, a relatively recent arrival, was out "three or four times a week [after first arriving in town]. . . . I did that for half a year. It was a rat race. I just had to cut back. I am still doing them here and there, but I am being a bit more selective."

Another criticism is that it is hard to showcase one's work when there is such a limited time to present one's material, or that the "interlude" process of passing the microphone to the next person after just one song interrupts their ability to "really get going." These criticisms, justified as they may be, do not prevent artist-songwriters from participating in writers' rounds because the networking is vital to staying "plugged in." And maintaining that network is important. One of the seasoned songwriters in Dan Daley's study quipped, perhaps a tad hyperbolically, that when he returned after being out of town for just one year he was "out of the loop completely."[39]

CO-WRITING

Co-writing has long been a part of making music across genres. It has certainly been a hallmark of the country music industry. Bobby Braddock (b. 1940) is a country songwriter of some repute who was a prominent writer on Music Row during the 1970s and 1980s;[40] he's had a number of solo songwriting hits but he also wrote many of his best songs with two other legends of the day, Curly Putman and Sonny Throckmorton.[41] Since the turn of the new millennium, single songwriting scores have nearly faded into oblivion. In fact, of all the hits in 2016, only two were written by a solo songwriter.[42] Everyone in this study agrees that co-writing has become the primary way of succeeding as a songwriter in Nashville. The co-writing aspects of songwriting today, perhaps even more so than in past years, reinforces the strong network ties necessary to get ahead in Nashville.

There are two types of co-writes. One is with the artist; the other is with another songwriter, or, more specifically today, other songwriters. The historical fifty-fifty split is becoming increasingly rare. Indeed, Thomas Rhett's 2017 release, "Vacation," lists fourteen songwriters,[43] but the tradition now is to have at least three, one of whom might well be the artist. The participation of the artist is relatively new. Bart Herbison says that when he assumed the executive director position at NSAI in 1997 it was common for the split to be 90 percent pure songwriters to 10 percent artist-songwriters. Today the split is closer to 40 percent pure songwriters (and fading fast) to 60 percent artist-songwriters.

A recurring criticism of the artist co-writing "team" among some of the seasoned songwriters in this study is their experience with "drive-by writers," referring to those artists who merely stick their head in a room and go, 'Oh, that's great,' and then leave behind only their name to mark their "contribution" to the song. The degree to which this takes place is somewhat murky, though it is hardly a new phenomenon. Mel Tillis signed over half of his song, "I Ain't Never," to Webb Pierce because Pierce wanted his name added or he wouldn't cut it.[44] In return for co-author credit, Pierce gave Tillis a pair of cowboy boots. It was, according to Tillis, his $800,000 pair of boots.[45]

Drive-bys happen. It appears historically to be limited to a handful of hungry songwriters and greedy artists. Drive-bys are less of an issue today because so many artists are legitimate songwriters: "Remember," says Mark Irwin (S), "Luke Bryan won ASCAP songwriter of the year before he became famous as an artist." The degree to which artists are truly songwriters is a subject of much debate among the seasoned songwriters in this study; nevertheless, all agree that having an artist involved in the songwriting process (other than "drive-bys") is crucial to getting the record cut and can have a major impact on its success in the marketplace.

It is not just that the artist is interested in the royalties he or she might garner by having their name on a song—though there is that; most artist income is driven by album sales and concert attendance. Artists involved in the writing are likely to be more committed to the song. In part, this is because they know what works for them. By being involved in the songwriting process they are also more likely to push for the song to be included on an album. A few seasoned songwriters brought up a particular drawback to working with the artist; they take things too seriously. No doubt, this is because if a song fails it is the artist who bears the responsibility in the public eye since the public often assumes that the artist is solely responsible for the song. This negative has a positive, however: because they are so serious about the song, their effort often leads to a better song.

Seasoned or young, most songwriters do not work at home, or if they do, they typically come in a couple days a week to run their songs by other writers or their publisher. Those with a publishing contract, and that includes a number of young songwriters in this study, prefer to work at their publisher's place of business. Those budding songwriters who don't have a publisher are likely to rely on workroom facilities at places like NSAI or one of the Performing Rights Organizations (PROs), such as BMI, ASCAP, and SESAC. It is not uncommon for people who have to trudge in to work every day to envy those who have "the freedom" to work from home. But working from home can be problematic.

A number of seasoned songwriters appreciate the structure imposed by the workplace; it allows you to "get your shit done," as one seasoned songwriter succinctly put it. This songwriter simply means that it is far too easy to slip into leisure mode at home, but "at the office" one is there to work. In this sense, it helps separate one's private and public lives. Additionally, while they are always "on" in the sense that ideas constantly flit through one's mind at all hours, the workplace keeps a person focused—you are there to write a song. It is fairly typical that this focus often produces at least one co-write a week, if not more, since, whether young or seasoned, writing 100 or more songs a year is fairly common.

The workplace also puts a songwriter in touch with other writers, and while they might go off and tinker with a song idea on their own at one of the publishing firm offices, other songwriters are always around and it is not uncommon to spend some time working with each other. Today, despite her mentor's advice to "never forget how to write solo," Jennifer Schott (S) always writes with another writer. Working with others is especially important because working solo from home increases the chances that, not being seen, one will simply fade into oblivion. It is also important because if one gets stuck on a composition, it is often helpful to have others around to run ideas by and share in (re) constructing the song.

Most of the small independent publishing houses employ between three to eight full-time songwriters. Many of the houses on Music Row are four-squares that would be very roomy for a family (4,500 square feet), but, for a business with a full-time support staff and four or five writers working there regularly, it is a relatively small work environment. This is why most independent publishers mentioned uppermost in selecting someone to join "the family" is how they will get along with others.

Still, many songwriters work with other songwriters from another house. One would normally think that it is to the publisher's advantage to have co-writers collaborate in-house since the publisher would reap 100 percent of their share of the song's profit,[46] but in at least half the cases, the co-writer is from another house. This makes sense because if there are three co-writers and each is from a separate publishing house, then each house is pitching the song to an artist or label, effectively tripling the chances of it being cut.

One often assumes co-written songs are a fifty-fifty collaborative split. This is sometimes the case because one songwriter's strength may be lyrics while the other excels at melody and each contributes equally to a song. But often the co-writing arrangement is asymmetrical, and no one has a problem with this arrangement. "Some days," says Michelle Pereria (Y), speaking for any number of songwriters in this study, "it is like pulling teeth [to get a song finished]. That is when having a co-writer is so nice. Sometimes I bring in an idea, and sometimes they do." Even when one writes most of the song themselves, sometimes that other person—who gets songwriting credit—is needed to just help finish the song: "I have written some really good songs by myself," says Benji Harris (Y), "but there are times I just couldn't get over the hump, and I'd bring someone in and say what would you do here. That is when the co-writer can get that last 10 percent and then you are at the promised land."

It would seem that seasoned songwriters who have made it to the promised land can rest easy on their laurels because they have an enviable track record that keeps artists and labels coming back to the well. The seasoned aspect, some suggest, also carries with it a liability. Byron Hill explains:

> When you have a few hits, the publisher can look at your songs and see what you've done. They can say, 'Oh, well, we know what he can do'. The older you get the more you run into this kind of thing. The track record that follows you around can be pretty impressive. But it also can let people jump to conclusions as to who you are and what you can do [e.g. he only writes this kind of song but we want another kind]. On the other hand, when a young writer has a couple of hits, he gets the, "Wow, this kid is great [and can go far whereas the older songwriter doesn't have much left in him]." That is what I am up against. Daily!

Hill's rationale is one of myriad reasons seasoned writers often team up with young songwriters. Another recurring reason among seasoned songwriters is that it keeps them young. "I write with young co-writers," says Thornton Cline "because I like to cross a couple of generations; you change and cross into a different age group, like Tony Bennett working with Lady Gaga." Some writers fall by the wayside, one seasoned songwriter says of his former compatriots, because "the world [of music] changes fast and they don't adapt." Working with others 1) "keeps you focused," 2) "gives you a chance to bounce your ideas off of [others]," often 3) "gives perspective" and, 4) can sometimes introduce you to someone who "has the most interesting way of seeing things." This is not to say there are not issues at times. After all, sometimes you don't connect, and while "the person is a great person, you may not need to write together. And that's okay [because it is the way it is; no hurt feelings]." The only serious lament seasoned songwriters have regarding their young peers is that younger songwriters are excessively tardy now and then, which prevents the work from "moving along" at the productive pace accustomed to by seasoned songwriters.

Seasoned writers occasionally liken co-writing to dating, but when they do, it is more likely to be related to the aspect of getting to know another person, rather than as a romance connection: "It's like first-time dating," says Jennifer Schott. "You have to get to know them, and them you. Sometimes it clicks, and sometimes you like the person but it doesn't work creatively."

Younger songwriters are more apt to compare cross-gender co-writing to the more romantic aspects of dating. In a way, it is because in romantic dating one slowly self-discloses, revealing one's private thoughts to another, which leads to intimacy. Self-disclosure typically unfolds gradually over a period of time as one person reveals a little about themselves and the other reciprocates, then more and more is revealed until a bond is established and one begins to talk about their most intimate thoughts and feelings.[47] This may be greatly accelerated when working with a co-writer because, although one may not know the other very well, many songs come from one's heart: "Sometimes," Marc Beeson (S) says, "you start sharing stuff that you may not have even told your wife."

This may be why a number of young songwriters have intimated that opposite-sex co-writing can often lead to relationships and relationship issues. Relating it to sex, one young female songwriter said you just "jump in and do it. It can be really really great, or it could be 'Oh, my gosh, I never want to do this again [with that person].'" A young male songwriter mentioned that, like dating, "it either goes well at first or it doesn't go anywhere. I have had a few [dates and co-writes] where we just stare at one another." The analogy is apropos: you have to connect with the person you are writing with, but sometimes, in the process of establishing that special connection, you may end up in a relationship—especially when you are a young, unattached person adrift in a new town. John Miller (Y), who is a little older (mid-thirties) and recently married, goes overboard to make sure that the relationship he builds with his female co-writers, "is a big brother kind of relationship. I don't want to send mixed signals when we are writing. I have seen some co-writing relationships [that evolve into romantic ones] go bad—really bad."

One expects seasoned songwriters not to be intensively competitive because they have "made it," even if they all know that one is only as good as one's last hit song. Young songwriters are likewise, somewhat surprisingly, non-competitive in a very competitive business. The small-town ambiance that pervades the Nashville music community and the co-writing collaboration among songwriters makes one's rivals one's friends. They feed off and fulfill one another. Benji Harris (Y) makes this point:

> One thing I have noticed about Nashville is that people like to help each other. There isn't a huge competitive thing like there is in New York or L.A. [Nashville music people] always say, like, "Oh, I love your record, if I can help you out sometime just let me know." Or, "Oh, you need a band tomorrow. Let me make some calls; I know this guy and this guy might be able to help you out with that."

LYRICS: PUTTING IN THE HOURS

Charles Simpson found that a strong work ethic separated the handful of successful from the abundance of unsuccessful artists in SoHo.[48] The same holds true with successful songwriters, even young ones striving for success. The music muse takes work. "People have no idea how much rejection we have to deal with and the brutal work it takes," says Marc Beeson (S). It's one thing to listen to great music, Beeson goes on to say, but writing it is another matter: "It's kind of like someone telling you how it is to have a baby, but you don't know what they are talking about until you do it." The popular book market, however, is dotted with any number of books that purport to teach neophytes the process. Some of these books have merit, but they can only go so far. Often, they are good at laying out some of the basics.

Jason Blume, for example, is a seasoned songwriter and a regular teacher at the BMI Nashville Songwriter's workshops. The title of his book, *Six Steps to Songwriting Success*, suggests that he is going to quickly inform the reader of six simple gateway truths to writing a great song; he takes nearly 300 pages to lay out those six "simple" steps. His first chapter is on the structure of the song, and it is very informative for the would-be songwriter who has not thought of this very basic dimension of songwriting. He writes of one young man who, after dabbling with songwriting as a hobby for twenty years, decided to give it a serious turn. He spent $20,000 to cut a demo. "The production was pristine. The [backup] singer as good as hit artists, and the musicianship was top-notch." Nevertheless, it became "painfully clear" to Blume that "the songs had no discernible structure... [They] were more like a musical stream of consciousness than an actual song."[49]

Bart Herbison with NSAI estimates that for every hundred people who come to Nashville as artist-songwriters, 50 percent right off the top don't have the talent it takes. Bradley Collins, head of creative at BMI,[50] elaborates: "I generally work with people very early in their careers. I have had people sit in these seats [across from his office desk] every day with crazy dreams—they want to play in a stadium with 18,000 people. And they're dead serious." It's Collins's job to help the neophytes put things into perspective and guide them to a more realistic route. This is why most newcomers hear straightaway that they should anticipate about seven years before they make any serious headway. The dream that they are going to dash off a song and make millions doesn't sound that thrilling when they find out just how much time and trouble the process of just landing a publishing deal can take. This culls roughly another 30 percent of new arrivals: a string of dead ends after even a few months can be mightily discouraging for anyone but those who are committed to success. This is why any number of those interviewed remarked on Malcolm Gladwell's supposition that it takes at least 10,000 hours to become an expert in one's chosen field.[51] This theory is now widely debunked since more than hours alone are necessary to make one an expert.[52] Nevertheless, the point those who have been in the business a while are trying to make is that it takes some time to make headway as a songwriter, however good one may be.

That leaves around 20 percent with a modicum of talent and a strong degree of persistence who "hang in there" to pursue their dreams. Many in this study felt 20 percent was an inflated number and that 10 percent was much more realistic,[53] with only about 1 percent hitting the jackpot and garnering a number one hit: "It's like saying you've decided to become a professional lotto winner," Kelley Lovelace only half-humorously quips.[54] This is why every songwriter in this study at some point in our discussion never failed to mention their luck.

John Berry reflects on a business dinner shortly after signing his deal with Capitol.

> One of the executives said, "I bet you are wondering why you didn't come to Nashville sooner. You come to Nashville, do two showcases [at Douglas Corner] and get a record deal." I said it kind of crossed my mind. He said it wouldn't have been the same because the stars lined up tonight. He said, "Tonight was your night. Don't worry about water under the bridge. Don't sit there and kick yourself and think you should have come here when you were twenty-three instead of thirty-three. It might not have been your time then. It was tonight."

One budding songwriter asked Bradley Collins at BMI how many songs he had to write to get a publishing deal, and Collins half-humorously replied, "Just one! One really good song will get you a publishing deal." Collins was only half joking because, while he knows that one good song will put you at the head of the line, he also recognizes there is a process: "The [young songwriters] that are really good realize they have to take steps to get to the goal they want. The others want to skip steps, and that is very difficult to do."

The steps are just plain, old-school hard work. One might get that great song the first time out, but that is extremely rare. "Before I moved here," says Byron Hill (S), "I had written about a hundred songs. A couple of them got recorded later on, but it was a learning process for me to get good enough to get my songs cut. Lots of trial and error, and writing with guys like Dennis Knutson [a seasoned songwriter]."

All the songwriters in this study, young or seasoned, put in the hours and generally work eight hours a day, five days a week. "Whether I want to write or not," says Thornton Cline (S), "I always show up to work." In separate interviews both Mark Irwin (S) and Jennifer Schott (S) said "perseverance." Jennifer Schott put it even more extremely: "I work! I don't cancel [a co-writer meeting] unless I am on my death bed." Schott goes on to explain how she had to overcome the romanticized inspirational mythos that she brought to Nashville:

> When you become a staff songwriter there is a different expectation. You work with other people, and all of a sudden you have to be creative at ten-thirty on a Tuesday morning. You have to adjust and change your idea of creativity. If you are writing with someone else you can't just write when inspiration comes along. You have to be writing down all kinds of things [before arriving at work], like thoughts, melody, and such. That way when you are in the room with another artist or writer, you can, hopefully, channel some of what you have down.

Most write a minimum of one hundred songs a year but realize that out of all those songs only a dozen or so might move along the pipeline. John Berry has an extensive catalogue (songs recorded) and despite having twenty singles on the country charts, six of which went Top 5, along with a solid number of Christian albums, his goal at age 58 (2017) is modest: "I really want to go out with five, maybe six songs that are just to die for."

Songwriters are always "on" outside their typical forty-hour work week. One of the most common "after hours" lyrical deliberations is to get ideas for titles, lines, or themes, and jot them down in a notebook or, today, smart phone: any number of writers in this study, when this subject was broached, pulled out their cell phone and scrolled through an almost endless assortment of titles or lines that had crossed their minds. Ideas or lines are one thing, resurrecting old unpublished songs another. Ideas and lines can be developed since only the germ of a thought is there and the idea or line can be taken in this direction or that, but old songs tend to have a structure that confines them.

Some songwriters go back and mine their old songs; some move along and allow them to pass into oblivion. Seasoned songwriters are split fairly evenly on which way they prefer to deal with their earlier tunes. Mark Irwin never goes back: "Despite all the songs that I have written, I never go back and think, 'Well that was a good [but unpublished] one, let's rewrite it and put it out there.' I never take an old idea and try to rewrite it. I don't know why, I just don't." Perhaps, as he later acknowledges, it's because "there is a shelf life to songs." Other songwriters feel that there was enough spark in the original to warrant reconsidering it and bringing it up to date. Byron Hill will sometimes go through his catalogue [of songs] if an artist is looking for something specific to see if anything that he's done might work for the artist, though after it's sat for a while he might have to tweak it to make it current.

One of the things most songwriters like about the "new Nashville" is that they are not locked into a country format. Most of the songwriters in this study like the crossover blend of modern music. This tends to be more prevalent among young songwriters than seasoned ones; still, only a handful of seasoned songwriters were 100 percent country,[55] but even these acknowledge there is no such thing anymore as pure country. "Stylistically the country music world is larger," says Mark Irwin, "the genre has blurred." Michelle Pereira says pretty much the same thing: "Country these days is so broad." Almost all tend to see themselves as songwriters first and then, perhaps, country songwriters: "I have never considered myself a type of writer—country, pop, whatever. I just write songs. I just want to write songs that are good enough to fit anywhere."[56] Jaida Dreyer (Y) had a number of country records hit the charts and, at the time of the interview, had a song on hold with rapper Eminem because, she says, "I write from all ends of the spectrum."

Indeed, a good 60-plus percent of those in this study, despite being in Nashville, don't define themselves as country songwriters at all, or only occasional country songwriters. In part, this is related to developments in the Nashville music scene as more and more artists and producers move to Nashville from other areas of the country that are not strongly committed to the country genre. This influx of "outsiders" is remarked on positively by most in this study. This may be at least partially attributable to the fact that few in this study, and none of the songwriters, were actually from Nashville. But it is also because these non-songwriting musical transplants are helping to revitalize the music scene beyond its country roots. There is nothing new about this since it was a part of the music crossover legacy of 1950s and 1960s country: the Everly Brothers, Brenda Lee, and Conway Twitty, for example. However, during the 1970s, and certainly during the 1980s and 1990s, Nashville drifted into a more narrowly defined country base which it is now (2010-plus) moving away from, though, of course, country remains the prevalent genre. It is worth pointing out that Christian music has a strong presence in the Nashville area,[57] and Christian music represents 6.6 percent of the overall U. S. market.[58]

One of the reasons for the broader base that even the seasoned writers are following is because the young people they work with are more open to other-than-country music. "When I was younger," Mark Irwin (S) says, "if you liked country, you listened to country. If you liked pop, you listened to pop. Now people listen to a little bit of everything."

"There are six or seven young writers," says Marc Beeson (S), "who really kick ass. I wasn't anywhere near as good as they are when I was in my twenties. They are much more aware of what is happening in contemporary music."

Benita Hill (S), who made her bones with "Two Piña Coladas," makes a respectable living today working with "self-sufficient artists who do it all themselves," and most "of the younger artists have a pretty good idea of what their direction is." At the time of the interview Garth Brooks had just recorded another of Hill's songs, and she was working with a young Canadian artist on some techno dance music.

The Transformation of a Song

The collaborative aspect of music production is addressed by sociologists John Ryan and Richard Peterson, but their definition of collaboration does not underscore the teamwork dimension so much as how other hands get involved and indiscriminately change the music. "Songs," they write, "are often rewritten or reinterpreted at several points"[59] along the continuum, and the songwriter appears to exercise little lyrical control over the song penned. "Words may be changed or whole verses cut," they say, quoting S.F. Siman,[60] and then go on to add that, "[e]ven if words are not added, cut, or altered at [the production stage], the meaning of the song is inevitably shaped and interpreted by the way it is recorded. As a courtesy, songwriters are usually allowed to be present during the recording session of their songs, but the writer is not expected to make any comments on how to render it properly."[61]

The implication of their study, even if the authors occasionally qualify their remarks, suggests that once the song leaves the songwriter's hands, it may be transformed into something unrecognizable by the songwriter. Such drastic changes do happen, but they are rare. The songwriters in this study all exercise at least a degree of creative control over their product.[62] Some changes they recognize as necessary, but these tend to be modest, and they all are concerned that the "integrity" of the song remains intact.

In fact, a recurring concern of the songwriters in this study was the necessity to maintain the integrity of the song, by which they meant the inherent meaning of the song. Thornton Cline, for example, wrote a song titled, "Bottom of the Fifth." It is a play on words about a father who drank too much and missed his son's baseball game. To change that to "Top of the Fourth," or even "Bottom of the Sixth," would totally destroy the integrity of the lyrics. However, Cline did have one song changed: a gospel artist changed the pronouns from the plural couple, "you and me," to the higher power singular "He." They had to get Cline's permission to change it.

Songwriters put a lot of sweat and tears into their lyrics and don't like them to be tampered with, in large part because the songs are a part of them. The songs, any number of songwriters said, come from your heart and are likened by John Berry to "the soundtrack of your life." This does not mean that once the integrity of the song is ensured, they are not open to stylistic changes. Most realize that changes may be necessary and that acceding to them increases the chances of the song being recorded.

Some artists Jennifer Schott works with might say to her, "'I am not sure this is what I want, can we look at this [this way or that]?' I love that because I want to write a song that feels right to the artist and that they want to record." Another seasoned songwriter mentions a song by Keith Urban on his 2017 album. He didn't know exactly what the problem was, but for some reason Urban had an issue with a specific verse in a song, so he had the writers rewrite the verse once or twice before finally cutting it.[63] More often than not, Mark Irwin (S) says, "artists are very respectful of the writers. They really know how valuable a hit song is. I have never encountered an artist that changed something without notifying me."

The changes that typically happen are not to the lyrics so much as minor modification in the song's production. The tempo might be increased or decreased to market likes and dislikes, or the artist might pace the song differently to his or her style. It was common in the past for studio musicians to add a riff to a song and the riff was kept because it enhanced the song, which is why Bryan Hill (S) is "not too picky about the vocals or [production] tinkering" of his songs, but, he hastens to add, "occasionally they will want to change the lyrics a little," and he'll try to oblige but "I like to have the opportunity to fix it myself."

Irwin is naturally concerned about his share of the royalties because if the artist changes anything the artist gets co-writing credit; nevertheless, Irwin is just as concerned that the song's integrity be maintained, though what stylistically takes place in the studio is not a major issue. The impact of studio musicians on the style of the song is less pronounced today because many of the younger writers are also adept at making a solid sounding demo by using home recording devices, and the demo sound may be so smooth that it is released intact in the final version.[64] Indeed, for Mark Irwin, the perfect blend is a three-way: a young person who can build the track, a writer, and a writer who can sing, so that the trio can have a demo at the end of the day with a vocal.

It should be pointed out that most of the young songwriters are just as adamant about maintaining the integrity of the song they've written. Drew Kennedy doesn't care how production "dresses up the song," but he doesn't want them messing with the lyrics that he's worked hard on to make them intelligent, creative, and unique. Adam Wood doesn't like to make compromises on the lyrics he is working on with a co-writer because "once you start making compromises, you end up with stuff that is very vanilla."

A number of songwriters, both young and seasoned, link a song's integrity to its commercial viability. These are not antithetic terms. "Hey, Jude," after all, Bart Herbison remarks, "was a commercial song." And, we might add, not only was "Hey, Jude" critically and commercially successful but also deviated in no radical sense, either lyrically or melodically, from many other songs of the day. Creativity does not mean that it involves the production of novel products, which Michael Mumford finds to be the general consensus of songwriters today.[65] Indeed, at least in music, something too novel is likely to falter. People like the familiar, so any song that steps too wide of what people are used to is not likely to succeed.

In a provocative article, "The Same Old Song," the authors argue that, "the emphasis on novelty in the music domain, by consumers and people protesting the current [staid] state of the music business, is misplaced."[66] Their pilot study found that, despite laments by music listeners that they'd like to hear newer music, they preferred the familiar. Their lyrical findings are based on a series of experiments conducted by Robert Zajonc in the 1960s,[67] and which have been widely replicated: people respond more positively to stimuli they are familiar with than to unfamiliar stimuli. This explains why people like similar but different music. The popular online video, "4 Chords," Derek Thompson points out, shows that the same chord progression (I-V-vi-IV) provides the backbone of dozens of classic songs.[68] Several critics have used videos like "4 Chords" to lambast the derivative nature of contemporary music, though Thompson appropriately counters that, while "Don't Stop Believin'" and "No Woman, No Cry," use the same chords, they don't sound anything alike. Successful songwriters, then, build on the familiar while at the same time varying the lyrics/melody/style to make them stand out from the crowd. To manage that is an art.

Professional Rights Organizations: Royalties and the Future of Songwriting

"The point is to make money, not art," Ryan and Peterson quoted one music publisher, as if there was something shallow with this approach.[69] One can still maintain the integrity of the song and make the song commercial; without the latter, the song is stillborn. One songwriter made the point quite nicely, at the same time refuting the starving artist myth: you cannot write if your stomach is growling.

The heyday 1990s was the high mark with many of the major publishing houses having a staff of one hundred-some writers because the recording industry was booming and needing songs to feed the machine. "When 2000 hit," says Benita Hill, "it was the end of songwriting as we knew it." Hill is referring to the collapse of album sales and the move toward streaming, both of which have cut dramatically into the ability of songwriters to make a good living, compared to the 1990s when, by all accounts, one could make $80,000-plus a year from newly released songs (even if they weren't a number one) with residuals from older songs adding another $20,000 to $50,000.

Most of the seasoned songwriters lament the issue with royalties today; the younger ones less so: "I've no experience as to how it used to be," says Adam Wood. "I wasn't around then, so I scramble with what is now." The younger songwriters in this study are getting their music out there through various internet sites, but compensation is thin to non-existent. The various platforms are used to garner attention. All of the younger songwriters except one were attempting to get a publishing deal. This would provide them with a steady, if modest, income stream that would allow them to concentrate on their craft in order to hopefully get enough songs placed to at least recoup the draw, and maybe make a few dollars beyond that.

There are three main reasons why the income stream has changed for songwriters. First, the number one slot has become more coveted because that is really the only way songwriters can make any money. Prior to 2000, a songwriter could have a song on an album and make some livable money off their song because there were 8-12 songs on an album. Now, unless the song goes to the number one slot, an album credit is just a plaque on the wall.[70]

Second, the labels have started to take cuts on aspects of the music business that once were outside their domain in order to shore up their bottom line in a shrinking market.[71] This is referred to as a 360 deal. The label now takes cuts of the ticket sales and merchandise, formerly the exclusive domain of the artists, and a share of the songwriting royalty—with three writers, often at least one being pushed from the producer's in-house staff writers, the label gets a bigger piece of the songwriters' cut. What might once have been fifty-fifty now is divided into thirds, with one-third going to the in-house staff writer.[72]

Third, of course, is the self-serving adage advocated by downloading and streaming sites such as Spotify and Pandora that "music should be free." NSAI, along with the professional rights organizations (PROs), as well as other songwriter advocacy groups (Recording Industry Association of America and National Music Publishers' Association) have been actively lobbying for responsible remuneration to songwriters whose songs are downloaded or streamed in much the same manner songwriters are compensated when their songs are performed on radio. This finally occurred when President Trump signed the Music Modernization Act (MMA) on October 11, 2018.

The MMA was unanimously approved by both the House and Senate. It is considered "the most sweeping reform to copyright law in decades."[73] There are multiple royalty issues the MMA addresses,[74] but its primary purpose is to adapt copyright law to the rapidly changing musical landscape. The new licensing system, Nate Rau writes, "will be better for songwriters and lead to better royally payouts when their songs are played on Spotify, Apple Music or other streaming services."[75] The MMA is a timely development and a major step forward for songwriters of country music because research by the Country Music Association (CMA) indicates country music fans, who have not embraced streaming to the degree fans in other genres have, are likely to do so in the not-too-distant future and that streaming of country music is "primed for significant growth."[76] The organizations with primary responsibility for collecting and distributing royalties to songwriters and publishers are Professional Rights Organizations (PROs).[77]

The three prominent PROs are the American Society of Composers, Authors and Publishers (ASCAP); Broadcast Music, Inc. (BMI); and the Society of European Stage Authors and Composers,[78] which since 1940 has gone simply by the acronym SESAC since it now represents authors and composers outside of Europe. ASCAP is perhaps the best known and largest of the PROs in no small part because it was founded in 1919 in Great Britain and began collecting license fees from broadcasters in 1931. Antitrust lawsuits in the early 1940s along with a period during which broadcasters refused to play ASCAP because of a dispute about royalties led recently launched BMI to gain traction. BMI focused on country and R&B songwriters and publishers since this group did not have a strong presence with ASCAP, who leaned toward pop music in the Tin Pan Alley tradition. BMI's initial emphasis on country gave it a strong presence in this market that continues today, though both ASCAP and BMI, along with SESAC, represent a wide range of genres.

ASCAP is a not-for-profit PRO while BMI is a non-profit. The distinction is a slim one for the purpose of this discussion;[79] the main difference is that SESAC, founded in New York in 1930, is a for-profit PRO and, therefore, is not subject to the same regulations imposed on ASCAP and BMI. SESAC is the smallest and most exclusive of the three PROs because membership, at least today, is by invitation only while the other two are open to registering anyone who wishes to join their organization, so a budding "songwriter" in WallaWalla, Washington, can register online with either ASCAP or BMI for a modest license fee and call themselves an ASCAP or BMI songwriter, even if they have only written one song and it has never seen the light of day.

Collecting royalties is one purpose of the PROs; another is to increase the royalties songwriters and music publishers receive. SESAC "Score[d] a Big Win in Radio Royalty Dispute," *The Tennessean* headline justly shouted in 2017 because its songwriters will see a rate 50 percent higher than the one set by a federal rate court.[80] The increase for SESAC members will likely be used by ASCAP and BMI to urge similar rate increases for their members. In related advocacy for its members, BMI won a drawn-out two-year battle with the Department of Justice which had earlier ruled that any owner of a composition's copyright could license it without the approval of the other owners of a song, a decision made under the Obama administration that those in the industry felt went against standard consent agreements. In fact, the Copyright Royalty Board ruled in 2018 to increase the percentage of revenue that streaming companies must pay to songwriters and publishers from 10.5 percent to 15.1 percent over the next five years. Amazon and Spotify have appealed the new rate hike: Apple Music, the world's second most popular streaming service behind Spotify, elected not to challenge the ruling.[81]

The primary responsibility of the PROs is to monitor broadcasts and performances of music by their members and to ensure that royalties are appropriately collected and dispensed (record sales, called "mechanicals" in the trade, are regulated under the United States Constitution and collected and dispersed by the record labels).[82] ASCAP had a record year in 2017; it was the first time it distributed over $1 billion in royalty revenue to songwriters and publishers.[83] In order to be compensated for the songs that are performed, a songwriter must be registered with one of the PROs, and they can only register with one of them. Music publishers, on the other hand, whose songwriters might be associated with any one of the three, can register with all three

PROs. The songwriters in this study tend to reflect the general composition of the various PROs in Nashville: both BMI and ASCAP were divided, roughly equally (45/45); the remaining 10 percent were associated with SESAC. If there was any distinction between members of the two giant PROs, slightly more of the seasoned writers in this study were associated with BMI, which is not surprising given their strong country-brand association, while slightly more of the younger writers were associated with ASCAP, perhaps because younger writers cross diverse genres and ASCAP is not as strongly associated with country as is BMI.

The PROs do not just monitor performance airplay; they actively solicit and help the writers who are their members. The focus of this section on songwriters is 1) why the songwriters decided to associate with the PRO with which they are registered, and 2) how the PROs actively recruit and help their songwriters. Since the two larger PROs vie with one another for members, more so than with SESAC, one would assume they are intensively competitive, which they are, but in the best Nashville tradition, in a very collegiate way. Both ASCAP and BMI encourage prospective members to "check out" their competitor before deciding which to join. They clearly "pitch" their strong points, but this pitching does not stretch to denigrating their rival.

The same friendly rivalry holds for SESAC which, because of its focus on established writers, tends to entice writers away from one of its rivals. The Nashville "network" is quick to spread information about writers who are dissatisfied with their existing relationship. This is clearly seen in the next chapter on music publishers. It holds here as well. In general, writers may feel they are not getting the attention they desire from their PRO and thus might be "looking around"—two of the writers in this study were considering changing their PRO at the time the interview was conducted. SESAC has a strong enticement: they are smaller and can accentuate their more personal ties with their songwriters more so than the other two, whose buildings straddle either side of the entrance to Music Row. SESAC can also enunciate its exclusivity, giving the writers the sense that they are special in even being considered for membership in the SESAC fraternity.

The rationale driving the songwriter's association with the PRO chosen is very ad hoc. One-third of the songwriters in this study, leaning more heavily toward the younger ones, "just picked" the PRO they did because they had to be registered with one to obtain royalties. Not that the other songwriters in this study weighed the advantages and disadvantages of their choice. More often than not, the PRO selected was based on a personal connection, which is to say, they "clicked" with the PRO rep they met. The breaking point for one songwriter was that he was offered a cold bottle of Coca-Cola on a hot summer day; another went with the one selected because the other didn't return their call while the one chosen immediately responded.

Sometimes inducements helped tip the balance: one of the PROs offered a $500 signing bonus to a seasoned writer; another offered a weekend songwriter retreat in Key West for a young songwriter. It should be pointed out that such enticements are still offered but only in those rare exceptions where the songwriter shows special talent. One representative at BMI recognized the talent of the young man she was chatting with and picked up the phone and started setting up meetings with publishers. This kind of proactive soliciting is done but it is not typical. When it is done, the rep has a strong sense of the person's talent and feels confident that he or she is not unnecessarily burning network bridges. This may be why many of the music publishers contacted by a PRO representative respond: they know that if they are soliciting on behalf of one of their writers, the person must have some solid talent. SESAC may be in the best position to establish these songwriter-publisher/label referrals because it is smaller and does not call on its contacts as much as might occur among the larger PROs, though the larger ones still cautiously make these types of introductions.

The PROs all staunchly support their active members.[84] They all have special events for their songwriters. All sponsor writers' nights at the Bluebird and other venues around town. ASCAP and BMI have very extravagant annual award nights for their writers. SESAC sponsors the annual week-long Tin Pan South performances put on by NSAI.

PROs also all provide personal and financial aid when needed, the former being more pronounced than the latter. One of the young songwriters in this study had a number one hit but couldn't pay the rent since it would be months before royalties would start to accrue; the PRO in question advanced her the money to pay her bills until royalty checks began to appear. In this sense, they not only work to get their writers, they work to keep them. And it is work, for those that think in terms of nine to five hours, or going out "partying" to clubs to catch new acts is all fun, fun, fun. Like the songwriters, there is a lot of work and effort involved in acquiring new writers and maintaining existing relationships. BMI and ASCAP reps, more so than SESAC reps, who rely more on referrals from one of their existing songwriters, are out nightly at shows trying to identify and sign new talent. Bradley Collins, head of creative at BMI, comments on his hours: "I work nine to five [at the office] and then from five to midnight [going to writers' rounds] five nights a week."

Conclusion

Songwriters in the popular arena are given sparse attention, largely because many people assume that the artist performing the song also wrote the song. In Nashville, the songwriter is widely acknowledged by other members of the artistic community as *the* most important individual who contributes to the making of music in Music City. This helps explain why a songwriter's lyrics does not undergo a dramatic transformation as the song moves along the production continuum. Minor changes might occur to accommodate the artist or popular taste (adding horns, for example), but these changes are more stylistic than lyrically driven.

Nashville has long been associated with music, and, for nearly half a century, with country music, even if Nashville has always supported a wide range of musical genres. The synergy that is associated with Nashville has fostered the making of music in the Nashville environs. Just being a songwriter in Nashville defines one as seriously pursuing one's career. The songwriters in this study, roughly 10 percent of the contemporary songwriting community in Nashville, all came to Nashville because they were serious about pursuing their career. Most came to Nashville after finishing college, though approximately 25 percent delayed their journey to pursue the artist side of the artist-songwriter dichotomy and made a respectable living playing clubs. To move further along in their career, however, these individuals eventually journeyed to Nashville because, to paraphrase comments made by innumerable songwriters, if you are serious about being a songwriter, you have to be in Nashville.

The Nashville connection is facilitated by the strong network that runs through the music community, and NSAI stands at the heart of helping young, recently arrived songwriters establish relationships. Connections are vital in many career pursuits but they are especially pronounced among songwriters, even more so today with the emphasis on co-writing. Young songwriters off the bus are encouraged to connect and write with other songwriters and perform at shows around town in order to get noticed. One would think that seasoned songwriters would not have to work as hard establishing a network because they have other songwriters they regularly write with, but seasoned songwriters find it productive to establish relationships with younger, up-and-coming songwriters. This relationship is advantageous to both parties. The younger songwriters get some input from the old hands that can help them hone their craft while the seasoned songwriters get to stay on the musical cutting edge. Any number of seasoned songwriters who mentioned some of their colleagues that have fallen by the wayside intimated that the once-prominent songwriters often faded into oblivion because they did not adjust to some of the new sounds the young songwriters brought with them.

The network for young and seasoned songwriters is strengthened by writers' rounds. The younger songwriters get the opportunity to present their material and see what their colleagues are doing. The seasoned songwriters are more selective in the rounds they attend, but they nevertheless both participate and attend rounds to keep their hand in. The small songwriting community lends itself to personal relationships. At the very least, rounds help people get acquainted with their colleagues. At most, they allow songwriters to establish co-writing relationships with people they didn't previously know, or only heard about. And, of course, co-writing helps strengthen ties with others, especially given the tendency to reveal one's inner thoughts while lyrically parading their lives in front of another songwriter. Indeed, the dynamics of opening up with a co-writer tends to accelerate self-disclosure, and this gets people to connect on a personal level quicker than they might in ordinary conversation. Co-writing with an artist, though it might cut into one's royalties, also has its advantages because the artist is more committed to the song and the songwriter works with the artist to make the song work for them, enhancing the potential that the song will get cut.

Since the public does not separate songwriters from artists, it is understandable that the public tends to feel they don't have to pay for downloads since the artist is handsomely rewarded through record and concert sales. NSAI feels that it is next to impossible to educate the public about this separation and how songwriters are not adequately compensated in today's market. This is why royalties have long been a big issue among songwriters and why organizations such as ASCAP, BMI, and SESAC stand as guardians to ensure songwriters are duly compensated for their works. Along with NSAI, they have been at the forefront of lobbying Washington to try to get compensation for songs on newer formats, such as Spotify, that don't fall under the traditional royalty agreement. Their joint lobbying effort resulted in the Music Modernization Act in 2018.

The PROs do much more than collect royalties, however. They are major advocates for their members and help them move forward in their career. Both the organization and their members benefit from the relationship: if their artists do well, they do well. And even though the various PROs vie for members, they do so with respect for their counterparts, which, considering the intimate interconnection of the local music network, is the way business is expected to transpire in the Nashville marketplace.

2

MUSIC PUBLISHING

The Bridge to Somewhere

It may all begin with a song, but the song has to get to someone who, in turn, will produce it for popular consumption. The music publisher stands at this critical junction. The days of walking into a label and handing someone a song are long gone, if, in fact, they ever existed to the degree some in the music business reminisce about. Executives at record labels don't have time to look at every over-the-transom submission. They, like others in the cultural industry, rely on gatekeepers to prescreen material.[1] The gatekeeper standing between the writer and the book publisher is the literary agent. Substituting for the literary agent in the music industry is the music publisher. However, unlike a literary agent, who screens a host of submitted manuscripts to decide which to send to a publisher, music publishers actually hire the songwriter and work with them to hone their songs before "pitching" them to a producer.

Considering the pivotal role that music publishers play, they have received surprisingly little attention outside some esoteric studies that have examined the role of music publishers in Renaissance England (circa 1500) and during the Restoration in England (circa 1660–1680), in Naples, circa 1780–1820, in France during the 1820s, or even in contemporary Lithuania after 1990.[2] What attention is paid music publishers in the United States outside industry reports is generally confined to brief excerpts of who's doing what in business trade journals, such as *Billboard* or *Music Week*. Industry reports, however, reveal the critical role played by music publishers.

Nashville, among major metropolitan areas, is ahead of New York and Los Angeles[3] in revenue generated through music publishing: $1.1 billion, 1 billion, and 725.8 million, respectively.[4] Much of the revenue in the Nashville market

(83 percent) is generated by the big three labels (Sony, Universal and Warner), all of which also have strong publishing arms. Still, the number of firms that employ less than ten people is comparable to New York and LosAngeles: all hover around 97 percent. The number of independents is one reason why this analysis focuses on small (less than ten employees) and mid-sized (ten to forty-nine employees) companies. Conversations with songwriters and music publishers suggest that the larger music publishers are not much different from the independents with the exception that larger music publishers employ more songwriters and those songwriters are more focused on writing for in-house artists. Interestingly, the in-house association only slightly skews the major labels to favor their own songwriters; they are nevertheless all open to considering songs by songwriters from the independent publishers. The reason for this is very simple: the best lyrics win, no matter who writes them or where they come from.

There are quite a few independent, small to mid-size publishers in Nashville. *Music Row Magazine*, a trade publication, lists 279 music publishers after the Big Three (and their subsidiaries) have been discounted. The listed publishers are largely located in the Nashville market. This is a fair number of publishing companies, despite what Arnold Broido wrote in a 1977 *Music Educators Journal.* "Someone [*sic*] recently pointed out that in the last twenty-five years, at least fifty-five publishing companies have vanished as independent entities, leaving only a handful of major companies still functioning."[5] Many veterans of Music Row today lament the same thing that Broido wrote back then: once, to paraphrase any number of people in the business who were interviewed in the course of this study, record producers and publishing houses were knee-deep along Music Row and ran without interruption up and down 16th and 17th Avenue from Magnolia Boulevard to Demonbreun (a one-mile stretch in either direction).

It is certainly true that there are fewer publishing houses along Music Row, but then record production has declined significantly, as well. It is not a one directional downward slide, either. While any number of music publishers have folded over the years, others have emerged, in no small part because the music business is still characterized by relative ease of entry. The lower cost of establishing a presence—more so than other entertainment formats, such as television and the motion picture industry—facilitates new ventures[6]

The bungalows and four-square houses along Music Row also do not provide enough space for many publishers today, especially for the increasing number of independent businesses.[7] Many publishers have moved off the 16th–17th Avenue South corridor to neighboring areas where real estate is somewhat more reasonably priced. For example, HoriPro, which only a few years ago was situated just a block off Music Row on 15th Avenue South, is now in the Berry Hill area, three miles east of Music Row, the same area as 3 Ring Circus. SNC Music is one-and-a-half miles northwest of Music Row; Tree Vibez, which is, ironically, promoting T-shirts embossed to "Save Music Row,"[8] is a half a dozen blocks north of Music Row on Hayes Street. As such, today's Music Row has less to do with a physical location and more a mentality toward making music. Regardless of where they are located in the greater Nashville environs, music business people in Nashville continue to embrace the cooperative, interconnective attitude toward making music that is generally lauded as a bygone facet of Music Row.

Aligning with a Publisher

All the seasoned songwriters looked at in the last chapter had publishing contracts, even if they might have changed publishers a number of times during their career. The younger songwriters, with one or two exceptions, either had a publishing deal or would give their eyeteeth for one. The primary attraction of a publishing arrangement for songwriters is that it provides a draw (an income stream offered by the publisher in advance against royalties). Both sides hope the income generated will go beyond the draw, and the draw today is modest.

Many seasoned songwriters and publishers intimate that a draw of $80,000 to $100,000 was common in the heyday 1990s, at least among the major labels. A draw today can range widely depending on the size of the company and the credentials of the songwriter. A young songwriter signing with a small independent publisher may get around $20,000; at a mid-size company a seasoned songwriter who has some solid success behind them and is still in vogue may command $40,000.[9] Most contemporary songwriters appreciate a modest draw because they don't threaten the company's bottom line if they have a soft year.

Songwriters who demand top dollar are likely to be the first to go when they don't produce since the money comes from the publisher's pocket. There is also a good chance that the publisher doesn't recoup any of the money advanced. "Okay, you have a new writer and you put them on a draw for $25,000 and sign them for two years," Butch Baker says. "You've got $50,000 invested in a writer but it's not just $50,000—you have demo costs involved, trip costs on places you sent them; you could have $70,000 to $90,000 invested and at the end of two years you have nothing to show for it, and they never have to pay back a dime." This is perhaps one reason that an alternative to a draw has gained popularity in the last few years (post-2015); rather than a draw, writers are offered a percent of the publishing royalties if and when a song is released.[10] This type of an arrangement may be appreciated by a new writer who otherwise doesn't have a track record sufficient to command a draw. Then there are co-publishing deals[11] where the songwriters get their share of the royalties for writing the song but they also get half of what the publisher gets. This means the publisher is making only 25 percent profit off of a charted song. These types of arrangements are most likely to occur when the songwriter has a solid track record and the publisher has confidence that they will pick up 25 percent, and 25 percent of something is better than zero percent of nothing. However the deal is cut, publishers recoup their draw from the songwriter's share of any royalties.

Performance royalties come from how often the song is performed publicly—on the radio, in a bar or restaurant, by the artist on a tour. Tour-generated income is a major income stream for artists, but the royalties from the songs sung don't constitute much for the songwriter or publisher. Mechanicals, on the other hand, are royalties collected and paid out by the record companies based on the sale of a song on an album or legal digital download. This seems pretty straightforward, but there are always qualifiers. John Barker, who makes his living keeping track of the intricacies of royalty regulations, hints at the complexities of mechanical royalties.[12]

> Mechanicals! Well, that can get complicated. Mechanical is reproduction rights for sound only. That can happen with a record company [that physically releases a record]. It can also happen with a car company that has a chip that they put in and you can play the music while driving. It can even happen with a music box: you pay mechanicals on the music played on the music box [or song ringtones on a cell phone]. And then there is streaming; that is mechanical, too. So, mechanicals are anyone who owns the reproduction rights of that sound. The record company, of course, makes money from the distribution of streaming. They don't call that mechanical, however; they call that record income.
>
> So, if I [as a record company] sell 10,000 units to Walmart, they are going to pay me, but I am going to owe 9.1 cents per unit[13] to the publisher, or co-publisher, depending if there are twelve songs on a unit and some of those writers have co-publishers, which mean there can be forty or fifty entities I have to pay. That's mechanics, too. But as a record company, when I receive my royalties from Walmart or Spotify, that is considered a product royalty.

The main source of income for songwriters and publishers today is performance royalties from terrestrial (AM/FM) radio, especially in today's market where album sales via Walmart and other retail outlets has drastically shrunk. A number one song, therefore, is the ultimate goal for both the songwriter and publishers, and in country music radio is king. "It's a very singles-driven market. You have to have those hits," says Mike Hollandsworth, who articulates the views made by any number of industry professionals. "It's the 800-pound gorilla," another publisher said. "Everyone wants a number one record. It solves a lot of problems" because it can keep the company afloat and pay for the draw the other writers receive until, with luck, one of them hits in their turn.

There is no hurry to reach the coveted number one slot, however. A "slow-burn" is preferred. A slow-burn is a song that doesn't slot too quickly to number one; instead, the song slowly works its way up the chart, peaks for a few weeks at number one, then slowly moves down and eventually off the chart. A song that "lingers" for 20 weeks on the chart generates some solid royalties for both the songwriter and the publisher. Performance royalty is monitored and collected by the PROs the songwriter and publisher are aligned with.

Publishers can also be reimbursed from royalties paid the songwriter for any expenses they might have incurred producing the record; usually, costs associated with making the demo, or related hard costs associated with making the record. A current number one hit could earn somewhere between $175,000 to $275,000. If the songwriter had a $40,000 draw and the publisher had laid out another $3,000 in costs to get a quality demo cut, the songwriter would pay the publisher $43,000 from his or her share of the royalties.

The publisher has to have a lot of faith that the writer they sign has the talent to produce at least enough to reimburse them for the draw paid out. This is especially important for small independent publishers who might have anywhere from three to eight writers under contract. Even with a modest $20,000 draw, the out-of-pocket expenses can add up to some serious money for the publisher even before normal overhead expenses necessary to keep a business functioning. To minimize their risk, contracts typically run for a year or two with a one- to two-year renewal clause.

The contract typically specifies that the songwriter write a certain number of songs during any given year—typically eight to ten "100 percent" songs, so if the songwriter co-writes a song with another it only counts as "half" a contractual song. This minimal commitment ensures that the songwriter doesn't go off and play golf all day on the publisher's nickel. Most songwriters typically exceed this minimal requirement. In fact, it is not uncommon for a songwriter to write fifty or more songs in a year. Since it's a numbers game, the more songs you write, the better your chances of getting one cut. Fifty songs give one a lot better chance of finding a song that "lands" than eight songs a year.

Another revenue stream is sync (synchronization) fees: money earned when the song is licensed for use to synchronize with television and movies.[14] The problem is that television and film don't use much country music and tend to rely more heavily on rock and pop, so sync revenues for country publishers are relatively modest.[15] Another issue relating to sync fees, pointed out by Marc Driskill at Sea Gayle, is that Nashville songwriters are not geared to sitting down to write brief fifteen- to thirty-second pieces to specifications; e.g., say this or that about a product.[16]

Publishers also gain from having songwriters under contract because they control the copyright to the song. This means the publisher, rather than the songwriter, makes decisions regarding where to place the song. The songs written are considered part of the publisher's catalogue, and every publisher, Butch Baker says, has something in their catalogue that they cannot believe hasn't been cut. Catalogues are the songs written by the songwriter while they are under contract with a specific publisher; these songs are owned by that publisher, who ultimately decides who records the song for the first time.[17] This is because the publishers are the ones with the inside track as to who might be looking for a song or who a song would "fit." Sometimes, to clinch a deal with a publisher, the songwriter will offer some preexisting songs to the publisher, who then effectively owns them. This kind of arrangement is called a "Schedule A."

Placing a song is, as will be demonstrated later in this chapter, a science in itself. The publisher's role in placing a song frees the songwriter from this tedious and time-consuming responsibility of shopping the song, which allows them to concentrate on their craft. As long as the publisher remains in business, it controls the copyright of the writer's songs, even if the publisher and writer have parted ways. John Ozier at Olé calls these "legacy catalogues."

In fact, controlling the catalogue is sometimes one of the attractions of a larger company buying a smaller one, because there might be some hidden gems—songs which haven't been mined but which the publisher might be able to exploit. Money from a sale like this only lines the pockets of the original publisher, who is effectively transferring any subsequent publishing royalties to the song to the purchasing company. After the sale, royalties go to the writer and the new publisher. The writer continues to garner 50 percent of the royalties regardless of who owns (controls) the song. A songwriter's song that a publisher later resurrects is advantageous to both parties: the publisher benefits if the song subsequently lands, as does the songwriter, whose song may have remained in limbo had the publisher not picked it up and run with it. John Ozier explains:

> When we buy a catalogue, we don't just sit on it. We get out and pitch it. Whenever we can get some of those unexplored songs recorded, it is cash. For example, I have a song [from a recent catalogue purchase] that is seven or eight years old that was cut a couple months ago by Kid Rock. We had another song that was written in 2008 that ended up on Chris Stapleton's last record that just blew up. Great songs are always great. What we do is repurpose them. We may have a song that was written in 1980 that might be great but the recording isn't, so it got overlooked. We might not be able to sell the song as recorded so we go back and redo it.

The purchase of a catalogue from another publisher is not without its downside, however. More than a few publishers referred to catalogue purchases as "fuzzy math." The fuzziness is the questionable merit of the songs in the catalogue. Songs that are hits have a drop-off phase. Profit from any hit song tends to go down from year to year, and it is difficult to determine how sharp that downspin will be, leading to a certain amount of "fuzziness"—it may be valuable at the moment but how long the value will be maintained is moot. It is also difficult to determine the potential profits from songs in the pipeline since just being in the pipeline does not mean the songs will be cut or, if they are, be profitable. There may be some hidden gems in the catalogue that the new publishing firm may be able to exploit, as John Ozier has done at Olé, but that is the great unknown. The new catalogue owner might notice an overlooked song that they are able to resuscitate, but the converse is just as likely and the song might be dead because it is a dud, which is why the initial publisher was not able to develop it in the first place.[18]

The songwriters themselves may decide to sell their copyright to a publisher when their songs are no longer providing an income, provided, of course, that the songs were written when not under contract with a publisher. John Chisum, a Christian music songwriter, had a catalogue of more than 400 songs he wrote or co-wrote. At their peak (1990s), the songs generated around $50,000 a year, but that had dwindled to $5,000 by 2017. He made an arrangement with a Denver-based company called Royalty Exchange to auction off his share of the songs he wrote over a forty-year career. It was, he tells Nate Rau at *The Tennessean*, a very emotional decision because of his attachment to the songs.[19] Chisum anticipated receiving about $15,000 for his songbook; the final bid was just over $45,000. The company that purchased Chisum's catalogue obviously felt there were some gems in it, or, more likely for institutional investors (versus publishing companies), songbooks have a fairly long shelf life and can generate a steady, if modest, income over time. Selling one's copyright goes against the conventional wisdom of the music industry but it is becoming an increasingly popular way for a songwriter to generate some needed cash when the songs are no longer producing a significant income.[20]

The Publishing Career Ladder

The average age for the publishers interviewed was fifty-something, and the majority arrived in Nashville during the 1980s, before the boom 1990s. Family background was not instrumental to shaping career paths. More germane to the publisher's career path was their knowledge of the industry. Family may have influenced their interest in music but it had little direct bearing on their ultimate decision to move into publishing.

In those instances where family background was raised, it tended to parallel the family history of most songwriters: a good two-thirds had a parent or family member who was either a professional or recreational musician or who was musically attuned: e.g., one publisher's father worked at a radio station. In contrast to the parents of young songwriters, only one publisher was encouraged to get a college degree in an unrelated area as a backup should their musical aspiration not work out. Back then, twenty to thirty years ago, a college diploma was not the necessary pathway to gaining entry into the workaday world, or at least not to the extent it is today.

The majority did go to college, however, and among those who did, three (12 percent) majored in music and another one went to a musical conservatory and went on to study classical music. At least a third who mention their initial musical aspirations performed as young artists in their teens (circa 1970s), the guitar being the favored instrument. Tony Harrell, now the general manager at MV2, won Keyboard Player of the Year a few years ago. When he reminiscences about his youthful infatuation with the artistic side, I am sure he speaks for many young men who followed this path in their adolescence. "In junior high I put my first band together; played at my first school assembly when fifteen. The girls went crazy. Knew then that [playing music] was what I wanted to do." Those who began their artistic journey as adolescents were more likely than the others in publishing to either continue their career as artists or became studio musicians after initially arriving in Nashville.

It is worth noting that there were no women publishers in this study. This may be attributed to the snowball effect, where men who were interviewed were more likely to refer me to other men who were publishers, though this was not a factor with young songwriters: a male or female songwriter was just as likely to refer me to another person of the same or opposite gender. More likely, it represents a historical male bias in the industry since one does not typically open a publishing house without some years in the business and a long, established professional network, and that network has been historically, albeit not exclusively, male.[21] This may be changing.

Many of the publishers had women in key positions on their staff and down the road these women, like the men in this study, might venture into publishing as they gain experience and make contacts. Bobby Rymer at Writer's Den hints that this may be likely when talking of his new, young creative director: "Sarah [Feldman] is out every night, sometimes multiple clubs in one night. I'm out some, but I'm not up to it like when I was young. She's very much on the cutting edge. She's making relationships; she knows the young writers that are out there. She's literally building her future right now."

A CROOKED PATH

The progressive ladder is laid out fairly clearly in many professions: one is employed as "x," works hard, is promoted to "y," shows their stuff, and moves up to "z." The only "progression" in music publishing—more so than book publishing—is that it is beneficial, but not necessary, to have some experience in the industry: you have to have an ear for the music and be able to recognize a potentially successful songwriter. The majority of publishers in this study had around twenty years of industry experience before they branched into publishing. Some stumbled into publishing because they were at the right place at the right time and were shrewd enough to take advantage of their good fortune. This study examines the career path of three publishers who took advantage of the break and three others who took the long way around. It can be estimated that between 50 to 60 percent fall into the former category with the balance in the latter. The ones critiqued are representative of those in their respective category.

Taking Advantage of the Break

Of all those in this study, Darrell Franklin took the most direct path to publishing. He had youthful aspirations to be an artist, but his father, a studio musician, sat him down and said that being an artist was not going to happen because he didn't have the passion to play. Franklin nevertheless credits his father with instilling in him a love for music; every Tuesday they went to Tower Records and selected music across a range of genres to listen to and discuss.

"You're passionate about music; I can see it in your face," his father told him. "You need to find your way in the music business." His father didn't know that much about the publishing business "but nudged me in that direction."

In 1982, Franklin attended the new music program at Belmont University and, of the three paths then offered, picked publishing. Though the program left something to be desired at the time,[22] he did manage to intern with one of the large independent publishers, which not only published country but also Christian and jazz music. He was one of only two people there who had a knowledge of music outside country, and his passion for all music served him well.

He was soon doing A&R but wanted to go directly to the writers. So he went to Windswept for a few years before BMG bought Windswept. Not long after, Franklin started 3 Ring Circus with producer Jeffrey Steele, who in 2013 was named to the Nashville Songwriter's Hall of Fame. The company is owned by Steele, who manages the songwriters that were with him before he started 3 Ring Circus, while Franklin concentrates on developing the other songwriters aligned with the company.

Michael Hollandsworth knew he wanted to be a songwriter at 13 because he loved music but, like Franklin, knew his limitation, which, he says laughing, meant he couldn't sing. Hollandsworth was one of the first to attend Middle Tennessee State University's (MTSU) then-new music program in the 1970s, which led to an internship at a Nashville publishing company. This experience made him realize that he also was not going to be a songwriter because he saw the talent he'd be up against. He stayed at Pi-gen for a while after completing his internship in the mid-1970s and when the executives at Pi-gen decided to start a small demo studio they asked Hollandsworth if he wanted to be the engineer. Although engineering was neither what he knew well nor the direction he wanted to go, he, of course, said, "Sure, I can do that." He was there a year when the company was sold and he "somehow" got the job starting the Nashville office of Dick James Music.[23] "I was just getting my feet wet as a junior song plugger," says Hollandsworth, "and here I was starting a company from scratch."

James died a few years later, leaving Hollandsworth looking for something new. His credentials running James's company led him to launch the Nashville arm of Fame, which was owned by Rick Hall from Muscle Shoals.[24] Rick told him when he took the job, "'Son, you and I are going to get into it and you're going to be so mad at me the next day you won't want to talk to me, and I'm gonna forget all of it.' Truer words were never spoken," says Hollandsworth, who was miserable for the eighteen months he was at Fame.

He left for a small little-known company from South Africa called Zomba (founded in 1975) that had recently opened an office in New York (1978). His timing was fortuitous because by 1990 Zomba was worth $225 million with over fifty companies, including Jive Records.[25] Besides his many ventures with Zomba, Hollandsworth was involved with Zomba's foray into the Christian music market with the purchase of the Brentwood Music Group in 1994 and, in 1997, another Brentwood Christian publisher, Benson Music.[26]

Hollandsworth was with Zomba for fifteen years, leaving in 2002: "It was a nice little run."[27] Toward the end, before the company was sold, Hollandsworth saw the writing on the wall. "It went from a comfortable, people-oriented company to a strictly money-oriented company." He lined up the songwriters' contracts to all expire within six months of one another and by the time he opened his own publishing company, Full Circle, six months after leaving Zomba, the songwriters who had been with Zomba followed Hollandsworth to Full Circle. "The agreement was, come over and have the exact same contract," in a more hassle-free environment.

During his tenure at Full Circle, the company claimed seven number one singles and twelve ASCAP and BMI awards, as well as cuts by artists such as Luke Bryan, Jason Aldean, Kenny Chesney and Tim McGraw. Full Circle is still a viable, functioning company, though Hollandsworth took a three-year sabbatical after selling Full Circle to HoriPro in 2014.[28] It was quite a run for a young man fresh out of the new music program at MTSU who only knew that he couldn't sing and, after a brief internship, also realized that he couldn't compete with all the songwriting talent in Nashville, and so stumbled into a long, respectable career in music publishing. In 2017, Mike Sebastian left relative newcomer Given Music to do independent consulting for music publishers[29] and Michael Hollandsworth reentered the game as Given Music's vice president and general manager.[30]

Bobby Rymer, like just about everyone in the music business, devoured records in his adolescence: not just the songs, but who wrote the lyrics, who produced the album, where the record was recorded. His first job in the business was in the mail room of Capitol Records, which may not sound like a very exciting job, but Rymer was thrilled: "It was like, 'Hey, man, I'm in the fucking music business.'" Capitol at the time handled Tanya Tucker, Barbara Mandrel, and Sawyer Brown; he was there when Garth Brooks was signed, and not long after was promoted to the A&R department. Then, around 1989, there was "a regime change," and he remembers someone coming in and saying, "'Welcome! You're now in the music business. You've been fired!' They pretty much let the whole staff go, so I was like, 'Uh-oh, what now'?" There turned out to be an opening at a small publishing company, Almo/Irving,[31] which Rymer looked at as a step back, since he would be returning to copying tapes, which was his entry level job at Capitol before he moved on to A&R. Still, he liked the people there and took the job, admitting "I didn't really know the publishing side at all. But it was a job, and I needed it."

Rymer's job at Almo/Irving was to copy tapes—make a cassette to showcase their songs so a label executive could hear them. "It's a really great job for anyone starting in a publishing company because you're going to learn the catalogue. Someone would come in and say, 'Put a cassette together for me in this order and get it ready to go.' There's only one way to learn a catalogue and that's to listen to it time and time and time again." After a short period being a tape copier, a position opened to be the one playing the cassette—the song pitcher, or plugger. "Then I got moved up to creative director, and eventually I was running the company." The progression from copying tapes to A&R might seem a leap, but Rymer says it really isn't since he got to know the catalogue and the writers. A&R, which is essentially promoting the songwriters, was a logical progression. The progression from A&R to publishing is a little more problematic. "I thought it would be easy because when you work in A&R you have your roster of things you need to take care of, but as a publisher you have to take care of everyone's roster," says John Ozier who, like Rymer, made the transition from A&R to publisher. Rymer was promoted to publisher by default after the then-president left to take a job at Mercury. When Rymer started with Almo/Irvin, the company had six songwriters; when he left fourteen years later, the company had twenty-six artists and writers. "Some you might know," he says modestly, "like Emmylou Harris, Patty Griffin, and Marty Stuart. I couldn't dream of a better training ground."

Then the cycle started over. He was at the helm for a little over a year when the company was sold in 2000 to Universal and, shortly thereafter, they merged their offices and "I was out [again]." Still, "they took care of me" with a nice severance package. He thought of starting his own company but a new label was starting up and wanted a publishing arm, so they brought Rymer in to start it. "Long story short, the owner of Montage closed the label but left the publishing arm alone." Rymer changed the name to Writer's Den rather than keep the name Montage "and be associated with the Titanic." But that was Writer's Den version one: the investor, an attorney from St. Louis, didn't fully understand the music business and decided to sell. Rymer, over a fortuitous lunch, found himself in sync with someone looking to invest in music publishing who appreciated the business and bought it, "lock, stock, and barrel." Rymer was able to bring the catalogue he helped build at Montage to Writer's Den, giving Writer's Den a solid foundation upon which to build. It is still Writer's Den, but as of 2013 it became Writer's Den version 2. "Life," Rymer insightfully concludes, "damn sure isn't a straight line." [32]

The Long Way Around

The individuals' stories in this section differ from the former only in that they did not as directly advance into publishing but had a somewhat lengthy career in other areas of the music business before they launched their publishing ventures. In that regard, they were more grounded in the music business before entering publishing. Nevertheless, there remains a certain amount of happenstance in their move into publishing which they, like Hollandsworth and Rymer, were astute enough to capitalize on.

It was quite some time before Barry Coburn started Ten Ten Music Group in Nashville. A New Zealander, Coburn learned a love for music from his father, who had a weekly radio show and a band that played in the Glenn Miller style. Coburn struck out on his own at the tender age of seventeen after the untimely death of his father. He played in a band for a while, then got a job at a record store, which led to him being hired in sales by one of the record companies. At twenty-one he headed to Australia and was soon lining up tours for Elton John, Duke Ellington, and Led Zeppelin. He arranged a fourteen-show tour for Black Sabbath, and that led to an endless stream of tours for acts like the Eagles, Neal Diamond, and Chuck Berry. He got in on the touring circuit just when the big tours were starting to happen and when "no one actually knew what they were doing." He got an early start because he knew "how to transport equipment, build stages, and do the big lighting." He did this for the next fourteen years. "I got a good reputation and I got to understand how to deal with people who were scarier than I and some who were crazier than I."

In 1984, he decided to venture to the United States. "I looked at New York, L.A., and Nashville." He ultimately decided on Nashville for the same reasons others have and still do: the social climate was better and the cost of living much more reasonable. He says he didn't really know country, but he had arranged tours for such luminaries as Roger Miller, Charlie Pride, and Emmylou Harris, so he did know something about country music. He was initially drawn to artist management and hooked up with Emmylou Harris's manager. "He managed Emmylou and I managed Lacy Dalton and together we formed Ten Ten Management." Coburn's big break came when his now-former wife[33] came back from Glen Campbell's studio where she had gone to pitch a Ten Ten song and said there was this guy he really had to hear. "This guy" was Alan Jackson at the beginning of his career. Jackson signed with Ten Ten Management in 1998 and released his first record in 1999. Coburn has also been involved in the careers of Diamond Rio, Suzy Boggs, and BR 5-49. Ten Ten Management morphed into Ten Ten Music Group along the way, a name more consistent with its broadened scope.[34]

Tony Harrell was inspired to go into music because he grew up in a musical family: his father played the mandolin, guitar, and banjo; his mother, the piano. He followed the traditional early path of many in the profession by playing in a high school band. Unlike Coburn, however, who soon abandoned playing for promotion, Harrell pursued playing professionally for the next quarter-century.

He did some studio work in Dallas for a while but then landed a gig at Billy Bob's, a hot new club in Ft. Worth, where he played five to six nights a week until one or two o'clock in the morning. It was a grueling schedule and Harrell felt he could do better. So he moved to Nashville in 1984, where a friend mentioned that Johnny Paycheck was looking for a keyboard player. Harrell got the slot and, laughingly, says he was immediately on a tour bus headed back to Texas, where the band played at Gilley's.

In between being on the road, he says he spent a fair amount of time "scratching and clawing to get demo work, trying to work my way back into the studio." In 1991, he was making enough of a living "so that I could stay in town and do sessions." The country market was just about to hit its stride, which meant that, for the next decade, he could make a very good living doing studio work in Nashville. He did strictly studio work until 2003 and then, while continuing to do studio sessions, also started going on the road with symphony shows. After two or three years of this, he was contacted by Amy Grant to perform with her group. "I was still swamped with studio work," so he initially declined. Since her group was all studio musicians, however, he reconsidered and, like the other members of the band, did symphony shows here and there while continuing to do studio work.[35]

In 2014, Harrell became the general manager of MV2 Entertainment, a new music publishing company. When asked why, he simply said, "Ownership." He met with an old, musically attuned Texas pal who had just sold his company to Halliburton and wanted to invest in something in the industry. They came to an agreement and over an old-time handshake entered into a partnership. They spent the next couple of months looking for a Nashville company to buy before deciding to start their own. Their vision statement harkens to the ideals he and his partner share: "to advance the art of music through inspiration, integrity and values." MV2 has a beautifully renovated four-square on Music Row with three writer rooms downstairs and a studio room upstairs. In addition to a staff of four, which Harrell expects to expand in the near future, the company employs a dozen songwriters, six of whom are also artists.

Tony Harrell went the studio route; Butch Baker took the artist path before veering into publishing. Like many young men, Baker wanted to be a singer. Unlike many young men, he has had four record deals. The first came shortly after his arrival in Nashville in the late 1970s. In 1982, he was playing a former furniture store that had been transformed into a dive club in one of the seedier areas of Nashville when a plugger from one of the local publishing companies stopped by. There was hardly anyone in the audience and the guy asked if he played any original songs. Baker played two and the guy asked him to come by later in the week. When Baker stopped by, he was signed to a record deal with Mercury Records.

He recorded some songs with other companies over the next few years: his best record hit number fourteen on the chart. He even recorded an album with another artist while at CBS Records, but it was never released. Of the four deals Baker had with various labels, the only record that was released was the initial one with Mercury. Baker was on the road 300 days a year in between record ventures and opened for some big names like Garth Brooks and Ray Charles. Between stalled record deals and the time spent on the road, Baker began to question the route he was taking and began toying with the idea of publishing or A&R with a label, feeling that in either case he could bring something to the table because "I've seen a lot of different sides to this business."

He landed with HoriPro and has been running the Nashville-based music venture of the Japanese conglomerate since 2007.[36] Though HoriPro existed before he took the helm, the company had become complacent. Baker was specifically brought in to get it going in the right direction.[37] Over the years HoriPro has had as many as ten to twelve songwriters. At the time of our interview, however, it "was down a bit" with only five songwriters. There were some deals in the offing, however, that Baker indicated would add to this number. His songwriters are on the young side: the youngest is twenty-one, the oldest thirty-two. That's because "it's a young person's game," though he acknowledges some of the best songwriters are around his age: fifty-seven.

DEEP POCKETS

Starting a publishing company requires a capital outlay that most small independent publishers cannot afford. The outlay is necessary to provide, at a minimum, a draw for songwriters placed under contract and an income for the co-owner or general manager who is running the company. Only a handful of publishers in this study started from scratch without a backer: Barry Coburn was one of them. The reader might recall that Mark Irwin, one of the successful songwriters mentioned in the last chapter, worked for Coburn early in his career purely on speculation, and though he did fairly well he still left then-struggling Ten Ten when offered a draw from another publisher (EMI), which was on firmer financial footing. Best Built Songs, run by Larry Sheridan and his wife Robin Ruddy, is another self-financed company that is augmented by their many other ventures, some of which are musically related while others are not.[38] This study would suggest that no more than 10 percent of contemporary independent publishers fall into this category.

Most of the independents, regardless of their size, had financial support that provided the basis for their business ventures. This support is divided roughly evenly between publishers that were backed by successful artists who wished to invest in the business they knew, while the other half were publishers who found music-minded backers looking for a business venture in the field.[39] Bobby Rymer at Writer's Den and Tony Harrell at MV2 are both excellent examples of those who made serendipitous connections with someone interested in music who wanted to become involved in the industry. Another example is SNG, a relatively new company Steve Leslie founded with financing from a senior partner at Edward Jones who is an amateur songwriter and guitar player but a diehard music aficionado.

Deep pockets can also be stretched to include those established companies that wanted someone new at the helm or are Nashville branches of larger musical conglomerates: Butch Baker at HoriPro is a good example of someone who was brought aboard to "take charge" by a well-established multinational entertainment corporation. The Nashville offices of both Olé and Kobalt are also parts of large media groups. Matt Lindsey at Big Yellow Dog, arguably one of the hottest independent publishers in town, was hired as vice president of creative after a long, distinguished career running Matt Lindsey Music. Lindsey felt honored to be offered the position because the president and active co-owner of the company, Carla Wallace, just had a child and wanted to step back some from the business. He certainly appreciates the financial stability it will provide in lieu of the *comme ci comme ça* income generated from a small, one-man run independent publishing company.

The other half of independent publishers were founded by successful artists: Sea Gayle Music was co-founded by Brad Paisley while Tree Vibez Music, a relatively new publishing venture, was funded by members of Florida Georgia Line. One might expect the artists to use the publishing company as their own publishing arm but they pretty much allow the company to function without their oversight. Brad Paisley did initially see Sea Gayle Music as an outlet for his songs as he began to hit his stride as an artist-songwriter. Despite this, explains Marc Driskill, executive vice president and general manager, Paisley is so busy today with the artist side of his artistic career that "we hardly ever see him."

The connection is important, however. While the artists at Florida Georgia Line are quite busy performing, their name association with the company helps open doors: "Just saying their name is a big thing," says Dane Schmidt at Tree Vibez. He then adds that the owners also "have a rolodex of artists if we should ever want to contact one of them [with a song that might work for them]." The smart artist-investors—and that certainly includes Keith Urban, a founding principal behind Boom—are the ones who don't try to run the company, says one old-time publisher, suggesting that their assessment of what works for them might not be in the best interest of a diversified publishing company, unless it is, of course, as some are, exclusively an outlet for their own songs.

Identifying and Honing Songwriters

There are two dimensions in publishing: the creative side and the business side. The business side deals with administrative details, and one of the time-consuming ones today is keeping track of the various royalty mechanisms. Some of the smaller companies with seasoned helmsmen have a foot in this side of the publishing businesses, but just as many smaller companies, and most of the mid-sized ones, also have people in-house who specialize in the royalty mechanism side of the business or farm it out to specialists. Numerous organizations, such as ClearBox Rights, are designed specifically to address the increasingly complex matters that revolve around royalty payments. ClearBox is a copyright administrative firm employing a number of specialists to deal with issues pertaining to royalty management, licensing management, and audio tracking management.[40] Nevertheless, all those in publishing who were interviewed, even when they dealt with administrative matters, primarily saw themselves as creative people. The creative aspect for publishers revolves around finding songwriters and helping them hone their songs. Still, at least one publisher mentioned contract negotiations with artists and labels on the creative side of the ledger rather than the business side, which is a logical association since each contract is a work of art in itself.[41] Finding songwriters is extremely problematic given the talented individuals who flock to Nashville. It is relatively easy to identify a talented individual amongst a host of lesser talents but recognizing an extraordinary talent among a host of like-talented individuals is no easy task. This is why the search for new talent has been likened to a daily treasure hunt.[42] For publishers, the inevitable "evaluation" of talent comes down to the "WOW factor," and the WOW factor in Nashville with its abundance of talented individuals must be fully capitalized WOW: something they see in the songwriter that blows them away, even in raw form. This is, naturally, an individual interpretation, and any number of publishers might pass over an artist-songwriter that another publisher is enchanted by. Butch Baker articulates a recent discovery.

> Wes Hightower, a well-known backup singer, gave Baker some songs he had written and asked that he listen to them. Baker said sure, not expecting anything but not wanting to hurt Hightower's feelings. He was going to East Tennessee that weekend so thought he'd just slip them into the CD player to kill some time. "I listened to the tape all the way there, some two hours. I couldn't get the songs out of my head. Played it for my wife, anyone else [there] that would listen. I called him and asked who he wrote with, and he did all the songs himself, and I said, "I have to do a deal with you. I have to be your publisher. Told him I hadn't listened to anything like this for a solid weekend in a long time," and that, Baker concludes, "is what you show up [to work] for."

Just what it was that Baker liked is hazy. Relating another, similar experience, he goes on to say, "The song is a gut feeling. If the bones of the song are not there on the work tape, you can smoke and mirror it all you want but it won't make any difference, you're still going to have a B-song." Bobby Rymer says it differently but the point is the same:

> Couple things I look for in songs, in songwriters. Can I close my eyes and see the movie that you're painting, or can I close my eyes and feel the emotion you're trying to create? "Can I see it; can I feel it?" If I can, there's something there that I want to pay attention to. That's what I'm looking for. And for a young writer, it doesn't all have to be in place because it often isn't, but you still have the, "Wow, that was a great line" or "Wow, that was an incredible hooky chorus."[43] That's the genesis of something we [at Writer's Den] can work with.

The process of identifying a prospective hit songwriter is even more of a creative endeavor for small and mid-sized publishers because they are looking to position their songwriters ahead of the curve while major houses tend to chase whatever is successful at any given moment.[44] This makes it difficult to define exactly what the WOW factor is. Yoshitaka Hori, the owner of HoriPro, was once asked if he liked to gamble in Las Vegas, and he responded that he goes to Las Vegas for the entertainment because he gambles every day in the music business.[45] It's not totally a gamble, however, or if it is, the deck is stacked. Identifying a new talent is not totally haphazard.

Identifying a new talent is typically predicated on the astute ear of the publisher, and that ear has been musically attuned since adolescence and honed by some twenty-plus years in the business. The "ear," however, is almost impossible to define: to paraphrase Supreme Court Justice Potter Stewart's famous quip about being able to recognize pornography, "I know it when I see it." The publishers in this study would all agree that "I know it when I hear it." Exactly what constitutes the WOW factor, therefore, tends to defy a clear definition. "If it was easy," Mike Sebastian says referring to this process, "everyone would be doing it [and they're not]." The one common thread is to be open to new talent since the next Alan Jackson or Taylor Swift, both identified early in their careers, may be around the next corner, or, more specifically, at the next artist-writers' round.

It is a tad easier today to identify new talented songwriters because most, at least in the early stages of their careers, are artist-songwriters.[46] This one-two combo is why publishers or members of their staff are common audience members at any of the host of artist-writers' rounds that take place regularly throughout the city. Some publishers mentioned talent shows such as "American Idol" and "The Voice" that have ostensibly brought new talent to the forefront. Despite the vocal talent of the performers, publishers tended to dismiss these shows because, while there are any number of contestants on the show who could unquestionably sing, there have been only a handful who have gone on to successful musical careers, such as Kelly Clarkson and Carrie Underwood. The general opinion is that most musicians on these shows simply milk what is popular and the artist-songwriters are anything but "ahead of the curve."[47] In the same vein, publishers are looking less to get their writer into an established artist camp than they are trying to associate their songwriters with identified artists before they make it big. In all these and related scenarios, the publisher considers themselves "creative" because they are seeking out the next trend before it happens, which is the very definition of creativity. "The curve is not what is on the radio right now. That was written one, two, maybe three years ago. The curve is what is written today and being played in the clubs tonight. That's what's coming and you better be on top of that if you want to succeed in this business."[48]

Dennis Kurtz at Big Spark Music adds this key caveat: "you have to be able to write just a little ahead of the curve," implying that if you are too far ahead of the curve the music listener has difficulty appreciating the songs. Staying ahead of the curve also holds with camps, that coterie of individuals who are "in" with an artist or "hit" songwriter. One interviewee explains: "I want to find the next thing [rather than camp on to existing]. I'd rather be on the front of a camp rather than chasing the back end. That ship's already sailed. That's why I don't subscribe to the 'Well, I'll put my writer with this writer just because they're having hits [right now].'"[49]

The WOW factor is not sufficient in and of itself. There are at least three pragmatics publishers have to consider when signing a new writer. First, publishers are looking for the right fit. This requires some time to evaluate the potential new member of the team. Many publishers will want existing members to provide input on the reasonable assumption that even a "creative genius" may do more harm than good by disrupting carefully nurtured dynamics within the company. Barry Coburn recently (2017) signed a sixteen-year-old that he'd been following since she was fourteen to make sure she was not an anomaly. He didn't want to repeat two earlier errors of judgment in signing someone too quickly. One of them, he says, "was a total disaster because he expected everything to fall into place [without any effort on his part]. He was a two-year deal, and after two months I thought, 'Damn, what have I done?'"

It doesn't always work that way. Darrell Franklin had just signed a young woman he heard in Austin while there for a songwriter symposium. Ninety percent of the people he critiqued "will never have a career [as a songwriter], but a few were very talented and one young woman I heard, well, she was something else, and she had written all her songs without a co-writer. So I signed her. First time ever did anything like that. I wasn't looking for a writer when I went down there, so just goes to show you."

It is much more common to "date" for a while to make sure the artist-songwriter is on an upward trajectory. Tony Harrell at MV2 recently put a twenty-one-year-old under contract after watching her for a good year, during which time "she just kept growing." Despite her potential, Harrell is cultivating her: "We are putting her in rooms with veteran writers, with young, established writers." He's trying to help her "find her sound," and they are "spending a lot of time in the studio with her." Her first CD was released in July 2017.

The second point arises from the first: newly signed artist-songwriters must fit the needs of the company and not compete with others in the company. This means that if the company has, say, a country rapper, another country rapper might be disruptive because it is difficult for the publisher to push two people who both tread the same path. Indeed, publishers are less likely to get excited by a new artist-songwriter no matter how good they are because they are tuned out by the publisher who is not looking for someone they already have.

This is not meant to suggest that a publisher has to have a widely diversified roster of artist-songwriters. Though most publishers are musically diversified, they also have a majority of artist-songwriters who are working in the country genre. There is, however, a wide variety of sub-genres within country. Therefore, in many instances, even with a staff of eight to ten country artists-songwriters, they are not necessarily all singing the same song—no one lumps together the country music of Chris Stapleton, Jason Aldine, and Blake Shelton, or confuses the country songs of Taylor Swift with those of Carrie Underwood.

Having a roster of country artists does not mean that they are competing stylistically or lyrically with one another. Indeed, the strength of the publishing relationship is in how the publisher works with the songwriter to enhance their song. The fit is not so much with other contracted songwriters but with the staff—the plugger, in particular—who has to support the new hire. The general manager at one publishing company says that he and his two creative directors "sit here and talk about [a new hire]. We don't usually sign someone unless we are super excited about them. It is usually someone all three of us really, really love."[50]

Third, and finally, a new artist-songwriter is likely to be a bit raw and needs to be open to constructive criticism. Even seasoned songwriters respect input because they may be too close to the lyrics and need that neutral third party to provide critical insight. Sometimes that third-party insight, which changes just one line, makes all the difference. We saw this in the last chapter with songwriters who co-wrote, but it is just as pronounced among relationships between songwriters and their publishers. Indeed, the relationship between the songwriter and publisher may be even more critical than that which exists between co-writers, because the publisher needs to be 100 percent vested in the song in order to push for its release by an artist or label.

All of the songwriters in this study, both new and seasoned, mentioned their openness to constructive input and recognized the importance of input from other songwriters and their publisher in helping shape their songs for the marketplace. This might be somewhat axiomatic, however, since those who are not open to constructive criticism are likely to be filtered out of the system before they even enter it. Sometimes the input is minimal. "It was all there," says Butch Baker regarding one of his writers, "but there was this *one* line. He asked which line it was and I told him. He got real mad. I told him not to be mad at me; I was just trying to help. He said, 'Yeah, yeah, yeah.' Told him to think about it. That night he called me up and said he'd thought about it and thought I was right. Said 'Check this out,' and gave me the new line. It made the song."

A more humorous anecdote is given by Mike Hollandsworth in his tête-à-tête with Brendan Croker, co-vocalist and guitarist with The Notting Hillbillies, a country music band formed by Mark Knopfler as an outgrowth of Dire Straits specifically to play smaller venues than was typical of Dire Straits.

> Brendan came to town shortly after making a splash with the Notting Hillbillies after they were guests on *Saturday Night Live*. He says, "Teach me to write a country song."[51] So, I say, "Let me hear what you got." I listened to him play a tune and said, "No, Brendan, you cannot do this, this, or this." "Okay, boss." "So, Brendan, what else do you have?" We did this for two hours. "No, no, no. Anything else?" "That's it, boss." "Come on, Brendan, you got anything else?" "Got a line and a lick." "Let's hear it." Strums: "I want to walk to no particular destination." "Brendan, that's cool. I like that. Now go in here and write that for The Judds." Twenty minutes later he walks out, '"Got your song, boss." "Twenty minutes?" "Nope, got it." So he plays this song and I go "Brendan, no. We've done all this. You cannot do this." "Okay, boss." Goes back in and 20 minutes later says, "Got your song, boss." "Brendan, you don't get a song in 20 minutes." "No, got it." "Okay, let's hear it." Same thing. Twenty minutes later, "Got your song, boss." Told him, "Why don't you go to lunch and we'll come back fresh, and you and I will sit down and do the song together."
>
> So we get back and we sit down. Now I don't write songs; I never put my name on songs [if I produce] because if my writer comes in and I do this then he's like "I'm not going to take my song to him because he's gonna take a piece of it." So, anyway, we sit down and in two hours we write this song. We had fights over the bridge and this and that, but at the end of two hours it was pretty good. So I said, "Let's type up the lyrics" and he came back with his name and my name on it. I said to take my name off. "Nope, not going to do it." Said I don't put my name on a song. "Nope, you wrote just as much as I did." Back and forth, finally said, "Brendan, I'll get in trouble." "Really, boss?" Well, that song was track one on Wynonna's first CD, which sold four million units. By my taking my name off it, it cost me $190,000. But it was the right thing to do.

Darrell Franklin basically says the same thing about his role as a publisher. "I am a partner in a publishing company. I get paid to help develop songwriters. I've never written a song with a songwriter. My job is to help them tweak their songs." Marc Driskill at Sea Gayle Music would agree. "The creative process is not always perfect. You have to find the good elements in every song and help the writer to see them. You have to encourage the good nugget in those songs and encourage the writer to go with it. You have to help them find their greatness."

Most publishers don't put their name on the song even when they often work as intently with their songwriters as Hollandsworth. Even those songwriters who prefer to work at home alone still come in to the office with some regularity to play their songs for the publisher and then, often, will go back and forth with them over this or that aspect of the song. The solo songwriter working from home without regular contact with her or his publisher is an anomaly, even if there is usually one or two at most publishers who work from home. More often than not, publishers prefer their songwriters to work from their offices, because the office social environment provides the necessary synergy to spark the creative process. Darrell Franklin at 3 Ring Circus explains.

> Most of our writers work every day, five to six days a week. In fact, I just finished a meeting. It wasn't scheduled, but then it needn't be. I have an open-door policy for my writers. They can come in and talk to me anytime, or vent. Earlier one of my writers wanted to play a demo of another writer, like "Hey, check this out." That kind of interaction [sparks creativity].

Another synergistic advantage of having songwriters in the office is elaborated upon by Mike Molinar at Big Machine:

> On Monday we listen to everything that was put together in the last week. We put together a hot sheet of who is up [to record] in the next couple of weeks. We send that list to our writers. Sometimes I'm very specific, like, "Hey, Rascal Flatts is cutting in two weeks. You really need to lock in on this. Next week your calendar is clear; why don't you give it a shot? Here is what I know about Rascal Flatts." Some of them react very well to that kind of direction; some are not good at it. The more they can do it, however, the more I will continue to give them that kind of information. And if they are in the office, I can give it to them directly and spend time discussing it with them, which helps them sharpen their focus.

It also helps to have your ear to the ground and be able to quickly mobilize your songwriters. All the publishers visited had a running board of who was cutting, where and when. The smaller companies had a white board; some of the larger companies had a very sophisticated computer screen. They were all positioned to take advantage of any last-minute needs by artists or labels.

> Tight deadlines are very common [in the business]. There is always the last-minute conversation [when someone is in the studio or going into the studio to cut]. Someone says, "Oh I wish I had [this or that on the record]." Well, we will see if we can get [what they are looking for] to them and if we meet their needs, the [new or revised] song has a pretty good chance of being included in the cut.[52]

The publishers in this study all spend an inordinate amount of time working with their writers considering all the duties entailed in running a publishing company. Then again, the songs that come from the publishing company are at the heart of their identity, so their often-intensive time investment is not only reasonable but necessary. The other major contribution publishers make to their songwriters is getting the songs placed. This is more fully explored in the "pitching" subsection that follows, but the expanding role of publishing today needs to be addressed first.

MULTITASKING: CONTEMPORARY MUSIC PUBLISHING

Publishers have historically concentrated on publishing songs. In the heyday 1990s this was possible because Nashville was cranking out country music albums almost hourly, and the labels were constantly seeking new songs. The need for songwriters during this heady period was exacerbated because the artists were not as invested in writing their own material, at least not to the degree they are today. This meant music publishers were kept quite busy supplying the system with songs. Album sales have substantially declined since 2000, and even "albums" (LPs) have given way to the shorter, three- to four-song EP.[53] The bottom line for publishers is that they have to broaden their historical role if they want to stay in business.

Multitasking has always been done to a degree: Acuff-Rose was primarily a music publishing company but they also provided management services to some of their artists and had a small record label (Hickory Records). The same with Zomba, which had numerous publishing companies and record labels across a range of genres: "The premise of Zomba was that if you were going to spend money, spend your own money. If you're going to have to use a studio, then let's be in the studio business."[54] Ditto Starstruck, whose ultra-modern building (1997) on Music Row was specifically designed to be the ultimate tool to nurture, develop, market and promote music for the 21st century: "We have the whole ball of wax here," says COO Cliff Williamson, referring to their artists and artist management staff, songwriters, studio facilities, and own record label (Starstruck Records).

Looking for alternative sources of income outside their traditional role of publishing songs has simply become more of an issue today as their primary source of income shrinks: "Being realistic about it," said one music publisher, "publishers these days have to be constantly thinking of other sources of income." Another addressed the same point but explained the driving force behind diversification. "I think the times we are facing—since we [independent publishers] are not getting [much] money from streaming—well, we have to compensate by trying to figure out other ways to make a little money. Production is a huge thing. . . ."

It is indeed huge. All the mid-sized publishers and a good third of the smaller ones in this study started labels to produce their own artist-songwriters or intended to move in that direction because dramatically shrunken production costs allow the independents to compete, at least modestly, with the majors. Chapter 3 addresses this point in greater detail when looking at the role of music labels. Chapter 4 examines the increasing number of publishing companies that have moved into artist management, a natural progression for publishers as more and more of their songwriters are also performing artists.

Multitasking in other areas outside production and artist management is more modest. Nashville is still a country music town, but publishers throughout the area are also broadening their musical scope. One factor accelerating the expansion beyond pure country is the fuzziness as to what pure country is. Americana, which was officially recognized as a separate music category at the 2010 Grammy Awards, seems to be filling this gap. A lot of Americana artists are recognizably classic country.[55] Early nominees in the Americana category include Willie Nelson, Lucinda Williams, Wilco, Rosanne Cash, and Emmylou Harris.

Beyond "classic country," country music today is extraordinarily diverse, which makes it fairly easy for publishers to "branch out" into country subgenres: e.g., alternative country, contemporary country, outlaw country, country rap, and urban cowboy, as well as the more traditional country subgenres such as bluegrass and country gospel. Country has long been associated with pop and rock, going back to at least the origin of rock with crossover artists such as Conway Twitty, the Everly Brothers, and Brenda Lee. In the last few years country has been returning to this blend of pop country with acts such as Florida Georgia Line and singers like Taylor Swift.

Today, the definition of country is hazy, except among the "classicists" who still hold fast to Hank Williams and Patsy Cline and those artists who followed their musical path, such as George Jones, Tammy Wynette, and Don Williams. The broad definition of country and ease with which country has long crossed into other genres, such as pop and rock, makes it easy for many publishers today to have a wide variety of "crossover" artist-songwriters on their staff. Even those handfuls of publishers that accentuate country are not talking about one monolithic style of music. SNG, for example, is "mostly country, but we do other things. One of our artists is really R&B; we do pop, too."[56]

Stephanie Cox at Kobalt has been in the business since the early 1990s and says the same thing when asked how things have changed in the city: "It is night and day from when I first started pitching. I mean, just our roster alone is amazingly broad. Artists are here that have never had a country cut. But they want to be here, and they want to write in this market because Nashville is a songwriter's town [regardless of the musical genre]. In fact, it is one of our main missions at Kobalt to not be just one format: we have film and television writers on our staff; pop, too." Cox nevertheless acknowledges that, while Kobalt is a global company, the Nashville connection does slightly skew artists in this area toward the country genre because, "Well, it is Nashville."

The internet, which practically every person in the industry decried because of its failure to produce significant streaming revenue, is also widely applauded by these same industry professionals. The cost of producing a record, once almost exclusively controlled by the deep-pocket major labels, is now widely available to almost everyone. The overwhelming majority of young songwriters are very savvy at making computerized album "cuts" that, at least in some cases, sound like studio cuts.[57] The internet also allows publishers, many of whom have media specialists on the payroll, to get their artists and their songs recognized beyond the confines of traditional radio. Indeed, the attention an artist-songwriter has accrued on sites such as Spotify is used to "sell" the artist or song to a "legitimate" producer who can give it even greater exposure.[58]

The internet also allows publishers in Nashville to reach further afield. Bobby Rymer at Writer's Den, for example, is following a relatively new income stream by shopping the Australian market. "A great thing about the internet: A little research and I can identify all the Australian record labels, who their manager is, their producer, and their A&R contact. It's quick and easy to send them a song electronically. Might not be a big-ticket return of six figures but [I] can pick up $100 here, a few hundred there. It starts to add up."

And industry people in other countries pay attention to these electronic contacts, Rymer goes on to say, because of the Nashville connection. "There's a certain cachet when they get something from a Nashville publisher. Ears perk up when you say you're from Nashville, and doors open pretty quick. 'What you got? Send me what you have.' They assume [rightly] that they are going to get quality stuff. It's not like Joe Blow from Poughkeepsie saying, 'I'd like to send you a song I wrote'".

One publisher might have summed up the expanding role for all the publishers who participated in this study. "There is no going back into just the traditional publisher role. I feel now that the door is open to all the other sides of [the publishing business], we will stay there."[59] The role of the publisher has undergone dramatic change since the turn of the millennium; the pivotal role of the plugger within the house, however, remains timelessly unchanged.

Pitching Songs

Pitching or plugging songs, terms used interchangeably in the industry, is probably one of the most misunderstood and least appreciated aspects of publishing by those outside the music business. "I call my mom [out of state] every day," Aubrey Schwartz says; "and she always asks the same thing," which is to again explain her plugging job at SNG, after which Schwartz is met with the inevitable rejoinder: "Well, I just don't understand your job and how you make money. I don't get it. I just don't get it." Schwartz now simply tells her that she loves her job and is making a living.

It is not surprising that her mother doesn't understand the profession since Schwartz herself was not introduced to the publishing side of the business until she transferred in her junior year to Belmont;[60] she didn't learn much about publishing until her senior internship with Shar'n Clark at Shake 'Em Up Music. At Shake 'Em Up Schwartz and a cohort also learned some of the more difficult dimensions of plugging. "They didn't teach me a whole lot about publishing in college. I didn't even know what a song plugger was, which is what I am now. Most of what I learned [about publishing], I learned during my internship."

Pluggers quickly learn that selling a newly written song by an unknown songwriter is not an easy task. Steve Leslie's (SNG Music) mantra for his plugger is "Persistence, persistence, persistence." One has to have really thick skin to endure all the rejections. "I'm told no two hundred times a week," says Sarah Feldman at Writer's Den, "and I have to sit there and say, 'Okay!' I don't get to argue with them [A&R person], like 'You should cut this song, it's great,' but [if I did that] that would be the last meeting I'd have with them. It is a very delicate thing because it is people's lives, and their lives [and songs] are very precious to them."

If that isn't hard enough to do, it is even harder when you have to tell your writers you cannot plug their song because it just doesn't work.

> Songwriters are very sensitive; it's their art; it's a piece of creativity; it's a piece of who they are, especially when they've just written it. I always try to say something nice, even if I didn't like the song at all, like "I love the vocals on this song." Then you have to tell them the facts. "Okay, I'm not picking on you, it's the song, and I want it to be the best it can be for you." Most appreciate the criticism and thank me for giving them honest feedback on the song because a lot of people don't. I don't like doing that but if the song doesn't work then I'm going to get beat up when I take it out there [to pitch]. The writer has to handle my trying to help them or they're not going to make it in this business because [the rejections] only gets worse.[61]

Not all pluggers work as intensely with their songwriters. David Harper, an independent plugger, doesn't have the time to devote to honing the writers' songs that he pitches. Still, he won't handle someone who doesn't have the creative spark in their songs. "I can only handle a few, and that few have to be of high quality. I like to have five or ten quality songs in a combination of styles." Defining quality is problematic. "I might not like the song" Harper admits, "but if they have a creative expression that is of merit, then I will follow that up and pitch it. Maybe it is the guitar [that doesn't work] but you see the magic in the lyrics, in the melody. It's pitchable."

The position today is generally considered as creative as the publisher's role, which is why the title in many companies has been broadened to creative director. The name more aptly captures the nuances of the profession than a pitcher or plugger, which tends to conjure up an image of someone who simply tries to "sell" an artist or label on the merits of a song. Creative director may be more apt because contemporary pluggers are as dynamically involved in the creative aspect of discovering and honing a songwriter's lyrics as is the publisher.

Pluggers are as strongly invested in the artist's song as the publisher since they are the ones who are trying to convince an artist or label of the merits of the song. If they are not enthusiastic about the song, it is unlikely that an artist or label head will get stoked by it. "I have to really, really believe in what I am doing," David Harper says about going to a pitch meeting. "They need to know that I am plugging something I really believe in. When you go to those meetings, and they are really big meetings, you don't want to screw up. I have to give them the best I have. It's my integrity that is on the line." Harper estimates that independent pluggers, such as he, have increased in the Nashville environs from 10 percent to 20-plus percent over the last few years, an increase he attributes to the growth of independent artist-songwriters, and the concomitant increase of small, independent labels.

Pluggers associated with publishers, being generally a good deal younger than the publisher, bring a fresh perspective to the table that all the publishers in this study tended to appreciate in the same way younger songwriters often mesh with seasoned ones, with each learning from the other. Sara Feldman at Writer's Den says that because she is younger than her boss, Bobby Rymer, she can "bring the sense of the younger generation into [discussions about lyrics]." As a female counterpart to her male boss, she also evaluates the lyrics differently. "Well, in my head, I'm like 'Would the girl feel this or that way?'" Rymer respects his young protégée. "I have the older, male point of view; she has the young female point of view. We complement each other very well."

The respect is reciprocal. "Sometimes we are listening to a song and he might look at one word and say, 'What if that word was this?' or 'You need to make sure that both characters in this song look good.' I would have never thought of those things. . . . He really picks the song apart." These small but important dimensions of songwriting, Feldman goes on to say, might flit right past her because she is relatively new to publishing.

Putting the song together is more than simply writing good lyrics. The timing of the pitch is critical, says Rymer.

> Timing is a big part of our business. You don't want to pitch something too far ahead. If someone is not going to make a record for six months, the song you play now that they get excited about may grow stale after they've lived with it for four or five months. Gotta be careful with a demo, too. If it is produced so well that you essentially have a record and you play it for somebody, a lot of times people can only hear it that way. They hear it the way it is presented, especially if it is really well produced. You need to give them a great song without the track being overly produced; they can sometimes hear it more than the way that it is. Had a producer tell me once, "Bobby, if you give me a fully produced track and I go in front of the artist and say, 'Okay, we're going to take this out and this out and then add this,' well, they look at me like I'm doing high math. If, however, you give me something that is sparsely produced and I go there and go, 'We're going to add this and this,' they get it. They cannot always do subtraction but they can usually do addition."

Matt Lindsey, formerly with Matt Lindsey Music and now with Big Yellow Dog, mentions another key factor that is critical to plugging

> You have to pay attention to who you pitch songs and what their reaction is. One thing about pitching songs is that you are always at the mercy of the listener. If you go into a pitch meeting and they just had an argument with their spouse, if you catch them on the wrong day or in the wrong frame of mind, you could have "Friends in Low Places" or "The Dance" and they don't want to hear it. I'm guilty of that. I hear so many songs that I have to re-listen to stuff a lot. Sometimes it's like "Wow, how'd I miss this?" Everyone is susceptible to that.

Conclusion

There has been a decline in the number of music publishers in the major markets (New York, L.A., and Nashville) but there has also been a concomitant decline in the number of record releases, especially when compared to the heady heyday 1990s for country music coming out of Nashville. Music publishing may look attenuated compared to the 1990s but it nevertheless remains robust. The major labels, despite having an internal songwriting staff, still look to the independent publishers to supply them with music. It's very straightforward: the best song wins, no matter who pens it or what house they are associated with.

There is an abundance of artist-songwriters in Nashville, but it is hard to make headway as a writer when one has to wait tables for a living. The attraction of a publishing house for both newcomers and seasoned songwriters is that the publisher provides a draw so the artist can concentrate on their craft. Draws today tend to be relatively modest, somewhere in the $20,000 range, enough for songwriters to pay their bills but not a lot more, which keeps them hungry to write quality lyrics in the hopes that one will get cut. It doesn't have to chart number one, though everyone wants that, but if it climbs and stays on the radio a while, the songwriter and publisher make their money, and, at the very least, the publisher recoups the draw and any other costs relating to getting the song placed. A song that "hits" not only allows the songwriter to pay back the draw, but to make a decent income, which is what both the songwriter and the publisher want since performance royalties are typically evenly split.

Mechanical royalties, which come from record sales, are not what they once were since fewer records are selling and more and more albums are being released in the shorter four- to five-song EP category, which simply means fewer songs are needed. Performance royalties from radio airplay is the real country moneymaker because, as we'll see in the next chapter, radio is king in the country format. Performance royalties also include money from the songs sung on a tour, but it is really the artist (and labels) who reap the rewards there with only a trickle coming to the songwriter. Sync—songs that are played on a television show or in a movie—is another way to generate royalties, but pop and rock are more often synchronized than country, so this, again, is a thin revenue stream, though as Bobby Rymer might say, "A revenue stream is a revenue stream no matter how small." That is why every songwriter in the last chapter and every publisher in this one said *the* way to make money in country is to have a number one hit played on the radio, though no one is scoffing if it charts.

There is another critical way publishers make their money and that is by controlling the catalogue of the writer who writes for the house. Catalogues are sometimes mined by publishers for gems, and if one is able to find one and transform it into a hit, then performance royalties and mechanicals come back into play. Some seasoned writers with a string of successful hits and some solid business savvy have their own publishing companies to ensure that they reap 100 percent of the profit, but this rare; still, it does happen, primarily because their continued series of hits opens doors.

The publisher's "ear" has been honed by decades in the business. Even the ones in this study who have only recently moved into publishing, barring one, have a decade or more in the business. They typically share the same music background as songwriters. One glaring difference, however, is that while the younger songwriters are relatively evenly split along gender lines, publishers are predominantly male. This tends to reflect a traditional male bias in the field, though this may be changing since a lot of publishers (60 percent-plus) have a preponderance of females in key positions within the company, and this will likely alter the gender disparity in the years to come.

The path to becoming a publisher for most was anything but straightforward. Some, like Hollandsworth and Rymer, worked in the music field and stumbled into publishing, taking advantage of their good fortune to subsequently carve out a career. Others took a somewhat circuitous path by pursuing a lengthy musical career as either studio musicians or artists before veering into the publishing world. When opportunity beckoned, however, they were quick to adapt since publishing, for them, as for most, is more a creative journey than a managerial one.

One reason for the less-than-straightforward path to publishing is that the start-up cost is fairly heavy, largely because it has to cover the songwriter's draw. The few that were solely funded tended to build their businesses slowly or had other business that shored up their publishing venture. The others either camped on to an existing house when the opportunity arose for them to take an executive position or sought someone with an interest in the musical field who was looking to financially diversify their holdings. This latter group would include those successful artists who decided to invest in an industry they knew. Despite the financial commitment of successful artists in founding a publishing house, few appear to interfere with the actual running of the company, in part because, being successful artists, they have plenty to keep them occupied and also perhaps, in part, because they realize that their musical taste, even if it works for them, might not be in the best interests in directing a diversified publishing venture.

The publisher's sharp ear and the financial viability of the house are important in identifying and honing songwriters. Identifying new talent for publishers is easy: it simply comes down to the WOW factor. Defining the WOW factor is another matter, however. It is similar to one frustrated publisher trying to explain to me what, at first glance, is the simple math of royalties: "We do this every day," he said, "and have been doing it for ages, but you don't realize how intricate it is until you try to explain [all the ifs, ands, and buts) to someone outside the industry"[62]

Deep pockets, on the other hand, are not complex since in order to put a songwriter under contract, the company has to have a strong financial bottom line. The publishers interviewed were generally in agreement regarding the importance of contracts since they commit the songwriter to the house and provide them with enough income to allow them to devote themselves to their craft. If it doesn't work out, the publishing company loses because the draw cannot be recouped. If it does work out, both the publisher and the songwriter benefit. The desire of both parties is to not just make enough to cover the draw but to get a song placed that is a hit, which adds lucratively to both of their pockets. Sometimes—and this is fairly recent and not widespread—the publisher may hedge their bets by asking for 1) a percent of the artist performance (tour) royalties, 2) a percent of the songwriter's share of the copyright royalty, or 3) forgoing the draw but giving the songwriter a percent of the publisher's royalty if and when the songwriter gets a cut.

The publishers in this study tended to emphasize their creative contribution over their managerial one. In this they bear a resemblance to Maxwell Perkins, the editor who published the works of F. Scott Fitzgerald, Ernest Hemingway, and Thomas Wolfe, amongst other literary luminaries. There were those writers, like Hemingway, who refused to have their works tampered with by an editor, but then there were the works of Fitzgerald and Wolfe, which would have never reached their literary heights without critical input from Perkins.[63] The publishers in this study follow the path trod by Perkins: there are those songwriters who work independently and are quite adamant about the shape of their lyrics, but there is the wider majority who appreciate the input provided by publishers because the publishers' experience helps fine-tune their works, not just to market demands but also, lyrically, to the perfect word, line, stanza, or chorus.

Few of the publishers in this study, except for some of the smaller, one-shop houses, have the time to pitch song themselves. This is largely because publishers today no longer just focus on placing a song with an artist. The sharp decline in record sales have forced publishers to be broader in their scope, and many, as we'll see in subsequent chapters, have also moved into artist management, since so many of their songwriters are artist-songwriters, or produce the album themselves. The increased demands on their time mean that they have relegated pitching the song to specialists in the area. The publishers can all pitch a song, of course, and have done it, but it is such a time-consuming aspect of the business that they rely on their pluggers to perform it. Plugging a song is not just a sales job: pluggers work with the publisher to make sure the right line resonates in the lyrics. Their job, much like the role of publisher, has become more multifaceted, and most pluggers at independent houses act as creative directors. The term "creative" is apt because their role goes well beyond that of salesperson, and they are often involved, alongside the publisher, in identifying potential up-and-coming songwriters and helping them fine-tune their lyrics. It is a relatively new aspect of their job that most in this study find exhilarating, and it is a key reason for their enthusiasm in their publishing job. It is these individuals that are working the ropes by honing their ears that will likely lead them, down the road, to the coveted position of music publisher.

3

GETTING THE SONGS OUT

Producing, Recording, Distributing, and Promoting Music

Recording music has largely been the province of recognized record labels, which also distribute and promote the record once it's been cut. The majors and their subsidiaries continue to dominate the market. Globally, MIDiA Research reports that in 2018 Universal Music Group, after its purchase of EMI in 2012, is at the forefront of label share with 31 percent of the market, followed by the independents (28 percent), Sony Music (21 percent), and then Warner (18 percent).[1] The Big Three are jointly mentioned in one breath by the media because they control 70 percent of the market.[2] This dominance is why they have garnered their share of attention. They have often been examined from a historical perspective. Sean Wilentz and Gary Marmorstein both independently examined the history of Columbia Records;[3] Warren Zane did pretty much the same by detailing the history of Warner Brothers Records.[4] These types of analyses tend to revolve around the artists who were involved with the labels, such as Sinatra, Streisand, and Dylan. Other works examine the rise and fall of legendary labels, such as EMI.[5] These studies, historically illuminating as they are, give precious little information detailing exactly what labels actually do.

The majors certainly deserve attention but even a cursory reading of the statistics regarding market share indicates that the independents are making a substantial splash.[6] Despite the rise of independent releases, the majors justifiably continue to deserve their fair share of attention because, as Paul Resnikuff wrote in *Digital Music News*, the Big Three command revenues of $9.3 billion from a total revenue of $14.9 billion."[7] The "leftover" $5.6 billion is left largely to the independents to divide amongst themselves. These sales figures suggest the independents may have closer to a 40 percent share of the market, as any number of recent music analyses suggest.[8]

The music industry is not just about money, however. The songwriters and music publishers that were looked at in the first two chapters want, naturally, to make a living, but their passion is to make music.[9] The independents—more so than the majors, which are corporately rooted—fall into this category: they are proud of their musical contribution. They are often the ones at the cutting edge. For example, Sun Records in Memphis, which was subsumed by Mercury Records in 1969, was at the forefront of the rock 'n' roll revolution when it introduced the world to Elvis Presley,[10] Carl Perkins, and Jerry Lee Lewis in the early 1950s. Motown Records (1960) in Detroit (initially Tamla Records) pioneered the "Motown sound" before it was bought by MCA (Music Corporation of America) in 1988, which, in turn was sold to PolyGram in 1994. Rap, too, was produced by a string of small, unknown independent labels for a good decade before it was recognized as a legitimate musical genre in 1989[11] and the majors started to join the rap revolution.

The independents have often been upstart labels that provide an alternative way to get music usually balked at by the majors to the public. Taylor Swift, for example, at the ripe young age of fourteen, was with RCA for a year and when it came time to sign her, RCA said they needed another thirty days to evaluate her potential. She and her parents basically said, "What are you going to learn in the next thirty days that you don't already know after a year?" They walked.[12] She did a show at The Bluebird some time later, and shortly thereafter Scott Borchetta announced that he was going to start a new indie label that would be built around Swift.[13]

Thanks to their pivotal role in launching new artists, independents have likewise been the subject of some attention: *Little Labels—Big Sound: Small Record Companies and the Rise of American Music*, penned by Rick Kenney and Randy McNult, devotes a chapter each to ten small labels known for making some musical noise.[14] Similarly, John Cook narrows the lens to one small company, Merge Records, to explore the rationale for the label's success in what he hyperbolically says is "a failing industry."[15] These stories, too, are illustrative and informative but tend to skim over the processes of production, distribution and promotion, which are integral to making a label successful.

Flourishing independents do not go unnoticed by the majors and are at risk of being absorbed by the majors. This was the case with Broken Bow Records (BBR), which launched the career of Jason Aldean. BBR, founded by Benny Brown in 1999, was approached numerous times before Brown, at 75 years of age, finally sold to BMG in February 2017.[16] Big Machine founder Scott

Borchetta had similarly been approached over the years by both Sony and Warner before finally selling to Ithaca Holdings in 2019, an umbrella company owned by Scooter Braun, the manager of Justin Bieber and Ariana Grande, among others.[17] Since Big Machine was not purchased by one of the majors, it remains one of the big-little independent labels. Executives from both BBR and Big Machine were interviewed in the course of this study.

Majors are quick to point out the "discoveries" they have made. Indeed, Randy Goodman, chairman and CEO of Sony Nashville, recently crowed about the effort Sony is putting into finding new, young talent, such as Maren Morris.[18] Despite the claims, Morris wasn't "discovered" and signed to Sony/ Columbia until after her self-released five-song EP had gained 2.5 million streams on Spotify.[19] The independents, more so than the majors, are the ones at the cutting edge, a point delineated in the last chapter in regards to music publishing, only in this respect the goal is finding the next artist who is ahead of the curve rather than the next song. "Ahead of the curve" is a key phrase in this regard: how else would one explain Universal's chairman and CEO, Mike Dungan, pressing Chris Stapleton to go in a more contemporary direction in line with other pop country bands under contract at Universal, such as Little Big Town and The Band Perry? Another example is the time he remarked that Sam Hunt's debut album "Montevallo," which sold 1.2 million copies, didn't sound "remotely country."[20]

Pioneering new artists is one reason for studying independent labels. The majors themselves often find new artists by inititating sub-label deals with independents. Entertainment lawyer Joe Huckaby Rideout remarks, "The major labels have embraced the sub-label arrangement in order to capture the millions of dollars they are unable to generate because of the increased fragmentation of the music market. Their immense size and bureaucratic structure hinder them from reacting quickly to new artistic trends."[21]

Indie executives are closer to the music; they are not hampered by the cumbersome bureaucratic layers that separate those at the top from the musician.[22] In his study of how the different label types were discussed in *Billboard* magazine, James Hearn underscores the distinction between the bureaucratically encumbered majors versus the creative dimension of the independents.[23] He found that the two labels were treated in the press proportionately to their market share, with 84.2 percent of the majors covered compared to 15.8 percent of the independents. However, the two types were referred to distinctly differently. The major records labels were frequently described as conservative, bureaucratic and businesslike, while independent record labels were described using the terms creative, democratic, organic, diverse and niched.

Another reason for focusing on the independents in this study is that their small size allows a closer inspection of how they produce, distribute, and promote the music they make, which is simply raised to a "higher" level by the deep-pocket majors. A small independent producer may have only a few people to promote their records; the majors have dozens. Nevertheless, the process of promoting records remains basically the same.

Yet another reason for concentrating on the independents is that they have been ahead of the streaming curve, which the majors are just now (post-2015) beginning to enter . . . with a vengeance.[24] Indeed, the early positioning of independents in digital space is one of the key reasons they are beginning to rival the majors who have historically relied on radio as their main source of revenue, at least in the country format.[25] The independents' streaming revenue is likely to be enhanced even more with the passing of the Music Modernization Act in 2018. The MMA will provide a more substantive source of income for streamed songs. Greater income could make it attractive for the majors to more aggressively enter into this market, which could, in turn, affect the position presently staked out by the independents.

Record Labels

Independent labels traditionally competed with the majors by not competing at all. Instead, they found undeveloped niches neglected by the majors, such as rock 'n' roll in the 1950s, hip-hop in the 1980s, and jazz and children's music today.[26] The majors left these niches alone because they were seen, at least initially, as not generating significant revenue, and for the majors, more so than the independents, it is often about the money. The big change is that the independents are now competing head on with the majors, producing music similar to what the majors are releasing. Historically the majors relied on the independents to discover new talent, often co-opting indie artists by offering them lucrative contracts once they proved their value. Today, however, more artists are staying with the independents. "It's a different feeling for an artist to be on an independent today" [late-1990s], said Lesley Bleakley, vice president of the indie label Beggars Group, "because we practice artist development [now], and we do give artists more control."[27]

Artistic freedom has become the indie labels' byword, and because more artists today are singer-songwriters who do not depend on the labels to feed them lyrics, they are attracted to the independents. In this atmosphere, it is not so much about the money, but recognition. Revenue from streaming has historically been relatively modest since a large proportion of people who stream do not belong to paying sites or apps. Hu reports that "at least 60 million of Spotify's 100+ million users are only on the free tier, and fewer than 5 percent of Pandora users pay for its ad-free services."[28] The MMA may enhance streaming royalties, but even if it does not significantly increase revenue for artists, streaming attention builds an audience base, and that can translate into turnout at tours, where artists make their real money today. A major artist with a major label will tour to larger crowds and generate a greater income, but with 360 deals today, the majors reach deeper into the artist's pockets. Formerly, the majors made their money from record sales, but with those sales slipping they now take a piece of everything the artist does. Not only do they profit from the tour itself but also from merchandise sold, sponsorships, endorsements, websites, fan clubs and their associated ads, literary rights, and even acting.[29] This is less pronounced with independent labels, so while the artist may play to smaller audiences, they get to keep a greater percentage of the tour income.

It is worth noting that the majors are far from dead, as some headlines scream. Universal and Sony's market share might be chipped at but between the two they control over 50 percent of the market. The artist's strong name recognition has traditionally carried the label, and big names still do. However, a lot of talented artists have parted ways with their label or chosen to eschew association with the majors. The majors are certainly not dead but the independents branding their own artists in their own unique way are increasingly moving into an area dominated by the majors. Independent labels come in many varieties. Some are sizable, some have some heft, and quite a few are run on a shoestring. All are getting their artists recognized and cutting into the majors' profits. Each is looked at in turn since each has a different business model based on their size.

THE BIG-LITTLE INDEPENDENTS

Universal is the top of the majors, boasting the largest and most name-recognizable artist roster. Universal Nashville represents thirty-nine artists, including Sugarland, Shania Twain, Luke Bryant, Lady Antebellum, and Keith Urban, among a host of other highly regarded, well-known artists. Big Machine is one of the larger independents and closest to the majors in its organizational dynamics, largely because it has a fair-sized artist roster and generates a significant income. This is why the majors lust after the big-littles. Big Machine has four nondescript proximate houses on Music Row: it represented twenty-nine artists prior to its sale in 2019, including Taylor Swift,[30] Ronnie Dunn, Rascal Flatts, and Justin Moore, to name a few. This is a fairly robust roster and actually surpasses Sony Music Nashville, which handles twenty-three artists.

Broken Bow Records (BBR) ranks alongside Big Machine and a handful of other Nashville-based large independents. At the time of the sale to BMG (Sony) in 2017, BBR had eighteen artists on its roster, including Jason Aldean, Tracy Adkins, and Thompson Square. BBR is BMG's largest acquisition since launching in 2008. BMG has announced BBR will maintain its Nashville headquarters and its four labels. They've also stated that all 48 staff members will remain in their current positions; Benny Brown and CFO Paul Brown will remain as consultants while Jon Loba, who was interviewed before the sale, continues as executive vice president, reporting to BMG's North American President of Repertoire & Marketing Zach Katz.[31]

Like most people in the business, Loba took whatever job he could to get his foot in the musical door. His first introduction into the business was part-time accounting-related work with BMI. They wanted to hire him full-time but Loba quickly realized that desk work shifting financial documents was not something he wanted to do; he wanted to be at the heart of the music business in Nashville. Loba landed a job with Warner. When the person who hired Loba at Warner moved to Atlantic Records, he enticed Loba to make the move to Atlantic. "Everyone said I was crazy for leaving Warner to go to Atlantic" because the word on the street was that Atlantic was going to be shut down. I knew though that if I could get at least six months of phone calls in it would cement some relationships. . . . We actually made it a year and a half before Atlantic closed." This was Loba's introduction to the realities of big-league music:

> Talk about an illusion. We had taken Atlantic from the red to being in the black in a year and a half. I thought, "Wow, this is great, we're not going to be consolidated. We are making a profit and will continue [as a freestanding label]." It didn't happen that way. So I thought I needed to be in control of my destiny. I was doing some independent promotion work for Sony Music when I got a call from Broken Bow. I really hadn't intended to go there: they didn't have a great reputation and they hadn't broken the top forty in twenty years. But they kept calling me to come in for an interview. I stiff-armed them for a while and when they asked me what it would take [to sign me], I named a ridiculous figure, and to my surprise they said, "Congratulations, you are [now] a member of Broken Bow Records." I went in on Monday and they made me the vice president of promotions, which was some jump because I had only Southeast experience. . . . I was twenty-nine.

At the time, Benny Brown was in L.A. and only half-heartedly committed to the label on the other side of the country. Things were not going well at Broken Bow. Loba finally said, "Fuck it" and called Brown, who he had yet to meet, to tender his resignation. "Benny said, 'I have been in that town for three years now and spent over five million dollars and all anyone has ever tried to do [to this outsider] was take my money. You are the first one that has tried to leave.' He asked me to hang around for a few weeks because he wanted to fly out and talk to me. We sat down and he asked what the problems were and what he needed to do to fix them. I told him, and I also said we needed staff. He allowed me to hire Lee Adams,[32] and we just started to build from there." The two built a solid relationship and a successful company.

Loba brought country artist Craig Morgan over from Atlantic, but Jason Aldean put Broken Bow on the map. Since signing with BBR in 2005, Aldean has had nineteen number one singles with another eight hitting the top ten, an impressive track record at just over a decade, considering that both MCA and Capitol dropped him from their roster. Jon Loba recounts his discussion with Benny Brown about Aldean.

> We were starting to build a track record. I was very much into promoting the label as well as the artists. I always preached to Benny that the one way we were going to be competitive was staying small and staying focused. We had a hit on Joe Diffie, and Craig Morton, and Sherrie Austin, and he said that he had heard [from a friend] about an act and he wants to go see him.
>
> I said, "Benny, we don't need any more acts. Our plate is full with these three." I told you we had to be small and focused. But he insisted, so I say, "Fine, who is it?" He says, "I don't know, it's a kid. He was signed with MCA and got dropped and then he was with Capitol and got dropped, and he's never released."
>
> "Oh, great," I thought. We are going to see somebody that at least two other labels have dropped. I asked where we were going to see him and he says the Wildhorse Saloon. I said, "Benny, we're going to see some act that has been dropped twice, and we are going where the acoustics were terrible. Benny said, "Well, we had to get him into a venue quickly because if he doesn't get a label soon he is going back to Georgia to drive a Pepsi truck. He has a family to take care of."
>
> He said he liked going to the Wildhorse and didn't care about the acoustics. "I don't want to go to one of those industry places where everyone tries to hype me up. I want to see how the people do and how the people react. I don't need all those Music Row mucky-mucks telling me what is a hit and what isn't." So we go to the Wildhorse and I sat at a table with my arms folded and a "prove it" in my attitude, because I did not want to have any more on my plate. The artist came out and after the first song, my arms fell to my sides, by the second song I was leaning forward and at the third song Benny asked me what I thought, and I said, "I think we better run back [to the

> office] before anyone realizes what they lost." He was thinking the same thing. We went backstage and Benny stuck out his hand and says, "Jason Aldean, congratulations, we would like to offer you a deal on Broken Bow Records."
>
> Benny nailed it. Jason's first single hit the town and exploded. We hit gold within twelve weeks and we went from a label that couldn't get air play to a label that can sell records. Jason won ACM [Academy of Country Music] new artist of the year. . . . We can now say to a new prospect: "There is nothing you can do at a major that you cannot do here."

Despite the success with Aldean, Loba left BBR in 2007. He had an offer from Scott Borchetta at Big Machine and felt he needed "to prove to myself that I can run with Scott." He told Benny he would be back in three years. It was his doctoral program, and after "graduating" he returned to BBR in 2010. One of the main things he learned was how to be tougher. "I don't like being confrontational. I am still that way, but Scott sharpened my sword. There are times when you have to stand up. If someone takes a swing at you, you have to swing back. He made me a better record executive."

BBR remains strongly tied to country, though they've had a recent crossover duet with Jason Aldean and Kelly Clarkson. Like many other independents, they have no pop section. Loba doesn't rule it out down the road, but it is not on the front burner. All of their labels are country, but each label is slightly different. The rationale for having separate labels at BBR is pretty much the reasons the majors have separate labels rather than one monolithic one. Loba's mantra at BBR was to stay small, even as they grew. Brown's solution to small was to open another imprint: each imprint had its own staff and their job was promoting the artist on that label. Brown opened Stony Creek with considerable success while Loba was at BBR working the Valory label. When Stony Creek started to fill up, they opened another. Broken Bow Records is BBR Music Group's initial label, but there are four groups under it; the most recent, the Everett, was added in February 2018. Stony River, Red Bow Records, and Wheelhouse Records each have five artists. Red Bow was a joint venture with Sony. While at Big Machine, Loba saw the way Borchetta successfully partnered with Universal. Since Sony wanted to buy BBR, but Brown didn't want to sell, Loba suggested a joint venture, which suited both companies. Each free-standing label pivots on and promotes their artists.

The labels are artist-driven, but also executive-driven. The executive aspect was a key reason for launching many of the labels. There was a lot of consolidation taking place in the early 2000s as the heyday 1990s started to fade and the majors started to cut back staff. Brown calculated that there were going to be some very talented record label executives out of work that Loba could get at a reasonable price. This is another reason the independents succeed. They are not just about the artist, but also the staff. Broken Bow was actually staffing up while the majors were cutting back. Loba says the majors have success but get bloated with artists and employees. Then there will be a contraction in the market, and then they will have to lay someone off. They then go through it again and, somewhere down the road, yet again. "I want people to be here long term and have security. We're family. . . . I know that is an overused term, but it's true." Indeed, family was a moniker independent executives frequently used; it is a term seldom heard, or at least not really believed, among the majors, since everyone knows that corporate is more about the bottom line and that when profits start to slip the bottom line is shorn up by cutting back staff. Loba underscores his point when he mentions a staff member who wasn't the right fit for the job she was in and she was being affected both physically and mentally. But she was at an age where she might not be able to get another job. So Loba found something for her to do within the company. "I wanted her taken care of. It has worked out too; she is flourishing in her new position." That's family!

MOVING ON UP: MID-SIZED LABELS

Sales figures are closely guarded, so hard numbers are difficult to obtain and therefore cannot be used as a measuring rod to differentiate labels by size. Mid-sized labels are here defined, then, as ones that have a fair-sized staff and promote a number of artists, but fly under the radar of the majors, often because they inhabit specialized niches. It is easy to distinguish them from the small independents, however, because the small ones are often one-person operations with a support staff of just two to three people. Small independents tend to be located in private homes or rent space in office complexes in and around Nashville. Two mid-sized labels are critiqued here. Both have carved out a sizable niche: one is the Christian label Daywind Records in Hendersonville, a city in the northeast corner of Nashville-Davidson County. The other is Average Joes Entertainment, which started on Music Row, but its rapid ten-year growth required a larger facility. Average Joes relocated to a more spacious and cost-efficient warehouse district off Nolensville Road, eight miles south of Music Row.

Daywind Records: The Christian Sector

Christian music is as much a mainstay to the Nashville music scene as country music.[33] Word Music[34] is a Christian music publisher of some heft that Curb

Music, another big-little independent in Nashville, purchased from Warner in 2016. Daywind is smaller than Word, but hardly a mom-and-pop operation, even if mom (Dottie Leonard Miller) started the company in her garage twenty-six years ago. Her son, Ed Leonard, now runs the company; he's been involved with Daywind since 1993.

Like many initial ventures, Daywind started small, finding a niche distributing Christian music, typically to small venues that were neglected by the major distributors. In the process, Dottie Leonard Miller found and developed independent Christian artists only to have them leave for one of the major Christian labels. To keep the artists she nurtured, she started her own label. Although 30-some percent of the business is now in production, Daywind is still strong in distribution. Distribution provides a relatively good idea of what people want to hear and thus feeds production. Daywind's "on the ground" distribution network also puts them in touch with potential artists for their label.

> We try to make records for what people want. . . . Instead of getting a new artist and spending millions on getting them promoted, we focus on someone that may have done it on their own for a while and has a track record. If we take a chance on a new artist, it is usually someone coming out of a group. [Christian music] is a lot like bluegrass because you can take bluegrass artists and, tracing their family tree, you usually find three or four artists that are popular in the bluegrass world. The same can be said of southern gospel.

Daywind presently has sixteen artists and a state-of-the-art studio, Daywind Soundtracks, on the premises. Nevertheless, despite its decent-sized artist and writer roster, Daywind currently produces only ten albums a year in-house. It is worth noting that Daywind Soundtracks releases fifteen songs a month, which is equivalent to roughly thirty or more albums per year, but Daywind's studio is often underused. In an effort to better utilize the space, the company recently launched "Live at Daywind," a program that transforms the recording studio into a television studio for the day. They film three artists, making sure to mix in new songs, to create three episodes for Christian television. They also rent out the studio to shore up their bottom line.[35]

To feed the artists with lyrics, they have a separate publishing company with sixteen to twenty writers under contract. Daywind's primary distinction is that their writers do not receive a draw, mainly because there is less return on the Christian product. Leonard adds that "there is less air play because the market is tight so there is less chance you get a song on an album or less of an opportunity to get airplay." The Christian market relies less on radio because the Christian radio market is not as broad-shouldered as the secular pop, rock, and country markets. There is, however, some indication this is changing: Berklee College of Music recently reported that while Christian album sales are a paltry 3.6 percent of all albums sold in the United Sates, Christian music played on Christian radio is on the upswing.[36] Streaming has also taken its toll. Leonard repeats a sentiment heard often in the business. "You used to have a collection of records, now you have a digital single. It is true that streaming is up; unfortunately, with streaming you get a fraction of a fraction of what you'd get on an album." The hope, widespread within the industry, is that this situation will change with the implementation of the Music Modernization Act.

The Christian artist, then, much like their secular cousin, relies on touring to generate an income stream. The tours are just aimed at a different demographic: churches and church-related festivals, revivals, and the like. These tours are sometimes just as large as popular secular ones. Christian music extravaganza Winter Jam brings in sizable audiences: one of its 2018 venues was the US Bank Arena in Cincinnati, Ohio, which holds 17,000 people. Winter Jam frequented forty-six arenas across the eastern half of the United States between January 5 and March 31, 2018. The average ticket price is only $15 (at the door). Costs are kept low because the Winter Jam Tour circumvents major ticket vendors; it is also more concerned about delivering the Christian message than reaping monetary profits. Nevertheless, Winter Jam's 500,000-plus attendees ensure a healthy bottom line.[37] In this case, the 360 deal is just as important for the label. It is particularly critical for Daywind because they have long had an exclusive gift line, and the gift segment (merchandise) is a major tour revenue stream. The 360 arrangement with the label, Leonard says, is more prominent in Christian Adult Contemporary (AC) than in southern gospel and gospel.

Most musical genres span a wide range of formats; so, too, does Christian music. There are three primary musical genres, each of which has a wide variety of subgenres, such as progressive Christian, Christian rap, praise and worship, inspirational, and so forth. Southern gospel is the smallest for Daywind at 15 percent, which is fairly hefty considering that southern gospel sales within the Christian format only account for 5.5 percent of the market. Southern gospel is followed by gospel both at Daywind and nationally (17.6 percent), with Christian AC riding high as best seller for Daywind and the industry (33.8 percent) at large.[38]

Southern gospel is rooted to country with four-part group harmony and gospel-laced lyrics. AC is pop-Christian with a gospel base. Gospel, says Leonard, is somewhere in between the two, with gospel leaving the country sound behind. It also tends to be embraced more by the African-American community: 93 percent of African Americans, more than 38 million people, listened to gospel music in the last year.[39] The distinction between southern gospel and gospel is easier to hear than to describe. It's like distinguishing between hip-hop and rock 'n' roll, says Jackie Patillo, president of the Gospel Music Association: "the rhythms are different, the syncopation is different, and even the harmonies are different."[40] The pop element of Christian AC clearly distinguishes it from the other two genres, as does its predominantly white artists and audience.

Leonard explains how gospel sells differently than Christian AC. Since both are strong markets, stronger than southern gospel, labels have to cater to both these groups to be successful. "If you take a choir, you need about twenty people. But if you take a guy with a guitar and mix a bit of sound, you have one person that can go and lead at a church. And that evolves into younger people attending services and then going out and humming the songs. The more it permeates the churches, the more it gets out and gets played on [Christian] radio."

The older generation, however, likes a different type of music, more gospel rooted. Daywind and others are not neglecting the aging Boomers at the expense of a younger audience.

> No matter what your business is, you're always chasing the young consumer, which is the future. But maybe at the expense of the big group of Boomers [1946-1965]. They like the hymns that harken back to their past. I refer to that as gospel-laced music rather than gospel-based.
>
> I sense a slight movement back to hymns in the churches. One of our artists is doing something called in-synchs. He will go into a church or community center, and churches will come together and he will lead them in singing hymns, and they are right back into the Church of God style, which is the music the Boomers grew up listening to. They just love it.

Crossover Christian pop doesn't work like crossover country-pop, however. "The profusion of 'glory', 'majesty', and 'kingdom,'" writes Spencer Ritchie in *Music Business Journal*, taxes "the patience of secular listeners, and is a barrier to the genre's projection. Finding ways to put faith on record in a more intimate and less jarring context, and with a different aesthetic, could make the form thrive."[41] Be that as it may, the method Ritchie advocates would dilute the Christian message. But then "pure" country fans aren't happy with the style of country pop, which is doing very well with its "watered down" country lyrics, so a crossover Christian pop (not AC) style is possible.

In the end, most in the industry tend to separate the formats. We saw this with John Berry in the chapter about songwriters. Berry has a well-established country career but does a successful six-week Christian tour over the holiday season. Something similar was done at Daywind with the country group Shenandoah after lead vocalist Marty Raybon rejoined the group in 2014.

Daywind had a relationship with Shenandoah through a contemporary music arm that was run by Jack Green after he left Word Records. The group wanted to do a gospel album and decided Daywind was a good home for that. They already had a secular publisher, says Leonard, "but wanted to concentrate on the gospel market because country music doesn't try to penetrate that market, at least as a radio market. You might get a [gospel] song played in the country market, but not a whole album." In fact, Shenandoah has had some gospel songs over the years (1987-present) that became popular in the secular market, "but this [project] was just something they wanted to do; they wanted to separate their gospel music from the country music. . . . If it works to their satisfaction, they may come back and do another one."

Average Joes Entertainment: Country Rap and More

Average Joes typifies organic growth, which is the traditional business model for many small independent companies. Organic growth bypasses inorganic acquisition in favor of steady customer base expansion by slowly evolving the initial product line. Average Joes was initially Atlanta-based. The company was formed in 2006; it released its first country rap album, which was by Colt Ford, the company's co-founder, in 2008. These two years are important, says managing partner Shannon Houchins, because it helped them fine-tune their business model.

Houchins had a basic idea of where he was going. He was a business consultant in Atlanta but, like many consultants, was frustrated because "as a consultant your success is dependent on people listening to you," which is often problematic. Someone said to him one day, "Why don't you start your own business?" And so he did. Houchins tapped long-time friend Colt Ford, an entrepreneur and pro golfer since 1992. Things just blew up from there, so they followed it: "The Colt [country-rap] thing just took off super-fast."

Houchins's own roots transverse both country and rap, so he understood what Ford was doing. His father was a huge country music fan, so he grew up listening to country music, but his age inclined him toward rap, which he "had a good understanding of culturally." Blending the two, however, is not that simple. "I get a lot of songs from country artists saying, 'Here's a song for Colt.' I listen to it and it's almost offensive." The lyrics are country but the rapping is forced. It works the other way, too. "I have rap producer friends and the songs are just as offensive from a country music point-of-view." He feels he's a conduit for that segment of the market—young country people who grew up with rap—because he, like they, grew up in both worlds. "I'm in meetings [with music executives] telling them about this audience and this world and it's just a blank stare. They don't want to admit to things they don't know anything about; it is a whole other world."

Since Colt Ford's roots were country, they spent considerable time in Nashville—so much so that it simply made sense to move the company's base of operation. They initially relocated to a 3,000-square-foot building on Music Row, but soon needed more room so moved into a 9,000-square-foot remodeled warehouse (Cummings Station) off Music Row. Unfortunately, because the warehouse was in an office complex, they could record vocals and overdubs but couldn't do any drum work. At the time of the interview in mid-2016, they had just moved into a 30,000-square-foot state-of-the-art facility. The spackling paste was hardly dry on the wallboard and Houchins was already thinking of expanding to an adjacent building because, with three simultaneous projects under development, they were already running out of room and he wanted to better accommodate television production.

The physical expansion grew naturally out of their musical development. They initially thought of themselves as a music label, but once in Nashville drifted toward being a country label with such country-rooted artists as Warren Bryant, Corey Smith, and Montgomery Gentry. With the burgeoning success of Colt Ford's country rap, the country rap subgenre started to take precedent and another label was added, followed by a classic rap label. While country rap is their dominant format today and country is their current mainstay, Average Joes moved back toward being "a label" with no identifying moniker. "It's circular," says Houchins, suggesting you "go with the flow."

Houchins wallows in the company's diversity. He was excited about a recently discovered artist who raps like Eminem but sings like Justin Timberlake. It's "something [you] never heard before. [It's] not what Average Joes does as a label," he says, "but it's good music . . . and it excites our marketing team because no one wants to do the same thing every day. People get into the music business because they don't want the humdrum life. One gets in the music business to be on the roller coaster. Humdrum doesn't inspire. If you go to Disney World every day, sooner or later you get bored with Disney World. Our office is set up so no one gets bored. . . ." The problem with the majors, he feels, is that you have to conform to fit into the musical system. Not his cuppa: "I'm always looking for something different . . . I just like things that are different." To ensure that ennui doesn't set in, Average Joes—besides being on the lookout for new, undiscovered artists across genres—is building a set to do stop-motion animation and a stage that allows for 360-degree (all around) camera shooting so one can simulate jumping off a one hundred-story building that is only actually six feet high.

Music still comprises 90 percent of the business, but that also looks to be evolving as the company starts to move into other production modes. They have between eighteen to twenty-two artists under contract at any one time and manage three to four artists who are not with their label. They also manage a few in-house artists, but this is not typical. The ones they do manage tend to be ones that started with them. Ford's records take longer to produce than the average country album, and his work, as well as most of their artists' roster, is produced in their on-site studio using mostly studio musicians, rather than electronic overdubs. They use whatever works best, however. "There's [all kinds of] different ways of doing [the music]; it's depending on what you are trying to achieve. "

THE LITTLE GUYS: SMALL INDEPENDENT LABELS

It is difficult to determine exactly what percent of the labels fall into this category; half, no doubt, probably upwards to three-quarters. Given the access to electronic programs, it is not unduly expensive to operate a small studio today. This does not mean it is cheap: a modest investment in quality studio equipment is at least $100,000, and this does not take into account normal operating expenses, which, even with a home studio, can add up. Unlike the independent artist, however, small independents labels tend to use state-of-the-art software programs in soundproofed rooms to ensure a quality recording. They typically use studio musicians but it is no longer necessary to gather everyone together at once to cut a record. Many of the small independents send music to the specific instrumental players or backup vocalists, who contribute their part of the song, or bring such-and-such player to the studio where their portion is separately recorded and then dubbed onto the final product. This method, as we'll see in the next section, has dramatically cut costs but it has also undermined the traditional contribution made by studio musicians recording together "live" with the artist. Still, it has certainly helped the small independents cost-effectively cut records.

There have always been small independent producers. Perhaps the best known is Cowboy Jack Clement (1931-2013) whose Tudor-style residence on Belmont Boulevard, a half-mile south of Music Row, was used as a studio and artist hangout until it burned down in 2011.[42] Zoning laws today tend to restrict the small independents from opening in residential neighborhoods, at least in the city. This is why one of the independents that is critiqued (AfterTouch Music) is situated within Davidson County but well outside the downtown urban core. The other two critiqued here have, until recently, been proximate to the downtown area; one (deciBel) was run out of an office building just off Music Row and the other (Infinity Cat) was run from a small one-story, Victorian cottage located in a mixed-use neighborhood.[43]

Dave Brainard of deciBel Productions represents the traditional country music path into independent production. The other two stand outside the typical Nashville county/pop window as they carve out unique musical niches. Roger Ryan at AfterTouch Music is a Trinidadian who focuses on producing Christian and Caribbean-influenced music. Robert Ellis Orrall at Infinity Cat Recordings has a long-established history in the Nashville country music community. Despite this, he is working with his sons, Jamin and Jake, to record post-punk pop music that, according to Steve Haruch in the *Nashville Scene,* is going far in helping to make Nashville a "city synonymous with a raw, restless strain of rock 'n' roll," and, like many of the small independents, is "doing it on almost no budget."[44]

Dave Brainard at deciBel Productions

Dave Brainard comes from a military family, which may explain why he joined the Air Force Band after a year in college. There, a friend who made regular trips to Nashville told him about NSAI and "kind of fueled this Nashville thing," so he moved to Nashville in 1999. Two years after arriving in Nashville, Brainard signed with Thom Schuyler at Balmur Corus Music: "Everything seemed to be moving quickly; it all seemed pretty easy." Unfortunately, shortly after signing with Balmur, the company folded and "it looked like it wasn't going to be so easy after all." Brainard signed another deal with Big Picture while continuing to play on the road with artists like David Nail, Anthony Smith, and Jessica Andrews. He also continued to develop his skills on the recording side of the business. "After learning Pro Tools, I went from doing $25 guitar demos" for the likes of Dierks Bentley and Chris Tompkins, to "making pretty good money doing full demos for hit songwriters and custom records for independent artists."

After making a name for himself, he opened deciBel in 2006 above Off Broadway Shoes on Demonbreun at the foot of Music Row. He brought in a partner, Brian Kolb, who had been working out of Famous Music's basement studio for a few years. "We were fairly busy that first year; by the second year, we had a very successful business going." Although Brainard was mostly producing demos, he branched out to produce a concept record[45] for his longtime friend, Jerrod Niemann, which included a little ditty called "Lover Lover." Niemann's publisher, Sea Gayle Music, pitched "Lover Lover" to Joe Galante at RCA, who signed the record as a completed work to Arista Records. When "Lover Lover," the first single, went to number one, Brainard "realized I had an opportunity to really develop my brand as a record producer."

Demos are a form of production, but not quite. "It is a different level," Brainard explains. "With demos, you work for hire. Being a producer comes with a different leverage in the industry. I needed to shut my demo business down so people weren't calling and saying, 'Hey, Dave, are you available to engineer a demo vocal or record a demo?' I wanted to change how people in the business perceived me." It was fortuitous timing because today artists are increasingly doing their own demos. The switch was not easy, however. Brainard had a very strong revenue stream from his demo work but starting the production side took a while. He made a few more records for some new artists and eventually hit with a Brandy Clark number that received multiple Grammy nominations (Best New Artist, Country Song of the Year, and Best Country Album), which is like "a big billboard sign that says, 'Here is what I do.'" It never hurts, he adds, when "you bring a Grammy into the conversation."

These two all-too-brief paragraphs should not be construed as depicting an easy road to success. Brainard hit some speed bumps along the way that might have discouraged someone else. He invested everything to take the financial plunge to open, which ensured a heavy work schedule. He was putting in fourteen-hour days, seven days a week. He is still in the office by nine or ten in the morning and often there ten to twelve hours later. Half his time is spent on the phone, lining up dates, scheduling sessions. "The job of a producer requires a lot of organizational skills and time-consuming paperwork. It's not all creativity. It's about keeping the process humming along so you get the final product to the finish line in a timely manner." In 2017, Brainard moved the studio from the Demonbreun location to Berry Hill, a part of town that has been nicknamed "Mini-Music Row" because of the increasing number of studios, smaller record labels, and publishers that have been attracted to the area.[46] His previous location had some limitations in space and acoustic treatment; the new space expanded to a larger facility better suited to track a full band, which is very important to Brainard. He claims his best instrument is his Rolodex of musicians he's worked with over the years.

The process of recording for Brainard is all about collaborating with live musicians. The traditional approach to making music is for studio musicians to all play together in a large studio with a big tracking room and isolation booths.

Brainard takes more of a layered approach to track building. First, there is pre-production, where an album and arrangements are sketched out, after which the drums or percussions can be added to existing guide tracks. From there he builds out each track with whatever instruments or textures are inspired next, until the track feels complete. Bringing in session musicians to record their contributions individually has its benefits: "You don't step on anyone's toes." The one-on-one collaborations with the musicians give ample opportunity to experiment and be creative. Brainard believes that the final product has a handcrafted feel because the artist is involved at every phase of the arrangement. This process sounds fairly straightforward but it is quite complex and typically takes from four to six months. Time constraints notwithstanding, Brainard is kept quite busy. He had already finished four studio projects at the time of the interview in mid-2017 and was in the midst of four more which, he said with a pleasantly exhausted sigh, "is an awful lot."

Roger Ryan at AfterTouch Music

Roger Ryan is from Trinidad but went to Hope College in Huntsville, Alabama, where he hung out with Take 6,[47] a gospel music sextet from Huntsville. Take 6 moved to Nashville and, after graduating in 1996, Ryan followed. "I would follow them around, do odd music jobs, travel with them, and even got into some of their sessions." The most important connection he made was with CeCe Winans: "I became her first music director, and that is kind of how I got into the music business." He connected with Winans in the traditionally fortuitous Nashville manner, which is to say he knew this person who knew that person, who knew another person, and that came together because he worked hard and has talent.

> I happened to know some of the guys that played with her, and I knew her brother-in-law. I was doing a job in Toronto with a group called the Toronto Mass Choir . . . I got them hooked up with EMI and stuff like that. While there, this man and his wife that I knew came to one of our rehearsals and heard me and watched me put this live recording together. They asked me to work on a record for them. In the meantime, [my brother-in-law] called and said that CeCe wanted me to play for her and be her music director. I went to where they were rehearsing and sat down and played, and CeCe asked me to go on the road with her, and I said, "Well, let me think about it." I was trying to be nice about saying 'no' because I had this commitment with this other group. I spoke with Mark Kibble [with Take 6] who is like my big brother, and he said, "Did you really turn CeCe Winans down? Really?"
>
> He convinced me to talk to the Toronto people and see if we could work

> something out. So I went back to CeCe and said I have this group I am working with in Canada that I am committed to, but if you will allow me to, I will go to Ft. Lauderdale with you and do the first concert, fly back to Canada to do the [live] recording, and meet up with you on the road.

Ryan was with Winans from 1996 to 1999. He always liked to arrange and produce and starting doing more of that. "I've always had a gift for arranging," he says modestly. He did some work for EMI, with whom he had a preexisting relationship, and some freelance stuff. Then he got a call from Wynonna Judd, who was looking for some players to go on the road with her. "I went and auditioned, and three days later I was her keyboard player, and four days after that we did the presidential dinner for Bill Clinton; it was my second presidential gig."[48] Ryan hasn't toured since 2006, though he's still traveling a lot, only now as a producer and owner of a new label.

Arranging led to production; after all, Ryan says, "production is a medium for arranging." It was always there to some degree.

> It started in the beginning, like when you are playing a song and you change the beginning and the end. You change keys and modulate, and every time you change something you are, in effect, arranging. So production became my way of showing off my arrangements. When I was called in to do sessions, I wasn't being called to just play; I was being called so they could use some of my chording. I was being called for my arrangements. I wanted to be in the driver's seat because, frankly, I wasn't getting paid the way I should have been paid as an arranger; I was just [paid as] a session artist.
>
> I still do arrangements. Someone calls me for a string arrangement and I can do that here [in my home studio]. I'll put it together and send it back to them. Or I can get a four-string group and do a session arrangement, but if I do that, I am not involved in production. They can [just] pay me for the arrangement and I am fine. But then if someone calls me and asks me about this and that and [the] "that" means I am making the decisions on studios, music, producing, and all that, then they have to pay me [as a producer].

Producing also means knowing your artist. "The music is just a small part of it. Like when you are working on a track, the track has to fit the artist. It has to work for and with the artist. If you aren't doing that, then you aren't producing." He realizes that young artists build their own tracks today, but when a professional is working on a track, he says, it is no longer a track. "A track is an organic moving thing with a voice and a melody attached to it. . . . When you are putting an artist to a track, you have to decide, 'Is this the right key for the artist? Do we have a lower one? Is this the right tempo? Do we have to change it? Do we have to change some of the instrumentation? Do we have to add. . . ?'"

The production aspect is pretty much what Brainard does at deciBel. Instead of renting offices like Brainard, Ryan works out of his home. His work station and recording equipment is in the basement, and he has a fair-sized glassed-in soundproofed studio that is large enough to accommodate a small group. Ryan goes further than Brainard by producing videos and his own label. At the time of the interview in 2016, Ryan had four videos in various stages of production. He also uses a fellow in Trinidad for video work to make documentaries of his artists in Trinidad. He produces a range of artists and has four under contract with another three or so in various stages of development. He often visits and scouts Trinidad for talent: "Trinidad is unique. There's calypso, of course, but also gospel, as well as R&B and pop music." He was working with an artist from Trinidad at the time we met: "She is sort of pop rock. Her voice is amazing. I really love her work." Other acts from Trinidad include a reggae artist and a Christian artist

He laughed when I asked him how long it takes to develop an artist: "I think that is never done." He has two young artists who in 2018 were eighteen years old that he's been developing since they were thirteen: one is from North Carolina, the other is from Dixon, Tennessee, a city adjacent to Nashville.

Ryan's Trinidadian roots lead him to develop artists from the island that he frequently visits, but he is wide-ranging in the artists, and genres, he produces. This is typical of most independents—one goes where the music is, even if, like Ryan, most have a specialized niche. And like most other independents, he doesn't see the need to shop his artists to a major label. "Why would I sign an artist and then send them to someone else? It is why I have the label. They are all A-level artists here." And they are all given A-level attention!

Robert Ellis Orrall at Infinity Cat Recordings

Like many, Robert Ellis Orrall found his love for music in high school and, like some, his father urged him to go to college to have something to fall back on. He decided in short order that college was of limited interest and so started to pursue his music career. His first naïve step was to pony up $1,000, a substantial sum for a young man in 1977, to make a record, which he sent to the various record labels in search of a record deal. The only thing he collected was rejection letters. Some years later, while playing a club in Boston, he was discovered by a person from RCA England who had a new job as a scout and was looking to make his bones by signing his first deal. He made three albums for RCA, the first in Boston, the second and third in Monmouth, Wales, and London, England. He had one top forty hit before he was released by RCA after four years.

After his artist experience, he started songwriting. He had long piddled with writing songs but didn't know much about country music except that he noticed most of the songs were written by songwriters and not the artist performing them. Figuring he might get songs cut in Nashville, he started to visit the city. The first named group to pick up one of his songs was The Oak Ridge Boys. He and his wife decided to move to Nashville in 1991 after having a number one hit with Shenandoah, "Next to You, Next to Me."[49] He arrived just as the country music market was about to explode and rode the wave.

Shortly after arrival in Nashville, Orrall did a show at the Bluebird. The next day he got a call from the head of A&R at RCA who expressed an interest in working with him. He asked who the artist was that RCA had in mind for his songs and they said, "You are!" He did a country album with RCA that had a top fifteen song and then, as happens with the majors, the regime changed and he was dropped. Next Orrall signed with Giant and was nominated for a duo of the year at the CMA Awards, despite no longer being associated with his singing partner. Shortly thereafter "I hung up my performing shoes" and started writing full-time. He connected with a young Taylor Swift and wrote with her after school and on weekends. Orrall had three cuts on her first eight-million-selling record, which he co-produced with Big Machine. He, like many in the Nashville community, has nothing but admiration for Swift's talent, in no small part because, for Orrall, "the statements [royalties] keep coming in." He had a string of other hits over the years, including producing "Love and Theft" for Disney and launching the career of the Reklaws. In 2002, he started Infinity Cat.

His two sons had a punk rock band called The Sex, later renamed JEFF, which ultimately morphed into JEFF The Brotherhood. "They decided they wanted to start a record label. I thought it would be fun." He told them that they had to do it on a shoestring budget because he didn't want to have investors. Their first album was taped live at Guido's Pizza. They sold the CD on site, even though the CD box contained no record since it was being recorded that night. Orrall says they sold eleven albums and made $88.00. The next recording by the group JEFF had a color Xerox cover and was positively reviewed in the *Nashville Scene.* It was shortly after the second album that Infinity Cat really became a record producer: "We started putting out records for their friends." Profits were split fifty-fifty with the artist "but we didn't hold them down to long-term contracts." Orrall acknowledges that the no-contract arrangement may not be the best business model but it worked for them. "Some ended up with Third Man [Records] or Saddle Creek. They are our alumni. If they were ever on our label, they are still part of us. We are really in it for that [more than the money]."

The exact number of people who have passed through Infinity Cat is difficult to say with certainty, but Orrall does know that at the time of the interview (2016) they had released 110 records. Besides JEFF The Brotherhood, Infinity Cat's nucleus includes Music Band, Daddy Issues, and Diarrhea Planet, a name which, in itself, is sure to be off-putting to a major label, no matter how good the band might be. The staff consists of himself, his son Jake, Ale Delgardo, and Holland Nix, who manages the four main bands associated with Infinity Cat;[50] as well as a few interns from Belmont University. There are no plans for growth, which is why they are no longer taking solicitations: "We don't want to get any bigger. In fact, we would like to get smaller. We want to shrink to three or four releases a year on vinyl."

JEFF The Brotherhood had a brief flirtation with Warner Brothers. Warner wanted to work with them. Orrall says they had a great time. "They worked with a quality producer and recorded at the famous Black Bird Studio. [Warner] spent twenty times more than we ever spent on a record. The sound was great, everything worked fine, but [the record] wasn't them." Warner wanted to "hear hits," and so pushed the group in a direction they were not comfortable with. Four weeks before the record was to be released, Warner dropped the band. The band didn't really mind. The music "was not them. They make music for themselves, and if you like it, great, and if you don't, that's okay, too. That's how Frank Zappa made records." And that's the tradition Infinity Cat wants to emulate, and they are doing it quite nicely without a major label.

Recording the Music

Studios are used less frequently today for making demonstration (demo) cuts of a song. Nevertheless, the major labels still use studios to record at least a portion of their final project. The independents use studios, as well. The key difference between the major and independent labels is that majors are more likely to gather an ensemble to record the song with the artist in studio while the independents are more apt to record studio musicians' contribution to the album independently. This section discusses the changes that have taken place in the use of studios and studio musicians and then critiques how artists not affiliated with a label mix their music by using electronic platforms.

THE STUDIO SYSTEM

Despite music's long history in Nashville, studio development did not start until three engineers at WSM began to conduct recording sessions in 1946[51] and did not kick into high gear until the 1950s. It was during this period (1946–1955) that the major labels began to open offices in Nashville. The first was Capitol Records, followed by RCA, Columbia, Decca; BMI would open its offices nearby these labels near the foot of Music Row.[52] The studios brought with them the latest technology, introduced by Columbia in 1948. Prior to the new 33rpm LP vinyl discs, 78rpm records were made on the basis of "do two takes and choose the one with the fewer mistakes."[53] The new discs used tapes to lay down the music, and this allowed the recording to be edited: "embarrassing miscues . . . or wrong notes could be corrected by substituting snippets of tape from a different take."[54] Since the studio system itself came of age in the city at this time, Nashville quickly embraced the new system.

Two studio system developments nudged the music business in Nashville forward. One was the new studio operated by Owen and Harold Bradley. They purchased a house on 16th Avenue in an area that would subsequently become Music Row.[55] The Bradleys tore the floor out of the home so that when they recorded in the basement the music would rise; i.e., not sound like it was made in a small space. This really didn't do all that much, so the Bradleys bought a surplus, prefabricated metal World War II Quonset hut that they put behind the original building and moved studio production there.[56] This too was a bit primitive. Still, the recordings improved. They found that covering the ceiling with a curtain buffered the sound. Two other interior changes also improved the recorded sound: 1) wood paneling installed around the interior walls significantly reduce the "ping" echo caused by the tile floor, and 2) a waist-high wooden panel "baffle" placed between the bass microphones decreased the amount of bleed between the two.[57] Brenda Lee recorded her first major hit, "Sweet Nothin's" (1959) in the Quonset hut.

The other major recording development of the time was the new RCA studio, located a block down the street from the Quonset hut, known at the time as "Studio A." However, RCA built a second studio adjacent to the first in 1963. The original "A" studio, which produced a stream of legendary artists (Hank Snow, Jim Reeves, Elvis Presley, Charley Pride, and Waylon Jennings),was subsequently "demoted" in status and to this day carries the name "Studio B."

Legendary Chet Atkins oversaw RCA's Nashville operation. The new, nondescript studio was the first Nashville built-from-scratch state-of-the-art studio. When it was finished, however, writes longtime veteran of the Nashville music community Michael Kosser, "the sound was, just, well, *all right.* [*sic*]"[58] The sound vastly improved, Kosser goes on to say, when the studio's engineer, Bill Porter, "bought a number of two-foot-by-four-foot acoustical tiles, and cut and assembled them into pyramid-shaped devises that they hung at various heights." The acoustic tiles broke up the sound waves and served a similar purpose as paneling on the walls. After experimenting with microphone placement, the RCA studio "sounded like it was supposed to sound, a crystal-clear, neutral room, a blank page on which all sorts of wonderful music could jump from the artist and the musicians, into a mastering console, then onto a record. . . ."

In their article, "More than Microphoning" Steven Parker and Robert Davis cogently point out that it took more than simple microphone placement.[59] In this case, the sound system was vastly improved by John E. Volkmann, who worked his entire professional career for RCA and subsequently designed the sound system for the John F. Kennedy Center in Washington.[60] Volkmann added poly-cylindrical walls to the studio room. The cylinders—which can be seen in old photos of the RCA studio—look like humps on the wall. This rounded out the sound in such a way that, when it hit the wall, it reflected and rolled back so, according to former studio manager Sharon Corbitt-House, "you didn't have that big boomy sound like in a gymnasium. It was just beautiful."

The 1950s and 1960s also saw a dramatic change in the role of the studio engineers as they "evolved from craft-based technicians to creative artists."[61] Parker and Davis argue that this evolution "can be attributed largely to technological change, which allowed the engineer to gain a greater stake in the creative decision-making process."[62] In short, the engineer became part of the interactive song-creating team and not someone who simply manipulated dials on a recording device.

The interactive aspect of the studio is one of the key dynamics that marks the Nashville studio system. The studio promotes deep and personal ties between people, especially among those who have worked together intimately creating music over some years. Indeed, the bonds these individuals form may obscure the work put into honing their craft, because playing together just looks "natural." The synergy developed in the studio explains why musicians in Nashville can typically record a cut in a matter of hours when the same scenario in a Los Angeles or New York studio would take the whole day, if not longer.[63]

The famous Nashville Sound also arrived with the burgeoning new studio system. "Nashville Sound" started as a complimentary term by professionals outside of Nashville used to characterize the way musicians in Nashville came together to produce music. Their camaraderie remains a hallmark of studio performances to this day. Just about everyone in the business would agree with former studio manager Sharon Corbitt-House when she says, "There is a lot to be said about a group of people getting together and rubbing shoulders that spawns a feeling or an emotion that takes you in directions you [are unlikely] to go on your own."[64] A key part of the Nashville Sound—then and now—is the improvisation of musicians working together in the studio, rather than recording the music as it was written. Indeed, "what happens in the studio," Ron "Snake" Reynolds says, "is as important as the song itself. So all songs, to a great degree, are made or lost in the recording studio during the recording process."[65] Reynolds goes on to provide a few examples of times when cutting a song in the studio serendipitously improved the final product.

> While recording George Jones's classic, "He Stopped Loving Her Today," the string arranger, Bill McElhiney, had written the glissando (ascending) violin line at two places in each chorus to be only two beats long. When Billy Sherrill heard the first rundown of the strings playing, he immediately said, "Double the length of those glissandos to four beats." This became the musical hook and added a certain emotional lift to the song. Another example would be the bass riff in Johnny Paycheck's song, "Take This Job and Shove It." You cannot think of that song without hearing that riff. The same with Hargus "Pig" Robbins's iconic piano introduction to "Behind Closed Doors" by Charlie Rich. As soon as you hear the first few notes, you know what the song is. Both the piano introduction and the walking bass riff were improvised during the tracking sessions.

Reynolds also notes another aspect of the studio system that is critical in producing a quality album. "The singer(s) have to be cajoled, inspired, and put at ease so that they can deliver an emotional performance while standing in a room with no audience and listening to music over headphones." Sharon Corbitt-House echoes this sentiment. Her job working with artists is not much different from that performed by artist managers. Unlike the full-time job of the artist manager, which is taken up in the next chapter, Corbitt-House's managerial expertise is confined to the studio.

> I was good at taking care of creatives because you have to be part psychologist and part cheerleader. My role was to help them capture [in the studio] what they did live. I did a lot of homework before they came into the studio. I reached out to their managers to find out something about the artist(s). I would find out what their favorite foods were. I would find out what part of the country they were from and would have something there that would remind them of it so they'd be comfortable. I was always trying to be a bit of a distraction, a kind of mother hen. The idea was that when they [started to

perform] they would not be thinking about where they were and what they were doing.

It should be pointed out that while studio musicians' roles are obviously critical in a song's production, the producer also plays a key role. We've seen some glimpses of this with those small producers that are hands-on in the studio, like David Brainard at deciBel and Roger Ryan at AfterTouch. Pras et al. conducted one of the few studies to specifically address the producer's role.[66] The sample, small as it was with only six producers interviewed, is nevertheless instructive. They found five of the six producers in their study could also engineer recording sessions. Their conclusion is replicated in this study: "Musicians expect record producers to direct recording sessions artistically by providing guidance according to the aesthetic context, but without controlling the musicians."[67] The producer primarily served as a second pair of ears; e.g., making sure things are not out of tune and in the right tempo. Pras et al. mention another facet of studio work not previously addressed—tact! One does not say, "You are flat," but rather "the B-flat maybe could be a little higher."[68] This same sensitivity was discerned among all those interviewed about their studio work; it ensures that camaraderie does not turn to acrimony.

The comfortable camaraderie of the Nashville studio system, then and now, is a key component to making a quality recording. An offshoot of the Nashville Sound is the famous chord numbering system, created in 1953-1954 by Nashville native Neal Matthews, Jr., a founding member of the Jordanaires.[69] Musicologist Brian Kilian explains the Nashville Number System (NNS).[70] "It's similar to the Solfège system, which uses 'Do Re Mi Fa Sol La Ti' to represent the seven scale degrees of the major scale. In the key of C, the numbers would correspond as follows; C=1, D=2, E=3, F=4, G=5, A=6, B=7."

NASHVILLE NUMERICAL NOTATION	1	2	3	4	5	6	7
Solfège	Do	Re	Me	Fa	So	La	Ti
Common musical notation	C	D	E	F	G	A	B

Kilian elaborates: "The numbers do not change when transposing the composition into another key. They are simply relative to the new root note, so the key of C in the NNS would be noted as 1, 4, 1, and 5. These numbers represent major chords, and each chord should be played for one measure, so a 1 would be played in the key of C major (one bar), a 4 would be played in the key of F (one bar), and so on." Kilian provides the following example.

NNS	PLAYED IN KEY OF C	PLAYED IN KEY OF G
1454	C F G F	G C D C
1155	C C G G	G G D D

The NNS still reigns in the Nashville studios and among Nashville musicians in general, six decades after it was first introduced, but the same consistency cannot be said for the role of the studio musician.

Studio musicians have long ruled the roost in Nashville. Indeed, studio musicians are a key reason why Nashville is considered Music City.[71] The record labels, of course, relied on them. Before record sales began to decline at the outset of the new millennium, it was not uncommon for a studio musician to play on one cut at ten in the morning, record for another artist at two in the afternoon, and for yet another at six in the evening. During the heyday 1990s, says longtime Nashville studio musician Dave Pomeroy, studio musicians might do four sessions a day, every day. "We were so busy they'd even have a barber come in between session because there was no time to even get a haircut."[72] At that time, an album would release ten to twelve songs, and that took some time. Between cutting full-length artist albums and recording demos for publishers, studio musicians faced long days and frantic hours. The shorter formatted four-song EP "albums" and the move by many artists to create demos electronically leaves studio musicians and related studio personnel, such as the sound engineer, underutilized. The studio musician continues to be an important element of the final product, however. Of the seventy-five Top Ten country albums in 2018, Nashville studio musicians played on forty-six of them (61.3 percent).[73]

In a time when publishers typically created demos in the studio, musicians saw demo sessions as a key training ground for subsequent studio work and establishing a network. Other musicians got to know who you were and what you could do. "I learned a lot doing demos," says bassist Dave Pomeroy, who made his bones doing demo work for four years before graduating to the majors.

> Demos were the minor leagues. I learned how to be a studio player by doing demos. Songwriters who became producers, songwriters who became artists, we were all in there learning together. Suddenly the other guy is busy and then it's "Let's get that guy who did that demo; he was pretty good." There was always somebody who couldn't make it so it was "Who do we know [that can fill this slot]?" Sometimes it was literally the last person they worked with who might not be as busy as everybody else.

The quality of musicians available certainly helped bolster the Nashville studio system. Indeed, a key reason for the caliber of musicians in the city is that it drew extraordinarily talented musicians from other musical venues. Music was thriving in Nashville but started to falter in other areas of the country. Pomeroy explains the surplus of talented studio players in Nashville.

> Nashville became a magnet [in the 1990s]. A key element was that studio musicians from other recording centers weren't flourishing like they once were. So people who were very big in the Atlanta scene after it peaked were like, "What are we gonna do?" And the answer was, "Let's go to Nashville." The same with Muscle Shoals studio players, like Norbert Putnam, who tells the story of working nine to twelve hours and then getting a check for only three hours. [When the musicians complained] to their producer in Muscle Shoals, it was like, "I'm the only game in town so I'm going to pay you what I feel like paying you because if you don't want to do it someone else might." So, in Norbert's words, "We all moved to Nashville where an hour was an hour." The bluegrassers were also coming down from Louisville because they wanted to get on the Opry with [Bill] Monroe, and some of them became really good studio players. So Nashville was a magnet. The whole place was spreading out, horizontally rather than vertically.

Another key feature that bolstered the studio system in the 1990s was that the traditional dichotomy between studio and road musicians started to break down. "In the 1970s and 1980s, you were one or the other. There were very few exceptions. The studio guys were kind of a closed shop. [Artists] had their studio band and their road band. Road bands played the best they could. Standards on the road were not as high; you were just playing for fun."[74]

At the time, Pomeroy was playing on the road and when he was called to do a session, he said he was already booked. "I wouldn't say, 'No, can't. I'm on the road' because there was still a stigma [of a session player] being on the road." The stigma started to shift in the 1990s. He offers the example of Eddie Bayers, a well-known Nashville session drummer who toured with Wynonna Judd.

> Eddie played on all the Judds's records. Eddie was not a road guy; never his thing. But Wynonna loved him so much that she would pay him studio money to go out on the road [with her]. She fired a lot of drummers simply because they were not Eddie, and Eddie, being the kind of guy he is, would go 'Yeah, I can fill in for a couple of weeks (after she fired another drummer). Then there was Reba [McEntire]. After Reba's horrific plane crash, she had to reconstitute her band. By the late 1990s her band was pretty much a band of studio players.

Tony Harrell, a longtime studio musician who now manages MV2 Publishing, agrees with Pomeroy's assessment. Like Pomeroy, he spent his early days (1980s) on the road. He did some demo work and by 1991 started getting a name for himself as a studio musician, just when session playing was about to explode in Nashville. It was a hectic decade. "I was working five days a week—every week. It was an exception to have a day off."[75] He started returning to the road on weekends in the early 2000s, and in 2006 Amy Grant contacted him to play some symphony shows with her. "Amy's band was all studio musicians." The stigma had disappeared. "All during the 1990s there was a stigma. That was one reason I didn't go out on the road. You were either a road guy or a studio guy. Today, most of the top studio cats do live performances. You're viewed as an asset. You go out, mostly on weekends, do a great show, do great music, then come home and play on a Taylor Swift record. It's the best of both worlds."

The line today is completely blurred, says Pomeroy. For some of the long-time session musicians, it's like, "Man, this is relaxing. And I only have to work two hours a day. Others don't like the road." But today, concludes Pomeroy, "There is no longer a line in the sand." Today, the line in the sand between studio work and an artist self-engineering his or her work is starting to blur as well.

THE ARTIST AS PRODUCER/ENGINEER

Most in the industry recognize the benefit of creating one's own demos. The young artist-songwriters are very adept at doing this, and publishers applaud its cost-effectiveness. In fact, publishers tend to favor artist-songwriters who are skilled at making their own demo. Producing your own demo, however, does not typically give artists direct access to publishers or label executives, and even the independent labels tend to turn a deaf ear to unsolicited material.

Studio demos can cost a few thousand dollars (or more) to make; self-produced demos can be done for a few hundred dollars. Indeed, doing a studio-quality demo has its limitations. It may be too perfect, leaving the label's A&R guru or the artist unable to see how they can contribute to the song. "Producers especially," says song plugger Aubrey Schwartz, don't want a full demo and often "want to hear a lesser version because they want to do it their way."[76] A "lesser version" demo is fine since most producers feel that if the bones of a song are there they will be able to grasp how it might be tweaked to fit the style of their artist.

Doing your own album has historically been problematic. During the 1970s and 1980s even the studios found it nearly impossible to keep pace with the wave of technology spreading over the music industry. Studios invested millions of dollars yearly only to find their "cutting edge" technology already archaic after only a year or two.[77] At that time, home programs were particularly crude. In the last decade or so (post-2005), however, they've undergone radical transformation. Today there are a slew of state-of-the-art electronic programs that allow tech-savvy young artists to cut in a drum set or a guitar riff and release their own records. These same programs are also more modestly priced. "When digital came out it was prohibitively expensive," says Pomeroy. "Only the large studios could afford it. Now the kids can not only afford digital, they've grown up recording on computers. They understand the capabilities of recording on computers."

It helps that the younger musicians are not tied to one instrument. Dave Pomeroy played the bass, "And that's all I ever wanted to do." Eddie Bayers was a drummer; Tony Harrell played the keyboard. The younger generation "is not locked into one instrument. They play guitar, piano, drums. They know how to use the computer. And they're thinking from a producer's standpoint. I didn't know or understand what a producer did," quips Pomeroy, "until I'd been in the studio for some time. Kids are assimilating all this information at a much younger age." Maybe so, but "there's a big difference between demos and selling products to fans and trying to make it to radio," says Dennis Kurtz with Big Spark Music. "Every once in a while, a song will make it to radio that doesn't match up production-wise. You can hear it. The studio quality is just not there."

Making their own music also means they are not tied to a label. The artists can, like Amy Gerhartz, produce and sell their albums at shows wherever they perform.[78] Or they can, like Diarrhea Planet, find small outlets that might carry a local group's album.[79] Or they can upload their music directly to any one of a dozen music sites. The first two ways have limited reach. The reach of music sites is much broader but it is also the most problematic, because it is difficult to get recognized among the deluge of music available on the internet—difficult, not impossible. A decent home recording might garner a following on one of the music sites and, if it does, it could come to the attention of a publisher or label executive.

That's what happened to Maren Morris when her self-produced EP garnered 2.5 million streams on Spotify. Indeed, Cliff Williamson (COO) with Starstruck, one of the larger independents in Nashville, feels that sites like Pandora and iTunes have leveled the playing field because the marketplace, not the A&R executive, decides what's a good song. That is why companies like Starstruck monitor music sites. If an artist is getting heavily streamed, that person has a good chance of being recognized by a prospective producer. "[The artist] doesn't have to come knocking on my door when they're streaming," says Williamson, "we make the call to them."[80]

The problem lies in the massive amount of mediocre material on many of the music sites. If we apply the math for quality used for artist-songwriters in

Chapter 1, it is likely that around 80 percent of those uploading songs can be culled out. The remaining 20 percent might be good songs by serious artists, but these same individuals have to earn a living, which usually means taking a full-time service-industry job. In their free time they pursue their artistic career while, at the same time, attempting to master home-recording equipment. As tech savvy as some of the young people are, the sheer amount of everything on their plates makes this a formidable feat. Indeed, just learning the programs is, in itself, a time-consuming trial by-fire-process which, Adam Patrick Bell found in his study of the musician-engineer working from home, often still leaves the imprint of the program used on the final product.[81]

Byron Bell, who runs a small home studio in Portland, Oregon, emphasizes the difficulty in mastering just the technological side of the business. Bell talks about how he worked long-distance with two young artists to mix an album, while simultaneously working a day job.[82]

> [W]e used WebEx software, which is like Skype. [You can do a lot with Web Ex but] the one thing you can't do is sync the audio properly. . . . So we started writing in GarageBand and they'd record a piece of the song—a verse and a chorus, a bridge, sometimes . . . I was able to say, "Try a counter-melody here," or "Let's make the chorus twice as long," or "Let's move the bridge to the front," and because of WebEx, I could actually edit on their computer—I could reach into their screen and cut their GarageBand files. Or I might write a melody and say, "How about this for the cello part?"
>
> Once the songs were shipshape lyrically and musically, "[we] started working in Digital Performer. . . . We rehearsed for a few days [until] we got the tempos perfect [and] we got the scratch guitar and scratch vocal at the right tempo and the right feel. . . . We were recording in high resolution—96k—using groovy, expensive microphones and expensive preamps [until] we had four to six tracks pristine in my home studio.

It took six months to get to the finished product after Bell mixed in keyboards from here, guitars from there using various programs, such as ProTools, to make the twosome a band. "Amazingly," he says, surprised at the results, "it sounds like it was performed [live] by a real band playing together."[83]

The music community is split almost equally regarding the merits and demerits of recording at home in a quasi-professional studio. The largest drawback mentioned is the lack of feedback from producers or studio personnel that could help fine-tune the ultimate product. Most of the young artist-songwriters critiqued in Chapter 1 would not find this a problem. They regularly interact with other young artist-songwriters, and often co-write with seasoned ones, and this, they feel, gives them the necessary feedback to help them modify their lyrics or improve the delivery of their song.

Perhaps more problematic, at least to those in this study, is that the young music listener today doesn't appreciate a quality studio recording. Publishers and producers both tend to feel that young people are satisfied listening to less-than-perfect sound delivered by online sites. These assessments are largely based on anecdotal information. Though an audiophile himself, Andrew Scheps disagrees with the idea that only "weird audiophile(s)," notice the quality difference. In his own experience, he found when uploading a file that "I could absolutely hear the difference on my laptop speaker, and I wasn't expecting or trying to."[84] The inferior quality is due to the fact that "download services are not music companies. They're data delivery companies." His conclusion, however, is optimistic, and one shared by many in this study. "[T]he worse it sounds, the fewer people are going to like it enough to want to spend money on it. . . . Basically, the more people are aware that stuff could sound better, the better off we are. And I think that the idea of a home stereo is starting to take root again."[85] This means, in the context of this study, that demos will continue to be produced on laptops but the final recordings will still be made in a studio. Production, however, is only part of the picture. The labels also retain the distribution channels and promotional savvy to ensure artists that they represent get heard.

Distribution and Promotional Activity

Record distribution and promotion have been controlled by the major labels throughout much of the twentieth century. Distribution was where the majors made the real money. All musical genres have been affected by the surge of internet sites today. These sites have disrupted the traditional means of getting albums to record stores and other retail outlets, such as Walmart, neither of which are significant players today in the music distribution. The internet rules!

The majors have been fighting the loss of retail record distribution and significant income stress since Napster debuted in 1999. The Recording Industry Association of America (RIAA), a trade organization that represents record labels, filed a lawsuit alleging copyright infringement and successfully closed down Napster in September 2001.[86] Despite RIAA's success in a string of subsequent infringement issues against on-line companies,[87] Napster, along with related music sites on the internet, such as Kazaa, Limewire, and eDonkey, has "completely transformed . . . the model that ruled the industry during most of the past century."[88]

Initially, internet music sites provided the streaming and/or downloading of songs without charge. Obviously, most in the music business put up resistance because it circumvented payment to the artist, the songwriter, and, of course, the labels. Pharrell Williams' song "Happy," for instance, was streamed forty-three million times on Pandora but provided royalties of just $25,000.[89] The labels' knee-jerk response to piracy was to sue. This response was mostly ineffective because either 1) when one site was shut down, another quickly replaced it, or 2) the consumer wasn't intimidated by these idle threats—many of the participants in a study of internet piracy by Sinclair and Green "laughed at the attempts of the industry to inspire fear."[90]

Apple's iTunes Music Store (2001) was one of the first to provide legal sales and distribution of music online. In his analysis of the impact of the digital age on the music industry, Patrik Wikstõrm feels Apple's iTunes "was the first online retailer that was able to offer the music catalogs from all the major music companies."[91] Wikstõrm goes on to say quite categorically that iTunes Music Store is an enormous success and that, in the ten years since its launch in 2003, iTunes has sold more than twenty-five billion songs. Another key player today, Spotify, launched in October 2008. It bridges both the free and pay-for-music prongs. The free music streams are supported by advertisement; however, precious little of this income reaches the people in the music business, though the Music Modernization Act may help rectify this situation. Streaming aside, Spotify is putting more of an effort into growing its subscription services: 25 percent of Spotify's sixty million users are paying for the premium service.[92]

Subscription services are growing across the board.[93] The Recording Industry Association of American (RIAA) reports that full-service on-demand streaming services have grown from 7.7 million in 2014 to 50.2 million by 2018.[94] Jessica Nicholson reports that "playlists were [once] a hobby for music enthusiasts, they are now the primary tools used in an arms race to get music listeners to join one of the major streaming services," since streaming comprises nearly 60 percent (58.7) of the 12.5 percent growth in music consumption during 2017.[95] The majors might have initially dragged their feet but they have since entered digital space and are doing very well at it.[96] The majors initially resisted downloading; however, streaming is increasingly being co-opted by the majors. An exposé in *The Guardian* suggests the major labels received 18 percent of Spotify's shares.[97] Still, it does seem that streaming is the wave of the future; downloading, John Marks at Spotify proclaims, is "crashing and burning."[98]

Streaming is also a lucrative area for independent distributors to enter. The independent's angle is that they have a bevy of talented artists not covered by the majors who tend to focus on a select handful of label-contracted musicians. Indeed, streaming platforms are embraced by digital services, like Pandora, because 1) "it [is] a great place for independent artists" says Rachel Whitney, head of country programming at Pandora, since "I don't have to get direct communication from a label partner," and 2) "you don't have to be played on an official playlist . . . in order to become very successful."[99] To substantiate her point, Whitney cites rising artist Taylor Ray Holbrook as an example. "He was not on the platform and we found his name through search traffic on Pandora. If fans are searching for artists, sometimes we see them bubble up that way. He has now shown up several times on our Trendsetter Chart, Next Big Sound, and was on our Artists to Watch list last year [2017]."[100]

Pirating continues to be an issue within the industry, but it is not an all-or-nothing "let's steal it" matter. There are multiple reasons to illegally download or stream. Among the more innocuous reasons are that people want to sample music before they buy it. These "pirates" turn legitimate consumers because they want to listen to a quality recording and are dissatisfied with the sound quality of many digital platforms.[101] Sinclair and Green found that functional value is also important. Traditional illegal streaming/download sites dump tons of songs onto the market. The functional value Sinclair and Green refer to is the subscribers' ability, "to find out about and access music they may never have heard of before."[102] Sinclair and Green are cautiously optimistic about the future of legal streaming because, if one sets aside the steadfast pirates, there is a substantial body of individuals who prefer the quality of legal streaming services and their high level of content.[103] Indeed, the authors support findings by Weijters et al. that consumers "clearly and consistently prefer legal and ethical options if available."[104] The desire of consumers to want high quality material legally will help independent distributors because they are not married to a handful of contracted musicians for their bread and butter.

There are three primary ways independent producers distribute their product. One is those artist-labels who promote and distribute their albums at concerts and on their home website. This is what Shooter Jennings did in 2013 after parting with Universal. He follows a well-trodden path ploughed by many like-minded, label-disillusioned artists, such as Big and Rich,[105] as well as a host of other artists who either 1) didn't want to be affiliated with a major label to maintain artistic integrity or 2) who were released by the label but still maintained a strong fan base.[106] This is not an insignificant group, though it is impossible to determine their exact size or market cache. Using this study as an imperfect measuring rod, it is suggested that around 30 to 40 percent of independent producers fall into this category.

Another 10 to 20 percent of the independents rely on the major labels to distribute their records. Steve Norris with MondoTunes, an independent distributor in Los Angeles, uses Universal Music Group to help get his artists to a wide range of music sites.[107] A number of independent label executives camp on to distribution networks of the major labels. The majors charge a percent for distributing independents' artists and are happy to oblige since it incurs no real financial outlay on their part.

The remaining 40 to 60 percent of independent producers utilize the growing number of small independent distributors, who typically operate in the same way Emmanuel Zunz does at ONErpm. Zunz charges artists a nominal one-time fee to register. ONErpm uses web outlets, such as iTunes and MP3. ONErpm has started to distribute free packages on Grooveshark and YouTube, as well. Zunz does not just dump a host of artists onto these sites. "We review all [material] to make sure there is no problem, no fraud or anything. All of us [independent distributors] have to do this because if we didn't the market would be flooded with fraud."[108] To position his artists, Zunz tries to "create the right playlist for the right place and the right occasion." This is what Zunz finds "challenging and exciting . . . helping artists grow their channels and connect with a larger audience, and thus helping them succeed in doing what they love." ONErpm pays out 70 percent of the revenue, keeping only 30 percent. Independent distributors justify the (reasonable) 30 percent charge by working to promote their artists and getting their songs heard. If done right, promotion from an independent distributor will double the income generated for an artist who might otherwise get lost in the flood of songs available on the internet.

Promotion is an integral part of the independent distributor's role. Any artist with a modicum of technological savvy can upload their music on any number of sites. The problem, however, is that there are literary hundreds of thousands of songs on any of the various sites so consumers may have difficulty finding music that appeals to them. Independent distributors follow the majors in this area. They don't just put out the music; they attempt to position the songs so that consumers can find music that appeals to them.

In order for the independents to get their artists noticed, they have to rely on savvy promotional mechanisms. Steve Norris enhances his revenue stream by offering promotional press releases to young musicians who don't have a label or manager (which is most). Press releases help clients stand out among the bevy of artists competing for attention. While a press release would normally cost $300 to $400, Norris uses in-house writers and charges $99.99. "We not only write it, we put it out there. . . . The artist can also post the press release on their Facebook page or in other social media outlets." In the press release, "we talk about a gig in a club or something new happening with the artist, all kinds of little things the public wants to know." The press release "helps them grow their fan base."

Zunz positions marketers in different geographic areas to help him promote their artists. ONErpm has offices in Rio, where the company initially launched,[109] as well as São Paulo, which focuses on finding and signing new artists. ONErpm also has branch offices in Mexico City, New York City, Miami, and Los Angeles. Each office focuses on marketing to the region's Latino population. "A lot of companies have one big main office with smaller [outreach] offices that have only one person.... You need four or five people in each office to provide support. You need to be able to service the areas you are in." In 2015, ONErpm entered the Nashville market to tap into and service the country music industry. The country market is of particular interest to Zunz because he feels it is underserved by independent distributors.[110] He's been building relationships with artist managers since coming to Nashville and is optimistic about his foray into country music. "We changed the market in Brazil; I think we can here, too."

As both Norris and Zunz intimate, distributing new songs is only half of it; you also have to make the prospective audience aware of them. As the hand in the glove of distribution, promotion is one area where little has changed. This is perhaps truer of country music than other genres. Radio remains the primary means of making people aware of new artists and new songs. Former Sony Music Nashville CEO Gary Overton made this point some years ago when he quipped to a reporter, "If you're not on country radio, you don't exist."[111] His comment received considerable criticism from independent artists and country music bloggers. To quote Nate Rau, John Esposito, CEO of Warner Music Nashville, still felt, that "radio is the straw that stirs the drink for country music" two years later (2017).[112] Just about every person interviewed in the course of this study emphasized radio's dominant role in making or breaking a performer (and songwriter, and publisher).[113] Lee Adams, senior vice president of promotions at Broken Bow Records, explains more fully the prominent role of radio for new artists.[114]

> You can get only so much from social media. In country, radio is still the main way we introduce new acts. Radio is absolutely essential to make it to the level you need to make it to. [For example], Grander Smith [with Broken Bow] was selling out 2,500- to 3,000-seat venues on his own. But to get to 8,000-, 10,000-, 20,000-seat venues, it was not going to happen without country radio.[115] That's why, even though he had done phenomenally well on his own, he still wanted to be with a label. There was no way he was going to get the publicity [he needed], at least in country music, without radio behind him.

The majors still do promotion by going radio station to radio station to pitch new label-affiliated artists and soon-to-be released songs. Preliminary research by the Country Music Association indicates streaming is likely to grow over the next decade or two, but even then, it seems it won't challenge the primacy of radio among country music fans.[116] There appears to be only one small obstacle to the continued popularity of radio. Mike Dungan, CEO of Universal Music Group Nashville, indicates proprietary research finds only "the very, very young end of the millennials [born between 2000 and 2005][117] shows they're not intersecting with radio [and prefer] using online services and digital services almost exclusively. . . ."[118] It remains to be seen whether this group will change its listening preference, but even if they remain locked to digital services, their impact on the popularity of radio's staying power will be minimal, at least for the immediate future.

Interviews with individuals in promotions were obtained from independent producers and some of their promotional staff. I talked with a number of people in promotions at some of the major labels in Nashville, but it was impossible to work my way through the corporate legal maze to get permission to officially interview any of them. Their off-the-record comments, however, tend to reflect those of independent promoters interviewed. The only difference between the major and independent labels is that while the majors have dozens of individuals covering a limited geographical area, the independents have a handful of individuals reaching a larger territory.

This study explores three examples of promotional activity among the independents using the categorical division presented earlier in the chapter: the big-little labels (e.g., Broken Bow), mid-sized labels (e.g., Cold River), and the small labels (e.g., Infinity Cat). Robert Ellis Orrall at Infinity Cat explains the unique grassroots means he used to promote one of the bands with his label. Orrall wrote an anonymous column about Diarrhea Planet's second album for a small Nashville-area community newspaper.

> [The paper] has a column that people write in to and say what ticks them off. So in one of their issues a writer [Orrall] wrote in and said, "Dear Ticked Off. You are the first paper I read every week. Thank you for bringing problems to light. I am ticked off at a certain 8th Avenue [record store]. I brought my grandson there to buy a record on Saturday. I was pleasantly surprised that they still even make [vinyl] records anymore. But the record he wanted was from a group called Diarrhea Planet; the picture [on the cover] had a hand with a knife going through it. I told my grandson that both the name and the cover were vile and he was not getting the record. If we have to live on a Diarrhea Planet, show me where to get off." To my surprise, we got the headline. I didn't tell the band for about eight months that I wrote the letter. It got picked up by blogs all over the country. We don't have the assets [promotion money] and it was free publicity, so why not?

Self-produced artists and small independent producers primarily use social media and websites to get their songs recognized on the internet.[119] Social media is, of course, used by everyone in the business today. Starstruck, one of the big-littles, has a promotions department, and while some of their people still go out and knock on doors the old-fashioned way, they now have a social media department that increasingly exploits digital means to spread the word about new artists and new songs.[120]

Small independents, in particular, favor social media because, as Orrall points out, they don't have a substantial promotional budget. Orrall's diatribe in the community paper speaks to both: it didn't cost anything and was positively picked up by any number of bloggers, which vastly extended the scope of the paper he wrote it for. However, social media only goes so far. The personal connection remains important: the majors, and most large and mid-sized independent labels still rely heavily on promotional staff.

Just as the fans want to connect with the artists, radio personalities want a personal connection with the musicians they're playing. That's why country music still does radio promotion the old-fashioned way. Broken Bow's Lee Adams laughs when she sees an old movie, like *Coal Miner's Daughter* [1980] about Loretta Lynn.

> She literally got in a car and went station to station. It's not that different today. This is a people industry. If a program director [at a radio station] is going to invest in an artist [put their song on the air], they want to see the artist, they want to look at the artist and say, "Ok, I can see you as a stadium act." You can look at Twitter accounts [and such] all day, but you cannot really get a feel for the artist until you sit down with somebody and see who they are as a person and as an artist. And that requires one on one, and radio is a one-on-one business.

Kellie Longworth, Adams's counterpart at Cold River before Cold River suddenly closed its doors in late 2019 after 15 years in business,[121] sketches a typical day: "Sometimes my day starts at 5 a.m. trying to catch a flight so I can get to [an area] early enough to do three or more cities in a day. Say I am in Harrisburg, Pennsylvania. I see my station there, then go to Allentown for lunch and end up in York for dinner, after which I drive to Philly to sleep so I'll be there to visit my station first thing in the morning. It is a lot of time management."[122]

Adams oversees a staff of four others in promotions. Each covers a different region of the country: Southeast, Midwest, Southwest, and West Coast, plus the Northeast, which Adams handles herself because, she says, "I like to keep my feet on the ground." The artist(s) typically accompanies the regional promoter. "We put them on a tour bus for six to eight weeks and visit every station we can. Cannot do them all—there might be 3,000 stations in a region. But we do try to get the major stations in the major markets, plus we have someone working our smaller markets."[123] There may be forty radio stations to hit on a radio tour and it is typical to visit them twice on a tour, so a radio tour usually takes eight weeks. And when one of Broken Bow's artists is in the area doing a show, they usually make it a point to visit the local station(s). Radio is quick to give air time to well-known artists, like Jason Aldean; newer artists take a little more effort than established ones to get on the air.

> Promoting a new artist, we start out in an SUV going radio station to radio station. I like the chance to sit down with the radio people and answer questions they might have. Always go back and ask if there's anything else we can do to get entrenched in the region, like a benefit we might be able do, for, say, St. Jude's. After we've introduced ourselves to the program and music director of the station, we like to introduce ourselves to the audience—can we get on the station's website? Do a Twitter campaign? Very grassroots. It's building blocks. We don't just introduce [the artist], we reintroduce and reintroduce [him/her]. It's a constant circle.[124]

It's not much different at mid-sized independent labels. The promoter may have a little less experience, but they are just as enthusiastic about their job.

Lee Adams worked with Decca (1995–1999), Atlantic Records Nashville (2000), and a "couple stops in between," before landing with Broken Bow in 2001 after Atlantic closed. Kellie Longworth, director of regional promotions with Cold River Records, joined the company just out of college (2014). Cold River had a staff of eight before closing its doors in 2019, six of whom were involved at some level with promoting the company's three artists. Longworth was one of the three regional representatives when interviewed in 2017. While she officially covers the Northeast, Longworth also works in Texas, Florida, and Alabama because once she's built a relationship with the radio personality, she stays with them, even if they move out of her region. In a larger company, another person in the promotions department (PD) picks up the relocated radio person. Other than that, her job is similar to others in promotions.

> We have a new single that we launched three weeks ago. So a month before our play date, we go and add it to the list to play. There is about three months of prep to do that. Then it is heavy travel, and dinners, and meetings playing the new song. We meet with the directors of the radio stations. We try to book a show with the artists [at the station] because they're taking a chance on a

> new artist and a small label. I want [the people at the station] to get familiar with the artists and their music before they play the record.
>
> Sometimes we will bring the artist in and the station will do a listener showcase, which means they will give them about thirty minutes on the air. They will bring them in and talk to them and play their music. Sometimes stations will have venues they work with, and we will put a show on in those venues. Sometimes there is a jam the station is putting on with a number of artists, and our artist joins in on that. Every station has a different event, and we like to work with them [any way we can].

When asked how a small producer competes with the majors for song play, Longworth says that Cold River tries to have better songs and artists. Great songs and good artists cannot be ignored. "If we have a better song than one of the major labels, the station can't ignore it." It is not an easy task; there are a lot of songs out there. "A lot of new artists are coming out with good stuff. It's tough right now." Still, radio stations are open to the independents. Alex Kobrick interviewed the radio personalities who received *Music Row Magazine's* Reporter of the Year in 2007, 2010, and 2013.[125] The radio personalities all accentuated their openness to screen more independent artists and labels. One mentioned that he is "having more records promoted to me" by the independents than ever; another said that his station has revamped their playlist "to include more independent artists and [to] have more independent artists in station events and performances."

One way to build relationships and to ensure key people at the station are open to new artists or a new song is to help them out in an emergency. Longworth explains why she was late for our interview.

> Today is a perfect example. I was sitting [in the office] and one of my stations called me. She said that she had some artists lined up for a Saturday show but there was a last-minute cancellation, and could I get one of my artists there to do the Saturday slot. Well, today is Tuesday, our artist is in Vegas on Friday, and having to get him to Jacksonville on Saturday would be hard. We could probably do it by having him catch a red-eye on Friday so he'd be in Jacksonville on Saturday. That is the kind of thing [that builds relationships]; she knows we would move mountains for her. It also builds a fan base for my artist and a fan base for the station. It's a win-win [situation], but it's a lot of work. . . . We always hope we can do what they need.

An overlooked part of promotions is finding new talent. "Sometimes," Longworth says, "when we do shows with a station they might have a local opening [act]. That's one way we get to see new talent." Social media is another way; it was how sixteen-year-old Maggie Baugh first came to the attention of Cold River. Their VP, who lives in Florida, stumbled across her on YouTube and took Longworth to see her perform. Soon thereafter, Cold River signed her as a writer with their publishing arm. After graduating from high school in December 2017, she moved over to their artist side and is now one of their three premier artists.

Big or small, major or independent, the production process begins by finding the right artist to fit the label, then producing a quality record. Distributing the record has historically received little attention, largely because it was a straightforward process and the majors dominated the distribution channels. The internet has muddied the waters and anyone can upload a song, but a quality recorded song that is positioned to get attention is an art and takes some doing. Even then, one doesn't just put a song on a digital platform, which is why both the majors and the independents work to find the right platform and marry the songs to like songs (or artist styles) to reach consumers interested in a new song within a specific subgenre.

In country music, the process of identifying songs is still largely, albeit no longer exclusively, done by exposing the radio audience to new artists and songs. The process of how the gatekeepers themselves become aware of new artists and songs has largely escaped attention outside the payola scandal of the late-1950s.[126] As Longworth rightly concludes, "I think [the consumers] think, 'Well, that's a good song. They [radio station] did a good job picking it.' No, there is a lot [that goes into] getting [the artist/song] there. You travel and work, then travel some more. It takes a lot of effort. It is sometimes a little crazy. But I enjoy it." Her comments, while specifically addressing her own role in promotions, can be applied to anyone in the production nexus. It's a lot of work, it's often a bit crazy, but everyone loves it. Indeed, this can be said about anyone in the industry, as already demonstrated in the last two chapters about songwriters and publishers, and reinforced in the next chapter, which critiques the artist manager, talent agent, and tour support personnel.

Conclusion

It may start with a song, but for that song to make a dent in the marketplace it has to be heard. The chances of hearing it increase if the song is released by a major label. More often than not, however, the major labels only "discover" a "new" artist after that artist makes a splash. The independent labels historically served as "feeders" for the majors, who often enticed successful artists to make the leap by offering more lucrative economic incentives than the independent label could afford: enhanced royalty payments, an intensive advertising campaign, and/or more key market tours. Today, this same enticement extends to those who have established some solid streaming credentials. A key drawback, however, is that the artist may lose a certain amount of creative control over the music they make. In general, there are two reasons artists leave the majors to join an independent label or start their own artist-driven label that is embraced by their small but significant fan base. Either they want more creative control over their music or, just as likely, the artist is not generating the revenue the major had foreseen and the label terminates their label-artists relationship. Creative freedom is also why more artists today never even make the move to the majors. They prefer to stay with the independent label that fostered their career, and the independents are in a better position today to ensure their artist's music gets heard.

There are a lot of gifted artists who never make it to the majors, or don't last because the majors require a sizable market to generate a return on the millions of dollars they have to invest in developing an artist. On the other hand, the independents can generate a decent profit by producing artists who don't yet have a fan base. Some of the small labels get lucky, hit the jackpot, and move up the ladder. They are the big-littles. Initially small labels, the big-littles are labels who took a chance on an artist overlooked by the majors and struck it rich. Two big-little label examples critiqued in this chapter are Broken Bow Records, responsible for discovering Jason Aldean, and Big Machine, the label that launched Taylor Swift's career. The big-littles are a fairly exclusive group—including Curb Records, Big Loud Records, and Starstuck—and constitute about 10 percent of the independent labels. Their artist rosters suggest that they, like the majors, control a much larger market share.

The big-littles hold considerable clout in the marketplace and can be said to rival the majors, which makes them readily identifiable. Mid-sized independents are also readily identified: they have a decent-sized roster but are less bureaucratically layered than the big-littles.[127] It is impossible to determine with any accuracy the number of small independent labels since they are run out of small offices or homes, and thus do not announce their presence along Music Row with banners proclaiming their artists' hit records. A rough estimate suggests that about 30 percent of independents fall within the mid-sized range with the remaining 60 percent allocated to small independents. Some of the mid-sized independents (e.g., Average Joes) are actively positioning themselves to move into the big-little category. The small independents, on the other hand, are typically sole proprietorships where the owners make a decent living and are happy with where they are and what they are doing; they might add an artist or two down the road but they are not looking to significantly expand their client roster.

The advantage of affiliation with a label, regardless of its size, is that it has state-of-the-art recording equipment. The independents run their own studios and use studio musicians to record a significant portion of the material, if not all of it. Today's independents receive a boost thanks to the significantly decreased cost of making a record. In the "old days" (pre-2000), the majors were practically the only ones able to record a quality album. Electronic platforms today cut that cost to a minimum, allowing independent labels and artists to make their own songs. Downloading and/or streaming songs on the internet further enhances the ability of independent labels and artists to reach potential consumers.

If there is any downside to the vastly improved quality of electronic platforms, it is the synergy lost by producing music with talented studio musicians. Nevertheless, this downside is minimal since most final cuts are still made in the studio. Indeed, there is a growing body of contemporary research that indicates consumers are becoming increasingly dissatisfied with the poor quality of some streaming sites. This should not suggest that the old studio days will return with a vengeance, but it does intimate that the studio system is still alive and likely to remain so, at least for the foreseeable future.

Perhaps the greatest advantage the independents have over artists who produce their own material is their ability to reach the consumer. Like so much in the production nexus, this has historically been the domain of the majors. Some majors, such as Sony RED,[128] have opened their distribution channels to the independents in order to enhance their revenue streams. Others take advantage of the growing number of independent distributors that have arisen to serve the independent labels and independent artists. Still others, especially the smaller ones who are not looking for mass consumption, sell their albums while on tour or use their fan-based website to sell their artist-affiliated records.

Promotions is closely linked with distribution because promotion makes the consumer aware of the artist, song, or album. The playing field here, though not flattened, is more level. The majors still have the necessary deep pockets to ensure the word spreads about their artists and their artists' new albums. The demand for new talent remains strong among dedicated music aficionados, and the independents and the independent artists reach out to this group. This is one area that handicaps struggling musicians. Uploading songs is fairly easy. Alec Ellin correctly states that, "it takes about five clicks to distribute a song [on the internet] to the world."[129] Getting the song heard among the deluge of other uploaded songs is the challenge. Internet music sites can have some forty million songs "with a [hard-to-navigate] search box and a 'good luck' for ten bucks a month."[130] Independent distributors try to provide their artists with a leg up by not only making sure their songs are found on internet sites, but also by positioning and promoting the artist or song. For example, Steve Norris at MondoTunes writes and circulates press releases for his clients at a nominal charge.

Independent labels are better positioned to attract a radio audience than independent distributors because they have access to radio executives, and radio still is *the* way to make a wide range of consumers aware of a new artist or song. The majors have a leg up with their deep pockets. Nevertheless, radio executives are as open to independent promoters as they are to the majors, in no small part, says Mike Thomas at station KFAV in St. Louis, because the majors are not developing as many new artists today, and the station still has playtime to fill.[131]

For all the changes that have taken place within the production nexus over the last twenty years, promotion is still done the old-fashioned way: getting on the road with the label's rep and their artists and going station to station to make that personal connection that could open radio waves to their artist or song. If station "A" picks up the song and it generates some consumer traffic, it increases the chances that station "B" will be open to the promotional team when they swing through that market. "Hey, glad to meet you. Heard your song on WXYY. Loved it! Tell me something about yourself (or your artist)."

It comes down to the old tried and true: the best song wins no matter who produces it. But the song has to come to the gatekeeper's attention, and that's what people in promotions do in the best good-ol'-boy-slap-on-the-back tradition.

4

BETWEEN THE ARTIST AND THE AUDIENCE

Artist Management, Booking Agents, and Touring Staff

The literature on business management is extensive. To varying degrees, most writers touch on how managers need to connect with their employees to motivate them to accomplish assigned tasks within the company's environment. Artist management is another matter altogether, at least in part because one is not working in a defined corporate structure with clear-cut, measurable goals that employees must achieve (and on which managers are evaluated). Artist management books certainly touch on general managerial dynamics, like leadership and communication skills, as well as the importance of networking—a total of three pages in one artist management book. Instead, artist management texts tend to focus on those aspects of management that are unique to the music business, such as songwriter copyright laws, terrestrial versus satellite and online radio income streams, getting a record deal, and the like.

These complicated artist-relevant managerial dimensions tend to be oversimplified in many artist management books. This is not a serious concern in the classroom since the instructor can use the text as a bridge to elaborate on the issue under consideration. Artist management books are instructive outside the classroom because they serve as a guideline for some of the myriad dimensions facing an artist manager.[1] Like managerial texts in general, artist management books are helpful at giving the would-be manager things that they need to think about in their managerial role. A good 20 percent of those in this study leaned on artist management texts when embarking on their careers. Ross duPre, for example, found that he had a knack for managing fellow high school artists, but having little experience and no one to turn to for guidance, he "read every music business book I could get." Books, however instructive they may be in making one aware of things that need to be considered, only go so far, which is why duPre says that what followed was the inevitable hands-on, trial-and-error process many managers find necessary to "fine-tune" their book knowledge of the field.

One dimension books on artist management tend to skirt includes fine points of distinction. There is, for instance, a critical distinction between an artist manager and a business manager. They represent two different dimensions of the music business. Artist managers, as the name suggests, manage the artist and generally oversee the artist's business affairs. They are the ones who are often responsible for hiring a business manager. A business manager, at least in the music business, is, basically, an accountant. They handle the artist's finances. This is a very specialized accounting niche in the music business. Business managers take care of general financial matters, such as quarterly tax-related filings, but their knowledge of the industry allows them to also be able to estimate income streams from record sales, tours, and other sources of potential revenue. This is very important for artists because it allows them to estimate their income and plan their personal budgets based on realistic projected income estimates. Some artist managers may handle some of these business-related matters. This is most likely to occur when the manager is handling a young, yet-proven artist. Business managers are more typically utilized by established artists—financial matters get more complicated and artist managers have their hands full managing the artist's career.

Another key distinction is the sometimes-fine line between an artist manager and a person in artist development. Artist managers are also involved in artist development, and vice versa. In this study, those who enunciated their developmental relationship with the artist tended to be involved with younger artists who had yet to establish their brand: the types of songs they sang, where they performed their songs, and how they presented themselves on (and off) stage. The managerial side of artist development, which entailed "taking care" of the artist, was of secondary importance. Artist managers, on the other hand, were more likely involved with artists who already had a brand identity. Naturally, they worked to make sure the established identify was capitalized on and reinforced, but their primary responsibility was to "take care" of their artists, that is, to make sure the artist gets the best possible label deal and is booked at the proper venue. A certain degree of artist management is hand holding: helping the artist make connections between performance gigs when, say, the tour bus breaks down, or consoling the artist who has been waylaid by a personal event (e.g., the unanticipated dissolution of a relationship, the death of a family member) which can derail the artist from performing at his or her optimum level. In this study, the term artist manager is used to encompass those who are also involved in artist development.

Some managers directly handle booking arrangements. This is most likely done for those artists who do not have established credentials and are working in small clubs. As the artist gains a reputation and moves from small clubs to larger venues, booking agents are more likely to be involved. Artist management texts only glance at the booking issue, primarily because, while artist managers may oversee the booking agent's tour agenda, they tend to leave the complicated logistics to the experts. Nevertheless, the artist manager's job is to ensure the right personnel are hired to maximize the artist's performance. The complexities of booking tours and staging performances are addressed later in this chapter.

Artist Managers: The Accidental Profession

Managers tend to be very public officials. Their faces are well known to both the company's employees and the public they serve. The CEO of a corporation or the president of a university, along with their key management personnel—vice-presidents and the like—are the faces of their organization. Artist managers are a different breed. They tend to dislike being in the public eye. This made them the most reluctant of any professional group in this study to accede to requests for an interview. This is not to say other groups were not hesitant to be interviewed. Some publishers and label executives were also reluctant to be interviewed. Their reluctance, however, was often based on concerns about bad press. When the parameters of the study were sketched, many of these individuals acquiesced to an interview. This was not the concern of artist managers.

Many artist managers were likely to respond, as one highly regarded manager did, by stating "I'll be glad to chat about what little [*sic*] I know, but I think the focus needs to always be on the artist, not managers. I tend to take a backstage approach and probably won't ask to be [named] in the book." This was particularly the case with managers who had only one prominent client. Anything they said would obviously relate to their client, so even an innocuous comment about how they had to deal with even a fleeting artistic flare-up would reflect negatively on their artist. Those managers with three or four clients, which tended to be the norm, were more willing to be interviewed, especially if they had been in the business some years and had clients other than those on their current roster. In these cases, specific examples of artist-manager relationships could not be attributed to a specific artist.

OUT OF THE GATE

One manager quipped that artist management is an accidental career.[2] Indeed, few managers in this study saw this as their career trajectory when they started working in the music business. The accidental dimension is underscored in this section. The three managers interviewed came out of the box fairly quickly. They helped initiate the career of some solid artists and in the process launched their managerial careers.

Harmon Music Management

Like many college students, Rusty Harmon welcomed a little extra income, which is why he took a job doing security for a Joe Jackson concert at North Carolina State in Raleigh. Harmon overheard the young woman in charge of security for the event mention that all her DJs were graduating and she didn't have anyone to fill their slots. Harmon thought it would be fun. The next day he was an on-the-air DJ for the campus radio station. Harmon changed his major to mass communications.

Harmon soon became the programming director of the 3,000-watt station. The general manager, a graduate student, put him in charge of reviewing the unsolicited tapes that came in over the transom. Harmon found one that he liked and mentioned it to the GM, who thought that with a name like Hootie and the Blowfish "they are never going anywhere." Harmon convinced the GM to listen to the tape. The response was immediate: "Book them!"

Harmon hit it off with the band members. He helped them make a demo cassette and, when it was finished, they thanked Harmon for all his help, which, Harmon recounts, "was the first time that [any of the bands he worked with] ever thanked me for anything." The band wasn't sure what to do with the demo now that it was finished, and Harmon told them to "shop it." They didn't know what that meant so, "I told them they needed to send it to record labels." Then he asked who did the band's booking, and they said they did it themselves. Harmon retorted, "No, no, no." After three months of back-and-forth advice, they asked him to be their manager. He drove the three hours from Raleigh to the band's home in Columbia, South Carolina, where Darius Rucker played "Time," a song he just finished.[3] "I just flipped out. I knew then that I wanted to be their manager." Harmon graduated shortly thereafter and moved to Columbia.

The early years of management entailed just about everything: "I did the distribution and the PR. When their CD came out, I started going to radio stations and record stores. . . . I printed up 15,000 copies of the CD and every two weeks I had to do 15,000 more." Harmon's work and the band's talent soon got the attention of Atlantic Records, which released their first album in 1994. "The album came out in July and by November it sold 450,000 copies." Shortly thereafter, Hootie and the Blowfish appeared on *The David Letterman Show.* Harmon and Hootie were on a roll.

Harmon was with Hootie and the Blowfish for thirteen years. Then "it all started blowing up." The group went up too fast and couldn't sustain the momentum. "The first year we sold sixteen million copies; the second year, five million; the third year, a million. We were no longer selling out 30,000-seat arenas. It was frustrating [for the band members] who were now playing to half-empty venues." Egos started getting in the way. Some of the band members weren't getting along, and Rucker and Harmon "weren't getting along *at all.*" It was time to move along: "They knew it and I knew it. We sat down and had a talk, and we decided me moving on was best." They parted on good terms.

Harmon took a few years off to spend with his wife and two daughters in Raleigh before moving to Nashville where he started MTM management in 2004. He had a young country singer at MTM who he helped get a record deal. Right when the song came out, his client fired him. He was trying to be friends with the young singer like he was with the Hootie gang, but times had changed: "People were different and the work ethic was different." It was then that he realized how effortless it had come to him with Hootie: "Everything [with Hootie] was so easy, and everything fell [perfectly] into place. The timing was just right for us." He left MTM to become president of Average Joes Entertainment and after a break he founded Harmon Music Management (2015).[4] "It's a bigger struggle [now], but I am in a good place. I love my country staff, and things are going good here [in Nashville]."

Harmon Music Management presently (2018) handles five artists. Craig Wayne Boyd has been managed by Harmon for some years; the other four are relative newcomers.[5] This turnover is fairly common. Only about 20 percent of the management companies in this study have just one or two artists who are their bread and butter (see Slipshod Management). It is not uncommon for even solid management companies to have a revolving door of artists (see Hallmark Directions). This does not reflect on the management firm: artists come and go. Some, as Harmon himself pointed out regarding a client he handled at MTM, just don't have the work ethic. Others get discouraged because they find there is no fast-track to stardom or get disappointed when only a handful of people show up for a performance. Harmon enumerates other issues managers hear about from their artists: 1) the artist's career is not moving forward fast enough; 2) the manager is not communicating with them enough; and 3) the artists don't like the career plans the manager has laid out for them.

The artists who stay, the artists with whom the manager connects, have forged a bond. Harmon knows when he and his artists are on the same page: "There aren't many fires to put out." That's because "there's a [mutual] sense of respect." R-E-S-P-E-C-T is a refrain heard by all the managers in this study when they talked about the reciprocal relationship they have with their artists.

Workshop Management

Josh Terry went to college to study journalism. He quickly realized this was not something he cared for, but wasn't sure what he wanted to major in. He joined a number of organizations. One was hosting concerts. There were only two other people on the concert staff, and they were happy for some help because there was a concert planned for the upcoming weekend. "I worked that concert. I did everything from loading gear, parking cars, and putting water in the artists' dressing rooms." The campus ballroom held 600 people; 7 people showed up. The one young lady on the concert staff was so upset at the meager turnout that she quit; the other member of the staff, her boyfriend, followed suit. Suddenly Terry, a freshman, was in charge of booking concerts at the University of South Carolina. He did this for the next three years. "We started with a $33,000 budget and by the time I left we had $347,000 budgeted for concerts and 83 people working them. . . . We had a concert every week. Some were local, some district, and some statewide." He changed his major to public relations because "you have to set up events, and you have to be able to network with people, which, in essence, was what I was doing."

During the summers he did internships: one was with Rusty Harmon who was handling Hootie and the Blowfish; another was with a company in Chicago that was about to release Train's second album. His management internships enticed him to start managing artists himself. He found a couple local artists in South Carolina that he helped get record deals during his senior year. "And that is how [my career in management] started."

It was not smooth sailing. With little capital after graduating, he ran his company in "a small office the size of a closet for a year and a half," during which time he lost both his artists. He lost one for traditional reasons: the label changed hands and the band didn't feel the new people were that interested in their music, so, disgruntled, they quit the business. The other artist adds a new dimension to why management firms often have client turnovers: the artist had a drug relapse. "I was freaking out and didn't know what was going to happen." He received an offer from a friend in the business asking him if he wanted to sell merchandise for the group he handled that was touring. Terry felt selling merch was beneath him since he had a management business, "But part of me said, 'Dude, you are broke, you have no money, so shut up [and take the job],'" which he did. He flew to Boston and toured that summer with a group that was the opening act for The Dave Matthews Band. He had a few other month long music-related positions. One was from a friend who needed a tour manager because the one touring with the group had a nervous breakdown. Terry flew to Syracuse the next day; it was his first experience with punkers: "The lead singer had super long hair and one of the guys had a green Mohawk; everyone was [heavily] tattooed . . . and here I was with a baseball cap, baggy pants, and Nike shoes." He learned later that, "as soon as I walked off the bus, they called their manager and said, 'Who is this hillbilly you sent on the road with us?'" Still, Terry and the band clicked. He worked with them for two years at the same time managing a couple other bands while on the road. "I just had to have my hands in management."

Two years on the road and Terry was exhausted. He landed a job with Aware, a small artist management company in Chicago. He managed some forty artists during his nine years with Aware, most in the Adult Contemporary (AC) field.[6] "I managed between six and nine artists a year. That was a lot, but we had four interns and eight employees, which is a pretty good-size staff for a boutique management company." A Southern boy, he eventually tired of the cold and the expense of living in Chicago. He came to terms with his boss who didn't want to lose him: he could leave the city but stay with the company. Terry felt Nashville would be right for him and a good fit for the company. He moved to Nashville in 2011 and managed the Aware office for four years. He wanted the challenge of running his own management firm and parted company with Aware in 2015 to start Workshop Management. "It was the cleanest break I ever had. We've remained good friends. "

He started Workshop with his Nashville Aware clients. "I literally [just] changed the sign on the door, then called the phone company and said, 'Make the number Workshop now.'" At the time of the interview in 2016, he handled seven artists; his website shows six active artists in 2018, three of whom were there in 2016. It's a decent-size roster for a one-man management company—he relies heavily on interns and has a full-time administrative assistant who he hopes will eventually help out with management responsibilities. None of his artists are country. His roster, like his background, is eclectic: he has a producer, a folk singer, and a rocker; he was handling two punk bands in 2016. He purposely chose not to go the country route. He admits that he doesn't know country very well, but just as importantly, he recognized country was "a good old boys club," and that as an outsider he'd have difficulty making inroads. He likes "being the other logger in town. . . . It has given me a niche." Still, if the right country artist comes along, he'd certainly consider signing him or her. If one comes along, then the dance begins:

> We meet a lot, we talk a lot. We get to know each other. . . . It generally takes a couple of months. I always tell the [prospective signee] that this is as much you getting to know me as it is me getting to know you. You have to feel comfortable with me and accept where we are going. If we can't sit down and have dinner together and not feel like we want to choke each other, we shouldn't be working together. . . . In the end, they have to fit into the culture we are trying to build. It's also important they don't drive me crazy. My sanity is very important to me.

One of Workshop's strengths, at least compared to similarly-sized management firms, is the emphasis on sync fees. The placement of songs in film and television, he feels, are an artist's bread and butter: $30,000 for a movie sound track here, $10,000 for a commercial there. "The artist can make a lot of money [with sync rights] and doesn't have to be on the road 200 days a year." His website shows song placements on "Elementary," "Lost," "Cold Case," and Showtime's "Shameless," among a host of others. He is also heavily invested in getting his artists associated with corporate projects.[7] He did a project for Twix, for example. Twix wanted a young band for a company campaign. Twix was doing a radio campaign, and one of Workshop's bands had thirty seconds of their new song played on the Twix spot. This gave the band play time without Workshop having to spend money for active radio promotion. "I think it is the future and is one of the things that is going to keep bands alive. Bands are going to have to be smarter and more diverse. I think that is where it is going." Workshop hopes to point the way.

Maximum Artist Management

Mitchell Solarek enjoyed music but had no intention of going into the music business. Solarek ran a talent agency in San Francisco that handled broadcast journalists, actors, and models. He backed into the music business when some musicians came to him and asked if he could help them. He told them his agency didn't work in the music business, and they said "Yeah, yeah, yeah, but you know all these people, so maybe you can help us." So, Solarek called a friend who had a friend in the music business in Nashville at Reunion Records: "It was pretty easy. I called her and told her that I had this very talented group on the West Coast." He offered to buy her plane ticket and put her up for a few days so she could explore northern California if she'd just give him a few hours. "Little did I know she was a receptionist for the record company. Well, after she returned to Nashville I started getting calls from people who wanted to visit me in San Francisco: some of the people were in A&R, others were receptionists." He screened the prospective "producers" a little more diligently, and a number came out to hear some of the musicians he represented. The musicians crossed a range of genres but, because California had a thriving Christian music industry, the two picked were Christian musicians. At the airport, on their way to Nashville, one of the musicians asked Solarek what they should do next. "I told them they needed a manager. They said they didn't know anyone. 'How about you?'" Solarek was now a manager for Nashville artists.

It wasn't that big of a leap: "I'd been managing talent; I had also been developing talent. I knew how to spot talent and I knew how to get the talent in touch with people that could deal with their talent." The one thing he did not know about the music business in Nashville was that it is a very small community. "I didn't know what I didn't know. I just kept pounding away." For the next few months he took the red-eye to Nashville every six to eight weeks, took back-to-back meetings for 48 hours, and then flew out. He quickly learned "You need a lot of face-to-face in the music business." One of those meetings paid off. In 1998, he was asked if he could put together a boy band, like NSYNC and the Backstreet Boys. The group he put together was Plus One. Four of the five members of the band were preachers' children, and that became his niche: "The market was crowded with boy bands. But Christian music did not have any boy bands. It was an easy fit."

Plus One would soon become a worldwide success: "It was a tidal wave." That's when Solarek moved to Nashville to focus on the music industry. "I'm a Christian," he says, "but I didn't intend to go into that kind of music." Nevertheless, Maximum is heavy in the Christian market: beside Natalie Grant, they manage a Christian hip-hop group called Social Club Misfits that is with Capitol Christian. Maximum's artist roster is eclectic, however. In fact, not long after Plus One debuted, Solarek started to manage Blue Country, a country trio that was picked up by Curb Music in 2010. He's not that interested in rock 'n' roll, something he learned after a brief management flirtation with a rock group: "I don't want to live in that culture. I don't want to go to little rock clubs and smell twenty-day-old beer on the floor. It just isn't me." Maximum currently (2018) handles 10 artists and has a staff of eight: one staffer works extensively with business managers; another focuses on digital; another has a strong background in touring; while yet another deals with artists' merchandise—"You would be stunned," Solarek says, "how much these artists do in merchandising."

Most of the managers interviewed in this study have long-standing roots in the music industry. Solarek's advertising background sets him apart and has been helpful to his client's careers. His contacts in the fashion industry helped him get promotional spots for Plus One at Macy's and land Natalie Grant a clothing endorsement. It has also helped him think outside traditional formats, which he did with Mary Mary.

Mary Mary is two women who had some success in the late 1990s with a huge crossover song. They were in the gospel world but wanted to do less touring and make more money. "Instead of saying check please, I came up with a plan aimed at their consumer, which were those who supported reality television." Solarek came up with a television show that would utilize their music throughout the entire episode. He created a storyline about them touring and making music. The show was sold to a television network (WE Tv) and was in its sixth season at the time of the interview in 2017. It wasn't an easy sell, however. Rob Stinger, then with Columbia Music and now head of Sony, didn't think it would work. More specifically, he thought it might put money in the women's pocket but not Capitol's. Solarek disagreed. He felt that Capitol would sell their music after the consumer discovered the girls on television. "Long story short, I got to say I was right on that one. I don't get to do that often, but I did with them."

The point Solarek is making with Mary Mary is that there isn't a script: "There's no manual and you have to be creative. You sit with the artist and you connect with them personally. If I respect them, the consumer will too. When we move forward, I have to know as much about their consumer as I can. Then we plan things around the consumer and them." The biggest change he's seen in his 15 years in the business: "People used to get in the business to be rich and famous. I don't think it is that way now. I think the people who get into the business today are true music lovers, and they cannot think of doing anything else." Solarek is referring to contemporary artists, but his comments are just as relevant to all those who work in the industry today: publishers and their pluggers; producers and their pitchers; studio personnel; and artist managers like Solarek himself.

SLOW AND STEADY: TRADITIONAL CAREER PATHS

It is rare to come out of college and go directly into management. One young lady I spoke with, showing her youthful naïveté, was a self-admitted Wynonna Judd stalker. She was at Texas A&M and went to all The Judds' shows she could: "I always managed to make my way to the stage. Not in an appropriate way, but I would get there." She wanted to manage Wynonna, so she wrote her and said, "'You need to hire me. I am ready to go on the road, and I would be a great road manager.' I wasn't even sure what that entailed." Wynonna wrote back; her manager got off the tour bus and handed her the letter. She had written on the back of the letter sent to her, "If you want to do this the right way, go to Nashville. Go through the right channels and learn the music business." The young lady took Wynonna's advice to heart and transferred to the music management program at MTSU in Murfreesboro. She did an internship at a publishing firm, then worked at a few related music businesses. This process taught her that some areas of the business, including management, were not something she enjoyed doing. She subsequently found her niche in publishing and now works with songwriters at a national company with offices in Nashville. Paths to success in the music industry are not as neatly delineated as they are in most businesses, so it takes some time to get a feel for what fits. The two management tracks appraised in this section underscore the process of starting slowly and building toward a career in management.

Slipshod Management

Norm Parenteau was musically inclined at a young age and, like many in this study, played an instrument in high school. He soon realized, however, that while he was pretty good, the world abounded with more talented musicians. So, he started booking bands in high school and continued doing bookings in college. His school booking experience landed Parenteau a job upon graduation with a booking agency doing block bookings for colleges, which is when a number of colleges unite to get a better price booking an artist or band. He was surprised that the job was based in Nashville and not somewhere more cutting edge, like New York.[8]

Parenteau's story is yet another in this study that emphasizes the importance of one's social network. In college, and later, after coming to Nashville in the mid-1990s, he joined every organization that was even tangentially related to the music industry. One was the Nashville Entertainment Association (NEA). He was a volunteer on the entertainment committee for six years. Another member of the committee was Denise Stiff, who managed Alison Krauss. Krauss was just taking off with her career at the time (circa 1995), and Stiff needed some help for a few weeks. Parenteau was Krauss's day-to-day manager for six years, during which time he also worked closely with another of Stiff's clients, Gillian Welch.

Parenteau, who started with Stiff in 1995-1996, was toying with the idea of branching out on his own around 2000. He wanted to break someone into the industry the way Stiff had done with Krauss. His plans were temporarily stalled by the film *O Brother, Where Art Thou?*. He helped Stiff, who served as executive music producer on the film, find Americana groups to perform the musical score for the film.[9] He would subsequently manage a few new artists under Stiff before he found his breaking band in 2001 and started Slipshod in 2002.

A number of people had pitched some of the music by the Old Crow Medicine Show for the *O Brother* film, but Parenteau passed on it since they didn't have a good sound recording. He subsequently met Ketch Secor with Old Crow at the end of 2001 and they clicked: "He had a drive and a vision." Secor invited Parenteau to their performance the next night at the Station Inn, a venue long since deemed a Nashville institution that often showcases young talent. Parenteau was taken by the audience, a mixture to one side of older bluegrassers and on the other a cluster of college-age students with pitchers of beer on the table. Everyone was having fun and, when the band ended by performing "Wagon Wheel," everyone knew the words and sang along. Parenteau thought it must be a hit song that he was unaware of since everyone knew the lyrics. He asked the band members who wrote it, and they said it was a snippet from a Bob Dylan tune to which Secor wrote the verses and the melody.[10] Parenteau wanted to shop it but the band didn't have a recording. A few months later (February), Parenteau became their manager.

The band was ready to sign from the get-go but Parenteau wanted them to wait: "I knew from the past that you shouldn't rush into anything." Secor was ready to sign but Parenteau kept him at arm's length: "Let's get to know each other for a few months, let's do some more shows; let me bring some people [label executives] to the shows." The group wanted Parenteau to handle the money angle when they eventually signed (they brought their checkbook with $1,000 in it), but Parenteau said that was a bad idea and that they needed a neutral party, a business manager, to handle the money. "So we made an agreement. . . . I said I wouldn't take a commission for any gig under $500 and for any over that I'd take [the traditional] 15 percent." And until they started making enough money to hire a business manager, Parenteau told them they should keep a record of things, "But I'm not touching [your] money."

He told his other client, Parker Millsap, pretty much the same thing when Millsap was offered a record deal: "Get a lawyer. I won't ever talk to you again if you don't get one. It might not be a bad contract," he goes on to say, "but you need to protect yourself." Parenteau has seen too many people get the short end when they didn't protect themselves. And that's what good managers do—they protect their clients.

Parenteau discovered Millsap through the tried and true: he was a volunteer for Tin Pan South, a musical event NSAI puts on every year that showcases artist-songwriters. There was also, as there often is, a smidgen of luck involved.

Holly Williams had to cancel a planned (unpaid) Tin Pan South appearance because of a last-minute (paid) gig in Texas. Parenteau thought, "Oh, my God, what am I going to do?" He called his contact from NSAI at the Bluebird, and she told him about this 19-year-old "who has the voice of an old soul." She asked Parenteau if he wanted her to put them in touch with each other but Parenteau, under time constraints, said, "I trust your judgment." The young man showed up for sound check and Parenteau, who had his back turned away from the stage, heard him singing and said to himself, "Wow, who is singing that?" Not long thereafter, Millsap was opening for Old Crow. Millsap left his manager from Oklahoma and wanted Parenteau to handle him. Parenteau agreed, but only if he talked to two other managers before making a final decision.

Millsap made solid progress under Parenteau because he listened when "I told him it takes two years to set up a career. But nobody wants to wait two years. Just two lousy years. Everyone is in a hurry." Not Millsap; he listened, as did Old Crow. When asked if he'd like more than (just) two groups, Parenteau chuckles: "I have seven people with Old Crow, plus Millsap. That's plenty."

CTK Management

Another manager tells the story of an executive at one of the management groups he interned with: "Marty was yelling [into the phone] one moment, and then, a moment later, he was sweet-talking to some promoter. Then he would say, 'Hold on a moment' and start screaming into another phone. Then he would say, 'Wait a minute' and then [on another phone] he would make these very raunchy jokes."[11] Danny Nozell[12] might not be one to tell risqué jokes, but he is full throttle. He's 49 (2016), "not married, don't have any kids," is completely dedicated to his artists, and wakes up every day raring to go. "I love what I do. No matter how stressful it is. No matter how much drama there is, I still love it." He has 15 employees at CTK—four in marketing, two full-time CPAs, a director of operations, a touring manager who has three assistants, three full-time executive assistants, and one full-time personal assistant. "Except for church on Sunday, I work 24/7 so I need a lot of help." He likes having a young staff, "They keep me up on the technology. They run circles around me when it comes to that. We teach each other." He handles, among others, KC & the Sunshine Band, Kenny G, and Dolly Parton. Despite having an extensive staff, he always personally tours with Parton, who's been with him since 2005.

Nozell started in the business as a runner with Jam Productions in Chicago. From there, he moved up to production assistant, then into production management, then into promotion. "I learned a very valuable tool doing those things . . . I think the best managers [come up] from touring." He's old school and reflects the values of many managers in this study: "I have an education that money cannot buy. You cannot go to school and learn what I have. The only way you can [manage artists] is to experience [the business]." The experience he's gained makes it easy for him to handle artists from a variety of genres. "It's really a matter of marketing . . . it's an exposure game. The more exposure, the better. Even with Dolly, it was exposure"—he took her global, his strong suit: "I know global marketing, and that is what makes me different."

One would think, given Dolly Parton's iconic status, that CTK couldn't do much more than place her because her name, in itself, would draw crowds. Not so. At least not in the international arena, even though her name has global reach: "The guys in World Wide Touring didn't believe she would do well with tickets sales in Europe. I told them I had done my research and found that she had sold millions of albums in Europe. I said 'Let's put her in down-scale arenas and let's take a chance on this.' We went back and forth but they finally agreed to do it with down-scale arenas."[13] They should have been larger: Parton grossed $41 million performing 21 sold-out shows. Nozell explains how he worked with Parton to bring out her best performances.

> We've done six or seven tours (between 2005 and 2016). I got Dolly back into touring by getting her a brand-new bus. She won't stay in hotels. I went with a company called Beat the Streets [for design]. I had been using them for 30 years. Then I found a company in Europe that could make me the buses. They were the first buses made in Europe that had bathtubs and showers.
>
> Next I shipped all of Dolly's stuff overseas, because I wanted her to be comfortable. The last experience she had over there had not been great. So what I did, I took her blankets, her fans, her tea, her incense and candles, all of her stuff, and shipped it over there. Then I sent assistants over to take care of both buses.
>
> Next, I told Dolly we were going to fly charter. . . . I found out she had never flown charter; she had always flown commercial. She thought it was too expensive. Well, we've never gone commercial since. We go from Nashville to London in six and a half hours.

All this expense and attention makes it seem that Nozell pampers Dolly. In a way, he does. But that is the role of a manager. The comfort level of the artist affects the artist's performance. If the artist is comfortable, he or she will do a stand-out show. Still, there's more to planning a successful tour than simply making sure the artist is happy. The first European tour Parton did with Nozell involved a lot of strategic planning. This was critical because the contacts

Nozell had in Europe were skeptical about Parton's ability to attract an audience. Their skepticism disappeared after all 14 shows sold out in 60 minutes.

Researching helped Nozzell develop a promotional plan around Parton; it was also instrumental in helping Nozell move Kenny G forward in his career. "We are very systematic [here at CTK]. The first thing I did was to pull his analytics." This allowed Nozell to pinpoint where the 70 million records Kenny G sold both in the United States and in the international arena. This helped identify his diehard fans, after which "we can build on it to expand his fan base. . . . Everyone knows who Kenny G is but we want to reintroduce him to the millennials." Expanding the fan base to the next generation keeps the artist and his or her music relevant. David Corlew suggests the same thing in the next section about the vibrancy of Charlie Daniels's music today.

OLD SCHOOL

Management in any area is not a nine to five job. It is definitely not nine to five in the entertainment industry. The hours are long and arduous, which is why it is a young person's game. After a day filled with meetings, managers in the music industry often 1) hang around to support their artist by attending any events where they might be performing around town, or 2) are on the road with their artist when they tour to make sure everything comes together perfectly. Even when the manager has a tour manager to handle things, they are inevitably there to make sure everything falls into place.

Most of the managers in this study started in the music business in their twenties and have been in the business for twenty to thirty years. The key distinction for the two sketched in this section is the length of time they have been in management. David Corlew is sixty-something; John Dorris is seventy-something. Their experiences are similar to many of the other managers but their longevity in the field provides a sketch of how much things have changed, and, just as importantly, how some aspects of the business remain the same. Like others in this study, they started young. Unlike many others, they are native to the area.[14] This is more typical of "old guard" artist support staff than it is today. The key distinction, and the reason for addressing them separately, is that Corlew has been with one artist for his entire career—he celebrated his forty-fifth year with Charlie Daniels in 2018. Dorris runs an agency and has managed a wide variety of artists, including, among a host of others, Don Williams, John Michael Montgomery and Montgomery Gentry.

David Corlew and Charlie Daniels

Like many young (Southern) men back in the day, Corlew dropped out of high school to get on with his life.[15] He started as a "roadie" (aka roustabout) in a Nashville management company. The company brought the Rolling Stones to Nashville in 1971. Corlew did all the down-and-dirty jobs: making sure there was ice in the dressing room and plucking the petals off twelve dozen long-stems roses so Mick Jagger could throw them into the crowd at the end of the show. It was Corlew's introduction to the music business. It was not particularly glamorous, but it was the music business.

Corlew worked full time at a local record store. A member of Charlie Daniels's group came in looking for someone to help move and set up equipment. The job paid $50 a week and $5 per diem. The pay was less enticing than being on the road. Corlew set up the equipment and gravitated to doing the lighting; soon he was booking hotels and then handling the box office money. By 1989, Corlew was Daniels's manager because, after a decade on the road together "I knew *everything* about my client: I knew what he liked, what worked and didn't work for Charlie." Corlew's progression into management was boots-on-the-ground.

> I didn't have a formal education but now I'm great with numbers: additions, subtractions; do division and percentages in my head. Learned it all by sitting in box offices. Some rough guys, in some rough places. . . . We did a street festival in Chicago [Navy Pier] in the 1970s: carried out cash in grocery sacks. You don' have drunken roadies settle the box office anymore; today we have a road manager with a calculator, and tickets from computers rather than having them pressed.

Corlew does not denigrate the new way; indeed, he appreciates the new way of doing things.

> There's no need today for a manager or road technician to know how to fix a carburetor on a bus, or change a tire, or replace guitar strings. Today you need to know how to get social media out. There are some brilliant kids out there today doing brilliant things. My world today. We can track every ticket (sold to a Charlie Daniels show): know where it's sold. Don't have to worry about exchange of cash; no (hard) money's handled.
>
> Same with making music. Kids can mix from an iPad. Everything's electronic today. Days of sitting in studio playing together—all done by computers. We (recently) overdubbed some of Charlie's stuff ourselves sitting on the bus (between shows) and tied it to our studio. If I were an artist today and had an old guy like me show up and a young guy, brilliant with technology and

> able to reach out and grab massive amounts of data and put it in front of me—I'd pick the kid. It's his time.

Corlew is an old dog who has learned the tricks of the modern world, which is why he has so successfully managed Charlie Daniels's career for over forty years: "[I] can mix from an iPad today; [it's the] way of the [modern] world." At the same time, coming up the hard way had its advantages in helping move Daniels's career forward. "There isn't a road crew, road manager, or promoter who can bullshit me, 'cause I've been there; I know all the tricks."

He and Daniels have cut back in their old age—Daniels, at eighty-something, "only" does around 100 shows a year—being on the road is in his blood, Corlew says, as much about Daniels as himself.[16] Still, Corlew's priorities have changed along with Daniels: "When a painter first starts painting, their palette is bright and shiny, but as they get older, they start painting in softer colors, in pastel. Little things are important to me [and Daniels] now. Things we might have missed along the way."

Daniels's current interests are an offshoot of his conservative leanings, reflected in his recent string of patriotic songs, such as "This Ain't No Rag, It's a Flag" (2001), "My Beautiful America" (2002) and "Ragged Old Flag," an old Johnny Cash song[17] Daniels made into a music video (2017) co-directed by Corlew. Today, both Daniels and Corlew are mainly involved in helping veterans. "Twenty-four vets kill themselves every day, that's one every hour," says Corlew. Their cause "gives me [and Daniels] purpose." That's why "Charlie created a foundation [The Journey Home Project] which I'm on the board of. A big part of my time now is fund raising. We raised $500,000 last year," he says proudly.[18] "I'm [no longer] trying to figure out how to sell an extra 1,000 tickets." He could easily sell another 1,000 tickets if he wanted to, however; he knows exactly who Daniels appeals to[19] and how to market to them via social media when Daniels appears in their area.

It is hard to appreciate today because Daniels has become a certified country legend,[20] but Corlew laughingly remembers when Daniels was a Democrat and played Lynyrd Skynyrd-style rock music. Corlew recounts how Daniels didn't fit in with the Nashville community:

> Charlie's from North Carolina. He came to Nashville in the 1960s. He wanted to be a session player, but at the time it was very cliquish: his hair was too long, he played too loud, [he] couldn't see without thick, rose-tinted glasses. One of his first [professional] jobs in Nashville was to play fiddle with Earl Scruggs at the Opry. The person who ran the Opry at the time came to Earl after his performance and said he loved his work, "but [you] gotta get rid of the guy with rose-colored glasses who needs a haircut."[21]

Daniels's outsider status in Nashville probably helped his career. He was never co-opted into the Nashville "machine."[22] This meant he had to do things independently. The end result is that today Charlie Daniels is a mini-industry. There are no 360 deals. "Everything we do for Charlie, we control." Daniels owns the buses he tours on and controls the merchandise sold during a tour. He has his own production company and publishes his own songs. Considering the deep reach of labels today into an artist's pocket, Daniels is in an enviable position, and he made his way there because he was (initially) on the periphery of the country music industry and had to make his way largely on his own.

Daniels moved into country music with the song, "The Devil Went Down to Georgia" in 1979. "The Devil" underscores the benefits and drawbacks of fame that rests (primarily) on one song.

"'Devil' was a huge record," says Corlew, "but it pigeonholed us as a country act when we weren't a country act at the time. That put us in a tailspin," he explains, because country music was moving in another direction during the 1980s with "soft country, almost cosmopolitan country," with acts like Olivia Newton John, John Denver, and Barbara Mandrel. "We were *really* lost because we were thrown into a format we knew nothing about. Charlie's roots were country, but we hadn't made a living in the country music business." Nevertheless, "Devil" has had a long run beyond just being the requisite closing number on a tour. Corlew calls it their golden copyright. It was incorporated into the movie *Urban Cowboy* (1980) and then Mike Curb put it in *Coyote Ugly* (2000), a film about dance halls in the 1980s, and that made the song a hit again. "Devil" continues to be rediscovered. "It suddenly turned up on a computer game called *Guitar Hero* (circa 2005), and because it was the most challenging song to play we started getting fan mail from ten- and eleven-year-olds."

John Dorris and Hallmark Entertainment

At 21, John Dorris moved to Nashville from neighboring White House, Tennessee, with his newly minted degree as a certified public account and took a job with Price Waterhouse. He stayed there a few years and then took a job with LIN Broadcasting to launch its in-house tax department. LIN had contacts with a number of music companies, and Dorris did pro bono tax returns for some of their artists.

In 1982, Dorris accidentally became a manager. He was attending a funeral and someone asked if he knew that the deceased managed Don Williams. He "took a meeting" with Williams and they hit it off: "We had different backgrounds but similar values." Not previously having heard Williams perform, he flew ("a damn long flight") to Minneapolis where Williams was headlining. "Loved him!" He managed Williams for the next 15 years. To fully appreciate the connection between manager and artist in this context, it should be noted that Williams had a string of CMA and ACM (American Country Music) Awards for a series of hits between 1976 and 1981. Williams could have had his pick of managers but chose Dorris, largely because they connected.

Hallmark Directions was founded in 1982 with Don Williams as the first client. Over the next few years Dorris handled Butch Baker, who now runs HoriPro;[23] Dean Dillon, an artist-songwriter with Dorris from 1989 to 2000-something, who wrote some 30 hits with George Strait; and the Whites, a bluegrass act whose music would be prominently featured in *O Brother, Where Art Thou?*.[24] These were all solid musicians, but then he signed John Michael Montgomery. "Sales-wise, John was the biggest act I ever had: he had 17 No. 1 hits and sold over 20 million records."

On a business trip, someone Dorris met at the airport mentioned a young fellow who had a manager with no experience and who was looking for someone who might be interested in handling him even "if someone had papers on him" (a contract).[25] He heard a rough cut of Montgomery's song, "Nickels and Dimes and Love"[26] and "Just loved it. My life!" They "took a meeting" in Nashville and then Dorris went to hear him play at Austin City Limits in Montgomery's hometown of Lexington where his brother, Eddie Montgomery, played on drums and Troy Gentry played guitar. John Michael Montgomery was in the process of recording an album but wasn't happy with the process: "The in-house producer wasn't getting it done." Dorris found someone to finish Montgomery's album. He didn't think the lead song, "Life's a Dance," was that good, but "it had more meat in it than I gave it credit for. . . . It turned out to be a huge single."

He also connected with brother Eddie and Troy Gentry, both of whom wanted record deals. "I couldn't find them a single deal but tried putting them together and did a little demo," and so Montgomery Gentry was born. He added another big act, newcomer Blake Shelton, who he was hesitant to handle since Dorris was extremely busy with the artists he already handled. Still, he liked the song "Austin" (2001), so said, "Let's do it." Five No. 1 singles followed. They parted ways when Shelton was in the midst of a divorce and Dorris tended to side with the wife because he had a father-daughter relationship with her. Shelton initiated the break, but Dorris had no ill feelings since "my kitchen was a little full."

Dorris also lost John Michael Montgomery. Montgomery had recently married, and his wife's father, a very successful tobacco man, thought he could handle Montgomery's career. This is another reason artists sometimes leave their managers. After a while, they forget who helped them get where they are. The math gets in the way. Managers get 15 to 20 percent of the artist's gross; another 10 percent goes to the booking agent; another 5 percent to the business manager. Artists sometimes see large chunks of the money that should be in their pocket slipping away.

The parting was amicable, and that's another part of this story. The music community in Nashville is comparatively small and strongly interconnected. Dorris kept in touch with Montgomery over the years. In 2006, Montgomery gained a certain amount of public notoriety for a DUI arrest in Kentucky[27] and Dorris extended a hand: "I called to tell him I loved him and was sorry [about the situation]." He told Montgomery he was there if Montgomery needed anything. Montgomery asked what he was doing that night and "I said, 'What do you need me to do?'" They had dinner later, chatted, and "he asked me if I wanted to try it again. . . . Been 8 years now (2016); think all the bridges [are] built back up." Someone once told Dorris that he cared too much for his artists. Dorris's rebuttal would be widely applauded by the other managers in this study: "If I'm not their biggest fan, [then I] don't need to be their manager."

Today, at seventy-something, Dorris is cutting back—though he is in his office from 7:00 or 8:00 in the morning until 7:00 or so at night. If he gets tired, rather than fighting the traffic home to White House for the night,[28] he'll sleep on the office couch. For him, cutting back means being part of a co-management team,[29] rather than trying to do everything himself. His value to the partnership is that, after fifty-some years, he knows a lot of people in the business and can open a lot of doors. He likes the co-management arrangement because he realizes he's getting on and likes the idea of having a backup for his artists in case anything happens to him. He nevertheless keeps his CPA accreditation current, just in case he needs something to fall back on.

A Managerial Miscellany

The managers sketched to this point detail their progression into the managerial field and some of the issues they face in promoting their artists. The few selected only scratch the surface of the dozens interviewed. This section sketches some of the others in brief snippets. Their career paths are briefly touched upon. The focus, however, is on those issues that may be unique to their backgrounds and experiences.

MANAGEMENT PLUS

Greg Hill Entertainment.

Greg Hill had a few introductory-level jobs in the music business that didn't go far, which is why he pulled out all the stops when he learned there was an opening at EMI in the mid-1990s. The timing was perfect because country music was hitting one of its highs. He rose quickly at EMI from manager to vice president. Still, being young and impatient, he toyed with the idea of taking a lucrative position with another company. His boss and mentor told him he couldn't compete with the money offered but gave him some sound advice: "You need at least two more years here. You're just starting to click. You're just beginning to see how it's working. You need two more years here to understand the system." Fortunately, Hill says, he listened. He goes on to acknowledge that those two years were critical in helping him understand some of the intricacies of the music business.

Hill started Greg Hill Management in 2001 and rebranded the company as the Hill Entertainment Group in 2013. Like many others in the business, such as music publishers who are delving further into production, Hill is broadening his scope beyond management. He sees himself as an entrepreneur, not just an artist's manager. He manages artists, of course: he managed five artists at the time of the interview in 2016, including Naomi Judd. He recently moved beyond artist management when he launched "Legendary Coaches," a collective of former coaches that played for and helmed some famous teams. The coaches do radio interviews and appear at athletic events around the country. The idea sprang from an accidental event. There was a storm and the coaches gave a joint presentation, even if they were not initially scheduled to speak together. Hill was watching from the back of the room. He started thinking of his entertainment (versus management) model. "These guys are big," he said to himself, and "their brand has never been developed." And so, "Legendary Coaches" was born. The coaches are paid a fee for their appearances but Hill owns the trademark. "It's not on percent bases. I own the model." That's entrepreneurship!

Iconic Entertainment

Fletcher Foster is one of the few executives in this study who graduated (1985) from the music program at Belmont University in Nashville. Since the program was in its infancy, it is even rarer that he leaned on the management aspect of the music business. He did this, he says, because he came from both worlds: his father was an attorney and his grandmother a musician. The business side of music fit him well since "I had both my left brain and right brain working."

In 1990, Foster moved to Los Angeles where he spent the next decade in various positions in the music business. In L.A. he worked with Atista Records, which he rejoined on his return to Nashville in 1999. He moved on to Red Light Management in Nashville before leaving to start Iconic in 2014 with LeAnn Rimes as his first client. He presently has two artists, both country: the trio Runaway June and Levi Hummon. The broader entertainment dimension of Iconic is its extension into music publishing, primarily for the artists Iconic manages. What's more, Iconic, like more management companies, is multitasking: "We deal with the booking agents, the concert promoters, the lighting and set up, everything." This is relatively new in the management world. "It's much less divided today. It used to be the labels did the label job, the booking agents did the books, and the publishers did the publishing. Now there are managers and management companies that function like labels." The result is that "Management companies are taking on a lot more responsibility today than ever before." This may be why, despite having only two artists, Iconic also has a chairman and an artist manager to help CEO Foster handle things.

THE L.A. CONNECTION

Global Eyes Entertainment was founded in 1995 by Ramona E. Simmons, former director of international artist development of Arista/Nashville. Preston Sullivan joined his wife as managing director in 2008. The impact Sullivan has had on the group since joining belies his strong ties to Los Angeles.

Sullivan grew up in South Dakota. He attended Vanderbilt University in Nashville and immediately after graduating went to Los Angeles. He was the lead singer in an R&B band called The Drivers, which, along with Jack [Mack] and the Heart Attack and Billy [Vera] and the Beaters was one of the three "in" bands in L.A. at the time. He moved back to Nashville to continue in the music business, but his main reason for moving was to be close to his father in Alabama, who had cancer. He continued playing in Nashville clubs but gravitated to the business side of the music industry around 1985-1986. His company wasn't known for country music. "We were known more for pop and rock stuff." He generally pitched in New York and Los Angeles because Nashville was strongly rooted to country music. After marrying his second wife, Ramona Simmons, he joined Global Eyes.[30]

The entertainment aspect of Global Eye is much at the forefront today. "It's tough right now for managers. We don't just manage, we create bookings, and venues, and labels. Before, other people did those things. Now I am doing it all." Global Eyes had eight artists at the time of our interview in 2016, almost all of whom were new. Sullivan's "big city" contacts are still in play. One of his artists came to him from Brooklyn: "He came to me with this record and said he needed help [with it]; he also said he needed someone to manage him. I said, 'Okay, let's give it a shot.'" Another young person he is currently working with is from L.A. who had a big hit some years ago. Yet another artist he describes as "an L.A. girl. She is pop and jazz." Sullivan has an eclectic clientele and seems to attract artists from Los Angeles and New York, though he is quick to admit it is not something he consciously set out to do. Perhaps his background in an R&B band and his L.A. roots draw artists from outside country music, which, until recently, also meant from outside Nashville.

ARTIST DEVELOPMENT

Most artist managers do some form of development. They don't focus on development, however, because, as one manager put it, "it's finite"—meaning that one is paid a straight development fee, but if the artist takes off, they don't get to tap into the artist's career-generated income. There was only one person in this study who concentrated on development, and that is Stephen Linn, who started AmpliFLY Entertainment in 2014.

Linn fills a critical niche because many young artists cannot afford a manager. Since their payout only occurs if the artist takes off, a manager typically only takes an artist on when they see some long-term potential. The potential is still hazy for many of the throngs of young musicians who stream through Nashville. Many are floundering: their musical style may not be developed and thus their artistic identity is still in limbo, which makes it hard for a manager to promote them. "My goal is to help them get up and running." He prefers this over management, which he's done, because "I like building and growing things. I don't like maintaining things." He helps his artists learn some of the things that, if they were bigger, their manager would handle. "We go through branding exercises—ways to build the brand. We look at how to mine data—this is how the artist knows where to go and find places to perform." It's not like Linn is taking kids off the bus. He's worked with a number of artists who have or had label deals. One young artist, for example, was released from Warner. "He is a straight-ahead kind of rocking country. That sound changed and he lost his deal. Well, he kind of muddled around doing it himself, and that helped him realize that he knew what he needed. He knew how it was supposed to happen; he just didn't know how to make it happen."

Linn likes to have six artists in various stages of development, because those at the latter stage "can go off on their own." And with a firm identify of who they are, the artists may now be able to attract a manager who will help them move to the next stage in their career.

Recurring Managerial Themes

There are two main themes that dot practically all the managerial interviews. They are separately addressed here. One has been studiously avoided to this point so as not to put any one manager on the spot; the issue of babysitting an artist is something that occurs. For some managers, it comprises only a small percent of their time with their artists; for others, it can chew up to 50 percent or more of their managerial time.

The other issue has already been briefly raised. Here it is developed more fully. A manager no longer just makes sure his or her artists have a solid record deal and that their tours work to maximize their exposure. Corporate tie-ins with tours help shore up the bottom line, an issue of increased importance with labels cutting into the profits from tours. Another booster, endorsements, can not only add some nice change to the artist's (and manager's) income, but can be invaluable in helping to a) keep the artist's face in the public limelight, and/or b) expose the artist to people outside his or her fan base. Brad Paisley's "Jingle Sessions" commercial skit with Peyton Manning that airs regularly during prime-time football games is an excellent example of a country artist who achieves both these goals. So is Granger Smith's "Yee Yee Nation,[31] which now includes a "Dip 'Em and Pick 'Em" segment on CBS Sports, and spawned a line of energy drinks.[32]

BABYSITTING

Hand holding may be a more neutral term than babysitting; some prefer the term counselor or therapist.[33] The nomenclature notwithstanding, managers are often there for their artists. One manager says it is their primarily responsibility, in no small part because labels often treat the artists as products and don't fully appreciate artists' creative sensibilities.[34]

> Artists are living, breathing beings. It's not like making a thousand bottles of water—the water bottles are all the same; there's no difference between one water bottle and another. Artists [however] feel different every day: they put on weight, they lose weight; they feel sick, they feel happy, they feel sad; they're getting a divorce, not a good day; they are getting married, a good day. There are so many different components that come into play that a label is not set up to comprehend.

Artists have to perform, another manager says, varying the age-old catchphrase "the show must go on."

> When you are working with creative people, things come up that can impact their lives and that can affect their performance. Someone can be going through a breakup or a divorce; that can be a life changer. Say you are on tour and two weeks into the tour the artist learns that his girlfriend is cheating on him, or there's been a big fight [between the artist and his or her significant other]. It causes drama, and when you are in a dramatic situation it is hard to pretend nothing has happened. You are thinking, "I want to go home, I have to fix this." I get calls [from my artists] every day. Some deal with the highs: "We just accomplished something [wonderful]." Others are low points: "My records aren't selling. . . " You've got to be there [in both cases].

One young lady in this study, a songwriter with some credentials, illustrates the difference between a creative non-artist and an artist. Our interview was rescheduled because the man she had been involved with over some years suddenly packed up and disappeared. She was obviously distraught, which is why she took a month off before rejoining the creative world. This "luxury" is not available to someone who has to step on stage; they have no down time to adjust to a distressing life event. They have to go on, and they have to appear their cheery self. This is the integral role that a manager performs. They are there to nudge their artist forward, giving solace, but at the same time encouraging the artist to keep the preferable "stiff upper lip" and to do the best they can under the circumstances. A manager might have helped Scott McCreery, who just hours before he was to appear on *American Idol* was informed that he was being dropped from Universal Music Group Nashville. Fans of the show took to social media to bemoan his performance on the show that night. They didn't know that he, the show's winner in 2011, "had just been dealt the worst news of his professional life. . . ."[35] A manager might not have saved McCreery's record deal but he or she could certainly have seen that the news was dealt with at a more favorable time."[36]

Artists get their egos bruised. "Think about it," one manager said. "They are subject to rejection every time they step onto the stage." Another manager quips, "Of course they have egos. You've got to have an ego to go out there and stand before a couple thousand people."

An adoring audience can bolster an artist's ego. Unbridled applause puts the artist on top of the world, which can only serve to bolster his or her performance. A negative audience response, even a lukewarm one, suggests they are not loved and this can rock an artist's world. This is why a number of managers mention that they have had to help some of their artists through rehabilitation. The implication is that in order to cope with rejection—real or perceived—artists sometimes find solace in drugs, a situation exacerbated by the fact that drugs, alcohol in particular, are part of their social world. Drug use by performers is more problematic today because, writes Jessica Nicholson, "with increased time on the road comes increased isolation from friends, family and a constant routine, as well as the physical pain or discomfort that can develop from years of performing and traveling."[37] Al Andrews with Porter's Call,[38] a recovery program for artists in the Nashville vicinity, states quite categorically that touring is "an abnormal life . . . sexy to people when they see those cool buses . . . I don't know any artist who thinks being on the road is sexy."[39]

One manager, who's handled one group of artists over some years, confidentially remarked that alcohol was more of a babysitting issue during the group's early years because "It's [often] encouraged by the fans . . . this is, after all, a business that drinks and does drugs." Alcohol is less of an issue today for this manager with this group because the artists have married and settled down. It nevertheless remains an issue that surfaces with some of his younger artists. And when the situation gets bad, it's the manager who's there to offer a helping hand.

Fortunately, helping their artists does not have to be at the extreme end of the spectrum—drug rehabilitation. Everyday things are issues that managers have to deal with. "It's simple," one manager says: "People have their ups and downs and my job [for my artists] is to be their foundation. They can come to me and vent about whatever it is that's bothering them." "Okay," another manager says, "we are basically babysitters." This manager's job, he goes on to say, is to deal with everyday (babysitting) issues. When his artist is in the studio, he says,

> I want to make sure everything is okay. I like to make sure the producer and the artist are getting along. I want to make sure [my artists] are happy with the sounds they are making. I want to make sure the budget is where it should be. The last thing you want in a studio is for the artist and the producer to butt heads. So I'm around, and if there is an issue, [my artists] can pull me aside and talk to me about it. Hopefully, I can fix [whatever the issue is that is disturbing their ability to perform at their peak].

CORPORATE RELATIONS

In the 1960s and 1970s, artists distanced themselves from "the man"; they and their public would have looked at corporate tie-ins as selling out. The stigma associated with establishing a relationship with a corporation slowly dissolved during the 1980s and 1990s. Even then, it was not the lucrative money maker it is today. David Corlew with Charlie Daniels says that if he had brokered a deal with Budweiser in the late 1970s - early 1980s the negotiations would have revolved around how much free beer the members of the crew got.[40] It was not until country took off in the 1990s, Corlew goes on to say, that someone in corporate America figured out that music was reaching an awful lot of people and that they could promote their brand by sponsoring tours. There was a good payout for all parties. For Daniels, it "put some cash in his pocket," and all they had to do was "paint the [five Chevy tour] trucks with the Chevy logo. . . . The long-term payoff was that [Chevy's name] would be in front of two million people over the next couple years."

Josh Terry at Workshop and Rusty Harmon at Harmon Music Management both weigh in on the importance of corporate sponsorship today. "No one [today]," says Rusty Harmon, "blinks if you have a multi-million-dollar deal with someone like Coke. Toby Keith has a $20-million-dollar deal with Ford. The relationship artists have developed is amazing, truly amazing. Brad Paisley has Hershey's chocolate. A manager today needs to connect his artists to a big corporate partner."

Josh Terry's artists play to audiences of a few hundred to a few thousand. He's pleased if "I can get $50,000 to put up a Tide banner." It doesn't have to be the big-name brands either. "There are a lot of up-and-coming companies—shoe companies, sock companies, candy companies—that don't have deep pockets. I can come along and do [a sponsored event] for a fraction of the cost. If I can get someone to pay to advertise on one of the tour trailers for $10,000, we put some money in our pocket and the kids [artists] are stoked by it. . . . It's fun and easy [to do] and everyone wins." Terry shows his entrepreneurial side in this regard. "If we get enough of these campaigns, people [in the business] call and say, 'Hey, how did you get this or that?' Well, instead of telling them how to do it, I say 'Pay me a retainer and I'll do it for you.'"

Branding is somewhat different. Here one is linked with a commercial product. In this case, the artist is promoting a brand product as much as themselves, which is why both sides are concerned about associating with the appropriate other. Kenny G is a well-known (soft jazz) musician who belies a certain laid-back image; his image is reflected in commercials for Snickers.[41] The same holds with Blue Country, handled by Michael Solarek. Blue Country was his first band for Maximum outside the Christian format. Their first album went top ten and was covered extensively in *Vanity Fair* (versus *Chop Shop Magazine*), in no small part because of Solarek's extensive connections with advertising agencies.

Samantha Thornton at G Major Management elaborates on the branding connection. One of its clients, Danielle Bradbery, won "The Voice." G Major had recently (2017) finalized a "brand partnership" with Macy's for Bradbury to promote their American Rag line. The artist posted photos of herself on social media in the line's clothes, but it's a lot more than social media; "It is a lot of marketing." Thornton goes on to explain: "We had a deal for Danielle to wear [American Rag] clothes [at various venues, including her tours]. We went to Austin, we went to the CMA fest, and we went to the Governors Ball in New York [among others]. We sure didn't want her to be seen wearing anything other than American Rag." She was, in fact, the "face" for the brand American Rag.

Booking Agents and Concert Promoters

Booking agents are those individuals who book the tours for "the talent," which is why they are also referred to as talent agents, though talent agent is a more encompassing role that includes other artist relationships, including artist development. Booking agents (and artist managers) did not emerge until after World War II.[42] Prior to that, booking was done by the individual radio stations, and personal appearances were confined to the geographical area reached by the station's signal. This changed after the war when a number of major talent agencies emerged to book artists anywhere within the 48 contiguous states. These agencies were initially located in large metropolitan areas, such as New York, Philadelphia, and Hollywood.[43]

Booking agents and artist managers started coming to Music Row in the 1950s as more artists and labels started to cluster there. Promoters also began to gravitate to Music Row about this time. Promoters (also referred to interchangeably as tour buyers, tour promoters or concert promoters) are the ones who organize musical events. They may contact the artist, the artist's manager, or the booking agent who handles the artist to see if a specific artist wishes to appear at the event they are organizing. Conversely, booking agents may contact the promotor if they know a festival is in the planning stages to see if the promotor would like one of their artists to appear at the event. The relationship between booking agents and promoters is touched on by most agents and is addressed in some detail at the end of this section.

The primary function of booking agents is to match the artist with the right venue for their style and audience in a way that utilizes the artist's time to their best advantage.[44] Booking a show in Des Moines, Iowa, and then having the artist fly across country to Pensacola, Florida, to do a show on the following day is not utilizing the artist's time to the best advantage. It is far more productive to book the show in Des Moines and then have the artist do shows on the way to a Pensacola date. This is typically the way booking agents work since most artists drive to events. Bigger acts have their own tour buses; small acts drive their own vehicles. In either case, the best way to maximize an artist's time is to lay out a route that hits outlets where the artist can perform so they are not zigzagging across the country.

Some of the managers do their own booking. The larger management groups may have their own in-house booking agent to handle bookings for their artists; some of the smaller ones trying to manage the finances of their young, yet-unknown artists do their own bookings. Financial considerations are particularly important to cash-strapped young artists because booking agents typically charge a 10 percent fee. Booking beyond the local club level, however, is a specialized niche, so when artist managers do utilize outside booking agents, they tend to work closely with them, relying on their expertise. One agent interviewed quipped that anyone could do booking; nevertheless, he went on to say that "If you ask [musicians and managers] what is the one thing you would take off your plate if you could, they will all say booking. It's very time consuming."[45] Another manager in this study, who worked at a booking agency for a while, also mentioned the stress associated with the job and quickly decided a career in booking was not for him.[46]

Twenty-one talent agencies have offices in Nashville.[47] William Morris is one of the larger Nashville agencies with forty-some agents handling over 150 artists. Paradigm Talent has fewer agents (16) but a similarly sized roster. Some of the other large Nashville agencies are APA (Agency for the Performing Arts), Creative Artists Agency (CAA); United Talent Agency (UTA), and New Frontier Touring. All the large agencies have offices in Nashville as well as other major cities, such as New York, Los Angeles, Toronto, and London. Wherever they may be located, agents typically handle between three to five artists, though, as always, there are exceptions to this standard.

Three talent agents interviewed in this study worked for two of the larger agencies: APA and UTA. One of the agents at UTA is in New York City and focuses on working with alternative rock musicians. This agent is one of the exceptions to the normal-sized agent's roster because he handles twenty-five to thirty artists. The other UTA agent works out of the smaller Nashville location and deals more with country acts. The way UTA/Nashville and UTA/New York work with their artists underscores the dynamics of agencies that handle artists in different genres.

Among the smaller agencies, Keith Richards is one of the younger independent agents interviewed. Richards founded Brave World Artist Agency with

Warner Music Group in 2015 and moved to Paradigm Talent Agency eighteen months later. His experiences as an independent agent underscore the difficulties of competing with the majors.

The other three are old-timers who have been in the business for decades, which may explain why, in the current, heady period of booking and promotional consolidation, they continue to survive. These three agencies highlight the changes that have taken place in the industry. Each is distinctive: Buck Williams at The Progressive Global Agency, though based in Nashville, has long focused on booking rock bands; Ed Harper with The Harper Agency books Christian artists; and Liz Gregory, who runs Liz Gregory Talent, primarily books family acts at fairs and festivals in the Northwest. Liz Gregory is atypical because she not only acts as a talent agent but also doubles as a promoter who buys talent from other booking agencies. Her promotional activities provide a bridge to her promotion colleague, Dan Steinberg at Emporium Presents, which, since the initial interview (2016), has been folded into Live Nation.

THE BIG BOYS

APA opened its doors in 1962 in New York. It has offices today in New York, Los Angeles, London, and Nashville. The Nashville office opened at the height of the country boom in 1994. Steve Lassiter is the senior vice president of the Nashville office. One of the few Nashville natives in this study, he joined APA/Nashville in 1998 after spending thirteen years as an agent with William Morris. When Lassiter joined the agency, APA/Nashville had a staff of six and handled nine artists; they now have a staff of thirty and a roster of sixty-some artists. Most of their artists are acquired through a manager or a record label. Nevertheless, roughly 20 percent are developing artists who "don't have a record deal, don't have a manager, don't have a publicist." APA finds the talent the same way publishers find songwriters. "We have a lot of young, twenty-something agents here. Part of their job [after office hours] is to hit the streets [clubs] at night. They're out maybe two or three nights a week. Same thing I did when I was their age."

APA attracts talent—whether from a manager or directly—based on their organization's reputation, which means, "When we sign an artist, we keep them working, *a lot*." Lassiter feels this is APA's strength, especially for a developing artist. "Some of our competitors," Lassiter says, "sign fifty to sixty artists, but most sit on the shelf. . . . They say, 'When you get a top ten record, we'll put you to work.' We do the opposite. We put them to work and that may lead to record deals." Lassiter outlines the process:

> A car salesman sells cars; we sell talent. A whole lot goes into that. We're routing their shows. In other words, we route them from one city to the other, and when doing that you have to keep in mind the distance. There are regulations as to how far you can go overnight; how long a driver can drive. [Tour drivers] are monitored by the same regulations as truckers. A driver cannot drive more than ten hours. . . . So you have to pay attention to how far you can go—Charlie Daniels has gone 850 miles overnight, which is unheard of, but he has backup drivers who simply change seats.
>
> Most of our clients are weekend warriors: they leave the house Wednesday night and work Thursday through Sunday. They're back home on Monday. Some do tours where they leave on Wednesday and they're gone for weeks. When they get back [home], then they're off for a month or two. [Our] responsibility is to keep [the artist] working.

Weekend warriors are common to Nashville. Artist-songwriter Diana Jones explains why.

> Nashville reigns over New York and Austin for many artists. Look at where Nashville is on the map. You can get to concerts across the South, the East, North, into the Midwest with a max of twelve hours' driving time. You can cover the core region that supports and nourishes country and bluegrass and get back home—or to the Opry as Hank and a lot of the old school had to every Saturday night—without too much traveling.[48]

APA has five territorial agents to help cover the various regions. Territories tend to encompass a number of proximate states. "But we really have thirty [people working the territories], not just five," Lassiter explains. That's because each regional manager has agents who book some of the smaller venues; additionally, territorial agents have an extensive support staff. The territorial agents are responsible for booking APA's entire client list.

Besides routing artists to maximize their time, booking agents have to be sure their artists are placed in the right venue. This means more than just ensuring a country artist is not placed in a rapper festival. Lassiter explains:

> You have to keep up with the [venues]. New ones are opening up, old ones are closing. Outside the small clubs that seat 75 to 200, there are the big theatres, which seat anywhere from 300 to 800 up to 3,000. Then there are the smaller arenas which seat 8,000 or so. Nashville's Ascend theatre is 6,500, so it is one of the smaller arenas. This is the trend today. In the 1980s and 1990s most outdoor arenas [like Nashville's defunct Starwood] were 20,000 seats, with 7,000 or so seats under the roof with a big [open area] lawn. The bigger tours go to [places like Nashville's] Bridgestone arena [18,000 to 20,000 seats].[49]

The size of the venue is important. The smaller venues are often open to the agent's recommendation for an opening act, which allows the booking agent to find a slot for some of his or her lesser known artists. The big acts, like Madonna, Taylor Swift, or Luke Bryan can sell out the larger arenas, and have "pretty much already decided who is going to open for them." This is relatively new. "Years ago, the agent had a lot of say about who would open for the headliner. That's gone. The [big name] artists usually pick who they want. In some of the smaller tours, like the Ryman [1,462 seats], we might have a shot because [the headliner] may not need a named artist to open for them."[50]

This is an important consideration for APA, which handles mostly mid-level acts. Mid-level does not mean that the artists are unknown—APA handles Tanya Tucker, Clint Black, Crystal Gayle, and Lee Greenwood; it means that the artists don't fill 20,000-plus seat stadiums. They do book Dolly Parton's tours, and she is at the arena level. Lassiter does not handle her out of Nashville, however. A "responsible agent" handles her from New York.

A responsible agent is the one the artist has a relationship with, often because he or she is the one that brought the artist on board. The agent stays with the artist the same way promoters at record labels stay with their radio contacts, even when the contact has moved into another territory. This is not always the case. Leon Russell's responsible agent is in New York but his bookings are done from Nashville because "Leon doesn't care who books him, as long as he's getting dates." Russell is one of those artists who tours extensively. He, like Charlie Daniels, does a hundred or more shows a year. "It's in their blood," Lassiter says. Daniels is another one of those artists who "aren't going to fill up 10,000-seat venues. And he doesn't care, as long as he's working."[51] That's what booking agents do—they keep their artists booked.

Lance Roberts at UTA/Nashville does pretty much the same thing. His attitude toward booking is certainly the same. Echoing Lassiter's sentiment, Roberts says some agencies "put you on the shelf until they can get something going. I would rather sign someone and roll up my sleeves and get to work making them ready and building their career."

Roberts followed his father's footsteps and entered the family booking business as a young man. The Bobby Roberts Company primarily represented country artists. The Bobby Roberts Company would later be sold to The Agency Group (circa 2013) which was subsequently acquired by UTA in 2015. UTA itself was founded in 1991. Roberts adds some points not addressed by Lassiter.

> There are so many variables [when booking an artist]. It depends on the client. Each one has specific needs, or they might be at different spots in their

> careers. There are career-building gigs, and gigs that are for artists who are trying to get radio [time], and gigs for artists who are trying to hone their legacy. There are gigs that are for casinos, others for nightclubs, still others for arenas. There are rodeos and country fairs. The list goes on and on.

Roberts expands on booking in Las Vegas, which is hot on legacy acts. He uses Charlie Daniels as an example.[52]

> In a lot of casinos, the audience is there to gamble. In a rodeo, the entertainment is just part of the rodeo, not the main part of it. You have to correlate your artists to the place.
>
> Charlie works well in the casino world because he has a little older fan base that tends to have higher incomes. [His fans] are mostly Baby Boomers. They are likely to be retired, and they have the discretionary income to play the slots. A legacy act like Charlie is brought into a casino to cater to a specific clientele.

Legacy acts are easy to book because their fan base is often clearly defined. This allows the casino to target them for marketing purposes.

Younger artists who have yet to make their mark, Roberts says, are handled differently.

> A lot [of what we do] is career building. We look for the moments we can maximize the artist's chance to grow. Record stores are gone. People today are digitally driven. That's not necessarily a bad thing in my world. If you have a good team behind you, like an agent and manager, records are less critical. . . . Having a hit radio play is a good thing. But the way to build a career is putting music out and playing wherever you can. Engaging the fans at shows . . . that's where you build a fan base. That's what we focus on here [at UTA/Nashville].

One of the big changes Roberts mentions over the last few years is that today booking is not confined to certain times of the year. "It's constant." One reason for this, Roberts suggests, is that artists want to work all year. Another is that "more and more" new venues are opening, keeping artists employed. Yet another is that there is more crossing over in venues, with people from different genres performing at the same event: "We put Merle [Haggard] at a cool hipster festival. . . . When I had Waylon [Jennings], we had him with Metallica, and it worked. . . . There are a lot of multiple genre events out there today" that weren't there a few years ago. All these factors enhance the value of booking agents in today's market. "Lots of artists don't have a label, or they don't have a manager, but ninety-nine times out of a hundred they have a booking agent."

The artist needs booking agents in other genres, as well. But other genres may operate somewhat differently. David Galea at UTA/New York specializes in working with alternative rock bands. His interest stems from when he was a band member with Edna's Goldfish (1997-2000), a ska-punk[53] band from Long Island that had a fair amount of success, "at least as a 22-year-old would define success." He left touring behind in 2000, interned with a booking agency, and has been doing booking ever since. His artist roster reflects his interest in alternative rock; he handles X Ambassadors (rock), 21 Savage (hip-hop, gangsta rap), and Desire (synth-pop, new wave), among others. He books concerts but most of his bookings tend to revolve around festivals. Festivals, though seasonal, encompass a large swatch of the year. "The earliest are at the beginning of March; in the southern areas, the last ones are in late November in places like New Orleans where the weather is still warm." The eclectic mix of genres within alternative rock is perfect for the festivals:

> You don't want to have a metal act with a crooner, but you want some diversity in a festival roster because you are trying to attract tens of thousands of people. You need a mixed roster. You want some rock, some hip-hop, some indie rock. You want to create a festival with variety. You have to balance [your acts] with getting thousands of people into a festival. If you are too narrow, you are limiting yourself in terms of audience.

The alternative rock market is top-heavy in the Northeast, just as country is top-heavy in the South and Midwest. Nevertheless, country plays well in the Northeast, and alternative rap is well covered in the Southeast, part of Galea's territory. Hip hop and related alternative bands play well in large metropolitan areas (regardless of the region) because "you have an audience for everything." His audience is the younger set: "kids in high school and college, though they are kind of streaky in the artists they like. Older fans [thirty-somethings] seem to stick to certain ones." That's because alternative music "is more of a lifestyle for [the audience] than just a pastime," which explains why "younger fans are more apt to go out to a concert; they're more active in their purchases and their ticket buying."

Concerts and radio help enhance festival attendance. Alternative rock music "isn't as popular as top forty radio." At the same time, "alt-rock radio tends to take chances with new artists." It still remains "invaluable because alternative radio promotes my shows, and it gets people out and to the concerts. It is a very active tool in promoting concerts and festivals."

Galea has a musically narrow niche. He works with his clients to get them shows, which feed the concerts. Nevertheless, he tends to accentuate the larger festivals that allow him to book a large swatch of the artists he handles in one fell swoop. Still, he recognizes that the future depends on being a full-service agency. When he was with The Agency Group, before it was subsumed by United Talent, they specialized in music. UTA wanted The Agency Group because they "only had a fledgling music department" at the time. "It was a perfect marriage." The Agency Group "was a big music agency but we didn't have some of the bells and whistles of UTA." These "bells and whistles" are important for the larger booking agencies in today's market because "we need to go beyond just bookings and expand into the other aspects of the music world. Artists are multidimensional people. They want to be movie stars or own a vodka company. They might want to write a book or start their own company. Those are things we can [now] provide under the [broader] roof" of UTA. In the old days, concludes Galea, booking agencies would just make sure their clients had tours and concerts to play; "now it is much broader, and much, much more complex."

INDEPENDENT BOOKING AND PROMOTIONAL AGENCIES

It was not particularly surprising to learn that six months after our interview in 2016 Keith Richards moved to Paradigm Talent Agency. It was clear that he was swimming upstream with Brave World Artist Agency.

Richards has a solid background in booking, which was his first job in the music business after graduating from Belmont University in 2011. He worked at Elite Talent Agency (2011-2014), a small booking firm in Nashville that was founded by Marc Claassen. Slowly but surely, Richards made a name for himself. "I picked up a band out of Austin called The Rocket Band. We didn't make a ton of money, but it was great for me because they had toured for about five years, so all the talent buyers that knew them got to know me." Elite was going through some changes, so after a few years Richards joined The Fleming Agency (2014-2015) in Ann Arbor, Michigan. He was "looking for someone to take me under their wing and fine-tune me." He did not feel part of the team at Fleming and soon returned to Nashville, where he launched Brave World Artist Agency under the Warner Music Group.

At Brave World Artist, Richards worked with eight contemporary artists. Most of his artists were booked at small local venues. He rattles off the various clubs in Nashville according to the capacity: "The Basement has a capacity of one hundred; 12th and Porter [so named because of the cross streets], 200; 3rd and Lindsay [similarly named for the cross streets], 300 to 350; Exit Inn, 500; then City Winery, which has 350 seats, but if you took out the tables it can hold up to 850. The Cannery is 1,100; Marathon is 1,500; the Ryman, 2,000." Booking artists across a range of small venues is very time consuming, especially for a one-person agency. Dan Steinberg at Emporium Presents says that he books small clubs as a hobby, to keep his hand in, but he is glad that he doesn't have to make a living doing that anymore. "I don't have to book shows in 350-seat venues anymore because I would have to book 250 club shows to make what I do on a Dolly Parton [arena] show."

Richards would appreciate Steinberg's observation. He envied the agents at the big agencies, like William Morris,[54] because "opportunities come a little easier over there. That is a whole different network." So, when the opportunity came from Paradigm, an agency Richards voiced admiration for during our interview and one that a friend had recently joined, he made the leap.

Buck Williams is among one of the older agents (70-something) in Nashville who has never touched country: "I've always been in rock." Williams started booking in high school and eventually founded Frontier Booking International in New York (1981-1992). Frontier's new wave clients included The Police, Squeeze, and The Go-Go's. He sold the company in 1992 and moved to Los Angeles for two years before coming in 1994 to Nashville, a state income tax haven[55] —at least compared to New York and L.A. "The taxes in New York and Los Angeles were killing me . . . but there's no tax in Nashville." Arriving in Nashville in 1994, Williams started Progressive Global Agency. His client list includes Widespread Panic, who he has handled for nearly thirty years, and R.E.M., among a host of other rock bands. Progressive Global has around thirty artists on its roster with a staff of five people. Williams himself still spends a lot of time on the road because he wants to be there for his artists. The only thing he does differently today is "I don't ride buses. No buses. I did that when I was young. [Today] I fly."

In general, Williams doesn't follow country and do corporate gigs. "I don't go there. My bands don't do them. R.E.M. has never done a private gig, neither has Widespread Panic. We have turned down hundreds of opportunities, from Microsoft on down." For his bands, it is tantamount to "selling out." This is not to say he hasn't done them on occasion. He did book a private event with Yamaha and The Police, "and it got me a nice motorcycle." The problem, as he sees it, is that since you are taking their money, they control you. An artist may be picking up some nice change, but "How many meet-and-greets do you have to do? And on your day off, when you are touring—and touring is grueling, and you don't get many days off—you have to go to corporate headquarters and play a song on your guitar for five people who don't give a crap."

A point of booking that he mentions is how to sell a show. It's a variation of an old street organizer's trick[56] that is seldom covered in management texts.

Here Williams applies the concept of contagion to underselling an act. "It's about creating excitement," he says.

> Widespread Panic sold out fifty-one consecutive times at Red Rock [Amphitheater] in Denver [seating capacity 9,000-plus]. That will always be a standing record. . . . But there are places we appeared that we had to build and grow things. This is where it gets a little tricky. You undersell.
>
> For example, Widespread Panic did three shows at Philips [Arena, seating capacity 21,000] in Atlanta.[57] We didn't sell out the first one, and we got close on the second. We filled the third. I didn't like the first two non-sellouts, so I went back to the [smaller] Fox Theatre [seating capacity 4,665]. We did three shows there and sold out in twenty-five to thirty seconds for all three. There were some pissed-off people that couldn't get tickets. I started getting emails. I answered some of them. They were asking "How could you do that? Why didn't you go to back to the Philips?" I said, "Well, you didn't buy tickets at the Philips, so I went to the Fox."

The idea was to create excitement. If you put one hundred people in a 1,000-seat auditorium, it looks like no one is there and people wonder why they've bothered to come. If you put that same one hundred people in a small room and make sure there are only seats for ninety and the other ten have to stand up or sit on the floor, it looks like the event is a big deal. In short, the next time Widespread Panic plays the Philips, all those people who couldn't get tickets to the Fox will rush to get in to the Philips before it sells out. Williams goes on to add two other reasons artists like smaller venues. One is that smaller venues challenge them. The other is that the artists are closer to the fans "and that gives you goose bumps." Plus, he adds, "It's fun, and if we don't keep the artist doing fun things, what is the use?"

One of the big changes he's seen during his long career is the present trend toward consolidation—of record companies, promoters, and booking agents. In 1985, Williams recounts, 95 percent of the booking agents [and promoters] were independents, with the remaining 5 percent being large corporate entities; today it is reversed. "It's tough for the independents [today]." One of the problems with consolidation is that the big agencies have so much talent, "they have to push paper," which means "they cannot give as much attention to their artists." He survives because he got into the business before the push toward consolidation, and now, with his small roster, he "flies under the radar."

There has been a similar consolidation of booking agencies in the religious segment, but Ed Harper with The Harper Agency likewise flies under the radar in his small niche booking southern gospel.[58] The Harper Agency, initially called the Harper Booking Company, came to life in 1968 when then Oak Ridge

Boys bass singer Herman Harper grew tired of being on the road and away from his family. His son, Ed Harper, joined the agency after graduating from the business program at Belmont University in 1982. Although the agency had always dabbled in the Christian sector, in 1986 they shifted to gospel exclusively. He's been at it now going on forty years.[59]

> We're kind of a niche agency. Our area of focus is traditional and southern gospel, but we have some groups that expand out of that a little. [The] Martins do some inspirational things. We [also] book Mark Lowry. Mark is a comedian; we just signed him in May [2016]. Our focus, though, has been traditional southern gospel. We book those artists almost exclusively. We book their events, concerts, and fairs.

Harper's market includes fairs, outdoor festivals, and destination events, which is when people come to a specific destination and stay there for three or four days. "There are a lot of [destination] events in the fall. For example, next weekend [mid-August 2016] there is a ten-day run at Silver Dollar City in Branson [Missouri]. A big event. They have a lot of groups come in. In October, there's the Cattlemen's Association, which has moved from Louisville to Pigeon Forge. Dollywood Theme Park [in Pigeon Forge] also has a six-day-a-week festival in October." Christmas does okay, too. "We have some artists that do Christmas tours. There is one in particular called the Jubilee, and that one involves three of our artists." Jubilee relies on booking agencies such as The Harper Agency to provide artists; they otherwise promote the event themselves. One of the key distinctions for Christian gospel is that "you rarely see a gospel group with a country artist on a tour, though some festivals do that."

The Harper Agency presently has fourteen artists on its roster, all past the development stage. This is one of southern gospel's distinctions and one of the things that discourages consolidation. "There is long-term consistency [within our genre]. That is one of the things that is unique about our industry. The Kingsmen Quartet [is a good example]; they've been around for fifty years. We have artists [with us] that have been doing it for fifteen, twent-five years. Their names [in our market] become as iconic as George Jones, who [when alive] had a hard time getting air play but his name drew people."

Ed Harper and his agency are well known in the Christian community, which helps him get repeat business and new referrals. Ninety percent of new referrals come through the agency's website. Prospective buyers fill out a long form that helps Harper pinpoint the client's needs. Among the questions posed are: who the client has had before, what they want, and what their budget is. Through their answers he gets "a reading and a gauge" for what they want.

His goal, like all booking agents, is to keep his artists working. Some of his artists work 110 days a year, which "is on the low side." The average for his artists is between 140 to 160 shows a year. He elaborates on some of the issues in booking for the church market.

> A lot of churches are very selective. They know what they want and you have to know those things when you are talking to them [which is why the website questionnaire is beneficial]. They might not want the same thing as another church. There are no two buyers the same, so you have to know their personality. We have a responsibility to keep their schedules. You have to work hard to build a calendar. That is why we do one thing. We don't manage. We book venues.

Texas, he adds, is a growing market for The Harper Agency. But you have to know your market. "One thing I've learned living in the South is that you don't interfere with the local football. Trying to promote a concert on a Friday night in the state of Texas is suicidal, because high school football in the state is the biggest thing around. Those are the things you need to be sensitive to [in order to be successful]."

Liz Gregory founded Liz Gregory Talent in 1984. She also flies under the radar of the major booking agencies. Her niche is very narrow; it is lucrative for her and her artists but too small for the big agencies to bother with. She primarily books family acts into county and state fairs and community concerts. She recently moved to Montana because Montana, Colorado, and Wyoming are where a lot of her acts perform. Nevertheless, she books shows throughout the United States and still maintains an office in Nashville, largely for the Nashville connection: "Most people know I am from Nashville, but my people don't care where I live as long as I get the job done. I [sometimes] come back because I do the Tennessee State Fair [in Nashville]."

Her niche is fine for the time being but it is shrinking, another reason why she escapes attention from the larger agencies. "There are two types of fairs," she explains, "county fairs and state fairs. It used to be that county fairs got money from horse racing and other things, like rides and food. But that is going the way of things that used to be. Now [county fairs] need to get a sponsor [to have the money] to get talent. The county fairs don't have the expertise to do that; they're usually farmers or rancher volunteers." Because they are small, they are just as likely to utilize her knowledge of the industry and pay her to promote the fair.

State fairs have large attendances and deeper pockets, but there is typically only one state fair a year, compared to all the counties within a state. When she changes hats to promote the fair, Gregory goes to sponsors who might put up a few thousand dollars to have their name over an event. She is not talking about big corporate sponsors, but the local enterprises: "anything from a car dealership, a cable company, and local businesses." The one key difference for her fair acts is they are mostly family acts because one needs a band when you appear at a fair. She booked one act that "started out with two kids, and then there were four kids. I had them for thirteen years. Then they divorced and the family broke up and it all went to hell." Family acts tend to work well at fairs because of the fair's demographics: most fair attendees come with their family for a family night out. The same with community concerts.

Community concerts are also going the way of county fairs. There are community concert associations across the country that put on "concerts four times a year in the small towns; they charge $5.00 a ticket. People buy a pass for a year. They're a great value for a family. They don't know who they are going to see. There are all different kinds of acts. They could be classical, or country, or rock, or a comedian." Or they may be her famous racing pigs. "They are the best entertainment you can have at a fair or a [small venue]. I started them in the Northwest in the early 1990s. I had five units on the road. I went to a ranch and learned how to set them up and how to train them. People love them."

Her pigs are entertainment. And entertainment, she says, "comes in many different forms. My goal is to provide entertainment to a fair. It could be a pig race, a duck race, camel races, a rodeo, or entertainers." If they are entertainers, however, she is a very demanding person, whether wearing the booking or promotion hat.

Gregory is old school; she has no tolerance for the new breed of country artists. "I'm an authority on country music. I like some class with the artist; today they dress like crap and there is too much rock with it to my liking. It is all about the money today." She wants her artist to *entertain*.[60]

> An entertainer works the crowd, they work the stage. They get down to the level of the people. The audience wants to think they are singing to them, not the roof, the floor or the back of the room. I tell my people, when you walk onto the stage, you have twenty seconds to connect with the audience. I can walk into any place and look at the band and tell if they are connected. Some of [those in the group] don't even like each other [and the audience can tell]. I preach connection and connection is entertainment. I don't care if your mother died, if you are up there you better entertain. You [need to perform for] the people who are paying for you to do that. When you walk off the stage, you can go and cry or pout or do whatever you have to. But when you are up there, you entertain.

There is no hand holding for Gregory. "I am past that stage. They get one call to me, but that's it. No second call." She pulled one of her artists aside after a show:

> I kept him in my conference room for two hours. I wouldn't let anyone leave until someone coughed up what went wrong [on stage]. I did that because I do not tolerate drama. After thirty years, I don't have to. I pick who I want to work with. I'm choosy because it's my reputation. If someone says, "You cannot tell me what to do," I say, "Yes, I can, because when you are working for me, you better show up on time, you better look good, and you better put on a good show." If [my artists] cannot do that, then we are done.

Gregory holds the same stringent standards for talent she books as a promoter. She often does not have enough artists to fill out a festival lineup, and certainly not a headliner. Her artists usually fill the slot before the headliner, who she might get from one of the other large booking agencies. She often uses William Morris, but she's also used CAA and the recently closed Buddy Lee Attractions. She mentions an act she booked from William Morris. She docked the artist his full fee because he cut the show short. On the phone with the agent, she laid out the issue. "Your guy showed up drunk, he did a lousy show, and he cut it short. So I docked him." When you dock someone, she said, you hit them in the pocketbook and they don't do it again. The artist in question never got the chance to do it again because "he's out of the business."

Wearing the hat of a supplier (talent agent) and a talent buyer (promoter) is fine for Gregory because her niche is fairly small. Most have plenty on their plate doing just one or the other. Daniel Steinberg at Emporium Presents (acquired by Live Nation in 2018) nicely encapsulates the full plate dimension that is entailed in being a promoter.

Steinberg has worked in promotions for over twenty years. He started while in high school in Denver. At one point during his high school years he was booking the majority of acts for Denver's Mercury Café (450 seats), and "we were selling out the house." Most of Steinberg's early acts were in punk rock. He'd call them and say, "Hey, I'm in Denver. If you are going to play near here, I would be glad to help you out." He attended college for a brief period after high school but soon returned to the music world that he loved. Later he returned to college, but wanted a change. In 2000, he transferred to the University of Oregon in Eugene, where he immediately hooked up with one of the bigger punk metal promoters in Portland. It was a totally different promotional environment.

> Colorado was a much more competitive market. So I was a more driven buyer than most of the guys up here. A lot of them would take off at four o'clock in

> the afternoon. I was doing the whole day [and into the evening] so I had a better chance of booking. It was a friendlier version of the game up here. People were nicer and more polite. I was used to Denver where it was a tough rumble kind of thing.

In 2015, Steinberg joined up with Jason Zink to found Emporium Presents. The company promotes over 400 shows a year across the United States with a wide range of artists. Though his heart is still with punk, he books across genres. "We promote what we make money with. . . . I am not promoting my CD collection."

Steinberg is on the road "all the time. . . . I try to catch up with everyone we do business with, every artist, at least twice a year." He feels this is important.

> You need to keep the connection. You need to see people's faces. You need to let them know you want to have a beer with them. I think there is a connection in knowing the venues we work with and letting them know that we are part of it all. You don't want them to start thinking, "Hey, maybe we don't really need a promoter."
>
> We provide a really good service. We provide the money, the accounting, the catering, the promotion, the overall event production, and the marketing. We wrap all of that in a neat little package with a timely well-delivered service.

That being said, Steinberg also has to deal with the politics "that go along with the industry."

> For example, I am working on a tour in Norfolk. There is another promoter working on [a similar show] there and on the exact same date. This does no one any good. I know both [booking] agents and I know both managers; I'm trying to juggle around and see what act plays the market best so we don't play the same night. I am trying to see if we can trade out the market so we are not playing against one another. Otherwise it's a fuck you game and no one wins that.

In the short time since founding Emporium, Steinberg and Zink have done very well. During an interview with AEG, one of the big promoters, the company's CEO told Steinberg their base was $200 million. "That just blew my mind. They could not survive doing our [small] venues. We don't do Rolling Stones tours." Still, he is doing well. Emporium's corporate office is in Portland with regional offices in Nashville and Birmingham, Alabama. Though a national company, Emporium has a strong presence in the Northwest: "I probably do more volume in the Northwest than 90 percent of the promoters in the market." That may be why, even though his base falls short of AEG's $200 million, Live Nation picked them up in 2018.

Setting the Stage

There is a lot of razzle-dazzle in today's concerts: laser light shows; large, hanging over-the-stage screens highlighting the artist's performance; artists descending from the rafters to the stage on trapezes or appearing magically from below stage and stepping forward through a cloud of smoke; specially designed stages, like the claw-shaped stage used by U2, or Carrie Underwood's massive stage that stretched across the entire arena to ensure fans on every side had a great seat; and fireworks, sometimes real at outdoor events, or visually enhanced on screens during the artist's show. The razzle-dazzle is more high-tech today, but it has always been there, going back to the bejeweled costumes of the showgirls appearing before and during any of Sinatra's shows during his twenty-plus year run with the Rat Pack in Las Vegas between 1965 and 1985.

Then or now, audiences love the special-effect splash that enhances the artist's performance, even if they don't fully appreciate what goes into making it all seamlessly come together.[61] "Wow, that was awesome," is a remark often heard after any of these spectacles. To make an awe-inspiring show today, one constantly has to do more than just keep up with the Joneses. "Artists are continually seeking new ways of surprising audiences," writes Jessica Nicholson in *Music Row Magazine*.[62] One of those "wow" creators is Pyrotek, which provides pyrotechnical effects at concerts: flame projectors that can emit columns of flames or mortars that can eject fireballs. The biggest hindrance faced by Pyrotek is rules, says project manager Reid Derne.[63] It is necessary to obtain approval to do potentially dangerous special effects. Pyrotek's success rests, at least in part, on its ability to handle codes and licenses for an entire tour.

You need to do something spectacular in order "to have people come back," says tour management veteran Chris Lisle, whose company specializes in stage lighting.[64] "You have to have a memorable show. I'm not saying lighting makes a show, but [you have] to make a performance . . . memorable."[65] The three LED rings hanging over Carrie Underwood's Storyteller Tour clearly worked to enhance her performance as they "lowered, rose, and rotated during her concert to promote a dramatic focal point."[66] LED lights are favored today because they are bright, energy-efficient, and relatively inexpensive, an important aspect according to Lisle. "The biggest factor [in staging an event] is budget. The second one is space—how much room do we have to fit this in? Plus labor—who is going to set this up and run it?"[67] Lou Taylor, who heads up Tri Star's free-standing touring division states the biggest costs associated with production are sound, lighting and video elements.[68] Music is still the foremost ingredient for touring success, Taylor adds, but "fans expect elaborate production today" and if they don't get it, despite the music, they can be disappointed in the show. It's not easy, either. Chris Lisle says, "We don't always get it right the first time. Sometimes you have to downplay some fixtures or changes things to be able to make it all work."[69] Tour manager Chris Littleton would agree: "You try to anticipate everything you can and you just roll with the rest of it."[70] This section takes a brief look at some of the factors that help make a show memorable.

GETTING IT RIGHT: THE REHEARSAL STAGE

Groups have always rehearsed before a show to make sure their sound comes together. The artist's garage may still work to tweak the sound but more is needed to integrate the sound with the show. Artists need to work through their routine and ensure related technologies used in the act are synchronized to enhance the number being performed. In recent years, a growing industry catering to rehearsal space has blossomed to meet that need. Premier Global Production opened a 10,000-square-foot rehearsal room just outside of Nashville, in Madison, Tennessee.[71] Fort Knox Studios opened a 70,000 square foot 24-hour-a-day, seven-days-a-week rehearsal facility proximate to downtown Nashville in 2016.[72] With 160,000 square feet, Soundcheck is one of the largest rehearsal studio complexes in the world under one roof; its facilities are located in an industrial complex just across the Cumberland River from the downtown urban core.

Soundcheck owner and CEO Ben Jumper started his career at sixteen as a runner putting up posters around Chattanooga for shows coming to town. In the 1970s, he went on the road selling merchandise at Charlie Daniels concerts. Jumper ran stage production companies during the 1980s and 1990s; he took ownership of Soundcheck in 2004. Glenn Frey, one of the founding members of the Eagles, started Soundcheck in 1993, but Frey never had the time to develop it fully. The business was, says Jumper, "a diamond in the rough [that just] needed some love." The opportunity to polish the diamond came when then-owner-manager Bob Thompson turned 61 and decided to retire.

In recent years, Soundcheck has expanded into Austin (2010) and Houston (2013). Jumper's ventures outside Nashville are prompted by the same motivation for taking over Soundcheck: "If you see a need, you meet it, and you do it to the highest standards." His clients were the ones who prompted the expansion beyond Nashville. "Many of my clients came to me saying they just played the Austin City Limits festival and, 'we need you down there—your gear, your rehearsal space.'"

The loyalty of his clients was tested during the Nashville flood of 2010 when the Cumberland River overflowed and destroyed many of the buildings near its banks. Eighty-plus percent of his clients returned when Soundcheck reopened: "Kenny Chesney said that when we reopened, he'd take the first thirty days; Vince Gill called and said he wanted Locker Number 1 back—he was the very first (artist to rent a locker when Soundcheck Nashville launched)."

There are nine rehearsal stages at Soundcheck. The smallest are 20 x 30 x 19 (3) and 40 x 18 x 19 (4), with one at 70 x 80 x 19 and the largest (Studio A) at 100 x 80 x 24.[73] Rehearsal needs vary: "Some [bands] only need a few hours; some a few days; some a month, month-and-a-half." There is an on-site gym and shower for band members who need a break after a long day of rehearsing. There is 80,000 square feet of locker storage for bands to store their touring equipment, as well as 250 personal lockers ranging in size from 5x10 feet to 20x60 feet.[74] There is also an array of on-site manufacturers to meet the specialized needs of bands or band members, from cartage services, to building custom cases, to designing personal PA systems. Fender, Taylor Guitars, Hammond, Peavey, and Mayer Sound are just five of the companies that have a presence at Soundcheck. These on-site merchants are not competitive with each other: "If Fender has an artist come in and say [their Fender] doesn't work with the band, the people at Fender might go over to [the people] at Taylor Guitar. They help one another." The only thing Soundcheck actually retails is tour supplies: duct tape, batteries, gloves, even chalk to mark the stage floor. To keep abreast of the continued needs of their clients, Soundcheck is adding two sound stages that will accommodate full feature film production.

"Bands take time off," says Jumper. "Then need to get back in the groove. They need to work out new songs. They're perfectionists. They want to put on the best show possible, and practice makes perfect." Soundcheck and other state-of-the-art rehearsal spaces provide the opportunity to help bands achieve their goals by providing whatever they need to make their sound come together.

STAGING AN EVENT

Many of those who have been in the business for some years worked "grunt" jobs before finding their current executive niche. Some whose histories in the business have been traced mentioned early experiences staging an event. Danny Nozell—who now runs CTK Management handling Dolly Parton and Kenny G, among others—is one of those who started in production: he was a runner with Jam Productions in Chicago before becoming a production assistant, then a production manager. He's one from the "old school" who feels his early experiences in the field helped hone his current managerial style.[75]

Current Soundcheck owner Ben Jumper was president and CEO of Mid America Staging (1984-2004) before starting Crew One Productions in 1992.

Between them, Mid America and Crew One have designed stages for shows on aircraft carriers, did twelve of fourteen Alabama Jams, and eleven Nashville Summer Lights festivals. Mid America Staging was the first to have a certified load-bearing roof (over the stage). Jumper takes great pride in the fact he never lost a roof in a storm during his twenty-year staging career. Today Crew One Productions exists as the largest tech staffing source in the United States.

Despite being associated with two of the top four ranked staging companies in the United States, Jumper's pleased to be out of the business today. "It's very labor intensive and very equipment intensive. We once had forty tractor trailers running around [the country doing staging]. It just got to be too much. Just burned out after doing it for twenty-some years. You're the first person to arrive and the last to leave. No one ever thanks you. [I] wouldn't wish [the job] on my worst enemy. Definitely don't want my children doing it."[76]

Given this, Jumper decided to hold on to ownership of Crew One, but handed over the reins of leadership. This responsibility now falls to Atlanta-based chairman of the board and its general manager Jeff Jackson, who joined Crew One Productions three months after it was founded. Crew One Productions maintains offices in Atlanta, Nashville, and Memphis. Though Crew One has a division that specializes in festivals across the United States, the production arm focuses on the Southeast, close to home.

Like many non-artists in the music business, Jackson stumbled into his profession, because, he jokes, "I hung out with the wrong people in high school." A friend in school had "a little lighting company and did local things, like small clubs and high school dances. I hung out with him and I started helping set up his lighting system." The small business soon mushroomed and the company starting doing bigger things "likes arenas and stuff." He started touring with the Atlanta Rhythm Section in 1977 and soon became production manager "because no one else wanted [or knew how] to do it." In 1982, he went on the road as 38 Special's lighting and production manager. Jackson stayed with 38 Special until 1992. He also toured between 38 Special gigs with several other artists, including Cyndi Lauper and Twisted Sister, Stryper, and Triumph before joining Crew One. Jackson elaborates on some of the distinctions between different staging jobs and how they have changed over the years.

Lighting has always been important because, obviously, says Jackson, "you have to see the show." It also helps set the mood for the show by creating an atmosphere. "You could flick a switch [that would illuminate the artist when he or she appeared on the stage] and 20,000 people would stand up and scream." But there were no video walls back then and "everyone was looking at the artist." Now you watch the video walls. This also poses lighting problems. "It used to be that we had the lead singer all in white and you could bounce different colored lights off of them. You cannot do that anymore because of the close-ups—you don't want to have a green artist [appearing on the video screen]." This is why rehearsal facilities have become more important.

> I used to go out with the band for a whole day and [whatever needs arose] you worked it out. Now bands rehearse for weeks without the [featured] artist, and then maybe another week or two with the artist. [The time is needed] because it is all digital now. [The show] has to be programmed and reprogrammed. The audio as well. Everyone has to get together. The designer gets together with the video person, and the lighting director, and the set director, and they all have to work together [otherwise the show doesn't work]. Most of this is done during the rehearsals.

Some may find all this razzle-dazzle distracting because one is watching the videos and not the performance. Nevertheless, Jackson points out that videos have long been there to enhance the show.

> The Grateful Dead and the Allman Brothers had light shows. They would have a big screen behind the stage and they would use multiple overhead projections for images of weird shapes and designs—it was really good if someone was doing acid. There was [always] something else to look at besides the band. The lighting then, though, was not part of the show. These shows started to fade away and theatrical-type lighting came into play, and it grew, and grew, and grew to the point where the lighting became the show. It stayed that way for a long time. Then a few bands started using video[77] and they could show close-ups of the artists. Then someone started thinking, "Hey, we can show different backgrounds; we can show mountains and fields; we can show whatever the song is about. Then the video screens got bigger and, in some cases, moved on tracks and became the focal point of the show.

Finding qualified technicians is becoming increasingly problematic today.[78] In staging, the lack of qualified tradesmen is exacerbated by a growing need for stagehands. The average show coming to an arena, like Bridgestone in Nashville (seating capacity 20,000), requires from twenty to thirty tractor trailers to haul the equipment, where once the same size show would only require only seven or eight tractor trailers.[79] This means one hundred stagehands are needed to load it in and 140 to load it out. And if the Bonnaroo Festival in Manchester is taking place the same long weekend as the CMA Festival in Nashville, you need at least 600 stagehands. The problem is even more pronounced for mega-stadium shows (70,000-plus) since a week is needed just to load them out: "It takes three to four days to build a stage; at least another full day to get sound and lights up; another day to break everything down." Beyoncé, Jackson says, may have sixty-two trucks just for the production equipment. The cost for a mega-show like U2's 360 Degree tour (2009–2011), with its massive claw-like stage and spaceship-style dome over the stage, cost over $250,000 in labor to assemble at the Georgia Dome in Atlanta.

The problem of manpower is further complicated by the fact that even modestly sized arena shows are staged sporadically throughout the year and therefore don't provide a steady livelihood for stagehands. This means that one is relying more and more on students or part-time, inexperienced workers to work a couple of days a month.

The facilities themselves often complicate the ability of those involved to adequately stage a show. This is especially pronounced in some of the older facilities, like Nashville's Municipal Auditorium, which was built in 1962.[80] The place is "a beast to work," says Jackson. State-of-the-art that it might have been at the time, "no one thought [then] that you were going to hang 150,000 pounds of equipment from the ceiling." And hanging it is no easy task.

> The rigging is ancient. The Bridgestone Arena [built in 1996] has gridding hanging over the stage and beams that stretch into the house so riggers can climb out there, put a rope in, and pull up a motor with a chain, which they can attach to the beam. There are lots of places to hang [things] up there and it is easy to rig. At the time it was built they knew rigging had to be done. When the [Nashville Municipal] Auditorium was built, nobody thought they were going to be hanging rigging from the ceiling.
>
> If that isn't enough, the roof of the building is [for some inexplicable reasons] off axis with the floor by 15 degrees. In a symmetrical building, when you are calculating where you are hanging your chain motors, you do your algorithms so that the stage left calculations are the same as stage right. Not if the building is off axis. And that's just one problem.
>
> You cannot wrap the beams [in Municipal Auditorium] because they are up against the roof, so the riggers have to work around all the duct work, primarily in lifts. They have to hang beam clamps [to hold the equipment]. In newer buildings, it's easy because you can walk on the beams which are attached to fall arrest system[81] safety cable over each beam.

It's not that newer buildings are ideal for getting things in place for the stage so the show "works." Jackson acknowledges that Bridgestone "is a beautiful building" and very functional. He also appreciates that they are constantly upgrading the facility. Atlanta has done some good things with the State Farm Arena. They closed it down twelve out of the last twenty-four months for major renovations. Suites were replaced with an additional seating area; a new, massive video scoreboard was added, as well. "Most of the renovations are cosmetic, however; it's stuff for the fans." Nevertheless, Jackson appreciates that they also extended the rigging grid and added a few new rigging beams.

Some years ago, Jackson met with the staff during the design phase of a new arena that would be open in two years. During the meeting, Jackson had the opportunity to look at the blueprints. He noticed that the follow spot positions were located on a catwalk high above the floor near the sports lighting. Jackson pointed out that, at that elevation, the spotlights would not be able to hit the stage. He was assured they would be relocated.

A year prior to the arena opening, Jackson attended another meeting with the staff and saw the revised blueprints. The spotlight locates were still in the same place. After pointing this out, he was thanked and once again assured they would be properly relocated. During the load-in for the first concert at the new arena, Jackson looked up and observed the spotlights were on the catwalk by the sports lighting, just like it was shown on the original blueprint. He walked up to the catwalk, turned on a follow spot, pointed it toward the stage, and watched it form a perfect spot thirty feet above the stage in the seating. The staff was forced to admit that the spotlights wouldn't work (just as he told them), so the rig team had to lower all the spots from the catwalks to the ground with block and falls. They were then carried into seating areas where they could be aimed at the stage.

And so, Jackson says, "to answer your question: 'Do they listen to our suggestions?' The answer is ABSOUTELY NOT! If it doesn't have revenue stream attached to it, it doesn't often matter."

At various points throughout this analysis of the music industry, professions have been sketched that are seldom recognized by the public. They are, however, appreciated by others in the industry: publishers recognize the strategic role their pluggers play in getting their songs recorded, and record producers appreciate the role their promoters play in getting their songs played on the radio. Stage personnel may be the least appreciated profession within the industry. The audience may recognize that a show is well staged but it's just a given: they don't think of the effort involved in setting up a stage. Many just think of it as "there." It is not much different with the artists, who often similarly take the staging for granted. There are certainly some artists who might thank the lighting or stage manager for making things "work," but fans and artists are more likely to recognize staging features when something goes wrong. A circuit goes awry and some of the spots go dark. The show might go on because it is still illuminated, but not like it should be, and people get miffed. A good show, on the other hand, where everything comes together seamlessly, is "just" a good show, and everyone goes on about their business after the show ends, except the stage personnel who are left thanklessly behind to break it all down and get it loaded properly on the trucks for the next show.

Conclusion

This chapter looks at three professions that support an artist: artist managers, booking agents, and stage personnel. The distinctions are heuristically convenient even if they are not always firmly drawn.

Artist managers, the focus of the first section, should not be confused with business managers, the accountants who handle the artist's finances. There is also no clear division between artist managers and those in artist development. In this study, artist managers are those primarily involved with established artists. This is because their income is generated on a percentage based on the artist's income, and a new, unproven artist is unlikely to financially support a manager. There are, of course, those managers who take on an unknown artist because they see some long-term potential. Norm Parenteau with Slipshod Management saw the early potential of Old Crow Medicine Show, just as John Dorris with Hallmark Entertainment did when he first heard John Michael Montgomery perform. Management companies are able to take these risks because they often handle three to four artists.

Artist managers all deal with development to some degree, but since they are likely to take on a client who has some track record, and hence some identity, they focus on fine-tuning the artist's identity or ensuring it is capitalized upon. Only one person in this study focused exclusively on development.[82] Those who focus on development help the artist establish an identity. Then as the artist begins to establish some credentials (and generate an income), the development-focused manager passes the artist on to someone else to manage their subsequent career.

The majority of artist managers handle artists across a range of musical styles. They don't want to have two clients who are directly competing against one another. The artists may all be country, or rap, but their styles differ. This way the artist manager avoids any conflict of interest. The artist managers discussed in this chapter focus on artist management more so than publishing and/or production. Individuals who focus on management are a different breed than those who have multiple tentacles. Wearing multiple hats pushes the entrepreneur to the foreground while those who work largely as artist managers are very unassuming "behind the scenes" individuals. They may be very proactive on their client's behalf, but they push their artists, not themselves.

Artist managers recognize that theirs is an accidental profession. None of the managers in this study entered the music business with an eye on becoming a manager. They did find, however, once they began their managerial career, that they liked it and were good at it, which is why once embarked upon they stayed with the new career choice. Rusty Harmon ended up managing Hootie and the Blowfish, but it just sort of happened. The same for Mitchell Solarek who runs Maximum. He had a small talent agency for actors and models in San Francisco when some musicians asked him to manage their Nashville-bound music career.

There are two other aspects of artist management besides making sure the artist is booked at and gets to the best venue to reach her or his audience. Management, more so than development, entails a degree of hand-holding. This is not to suggest that artists are prima donnas. It is just that they are creative people in a business where a personal issue can disrupt their ability to perform, and a bad performance can substantially affect an artist's career. Someone has to be there to help the artist over the bumps. Another, relatively new, aspect that managers increasing deal with is to develop corporate relations with sponsors. Sponsorships at concerts in the 1960s and 1970s were looked at by many as tacky—it intimated the artist had "sold out." This negative association is no longer as pronounced. Sponsorship can also help with the bottom line, a financial benefit that has become more imperative as labels reach deeper into an artist's performance income with 360 deals.

Artist managers also act as booking agents, but this is largely limited to new artists who are booked into small local venues. Moving booking onto the regional level adds complications, and booking at the national level is an art. Artists and their managers are happy to hand over this responsibility to booking agents, who are sometimes called talent agents because they book talent. Booking agents have to know the different venues—their size, the stage, the demographics of the audience—in order to ensure the artist is booked at a venue right for them. Keeping track of all the different venues is a complicated task in itself because facilities are constantly changing. The booking agent is also responsible for the route the artist travels in order to maximize their time and avoid wastefully crisscrossing the country. There is little glamorous about the grunt work of booking; lining up all the dates and places perfectly is time-consuming and stressful. A number of individuals in this study worked in booking at some stage of their career before looking for something more creative.

Some of the bigger agencies, such as William Morris, are well known to the general public and book a wide range of artistic clientele. The larger agencies may have fifty or more artists on their roster and some added clout simply because they are so well-known, but even then, one agent typically handles only three to five artists. Three of the agents in this study worked at two of the bigger agencies. The booking agents at United Talent were particularly instructive because they underscored the contrast of booking for different genres in different sections of the country.

The other four were small to modest-size agencies. Free-standing agents offer a unique perspective in an age where largesse seems to be the booking norm; they underscore an "old-school" method of booking. Keith Richards, who launched Brave World Booking, enunciates the problem of being a sole-proprietary booking agent, which is why he made the move to one of the bigger agencies (Paradigm) when the opportunity arose. Dan Steinberg, who successfully ran one of the larger booking agencies in the Northwest, took the money when he was offered a buyout by Live Nation. The other two independents fly under the radar of the corporate booking giants because of their specialized niche: Ed Harper with The Harper Agency is cozily ensconced in the Christian music segment, while Liz Gregory with Liz Gregory Talent makes a decent living booking family festivals and rodeos in the Midwest. In an age of consolidation, Harper and Gregory may represent the quickly disappearing "old way" of booking.

The public may not know how much rehearsal time is necessary before going on the road. Even mega-artists need to rehearse to make sure everything comes together. And coming together today is more complicated than just hitting the right notes: lighting and video have to be synchronized to put the artist's "best face" forward. The complexities of staging a concert are a driving reason why providing rehearsal space, with all its associated paraphernalia, is becoming a mainstream industry within the music world.

Finally, there's getting the stage ready for the artist's appearance. Stages themselves are increasingly spectacular, so hiring a few local carpenters to nail some wood together is insufficient today. Complicating staging an event is the technical knowledge necessary to hang lighting and video walls, and to run the electrical cable. A one-night performance that requires a specially designed stage—which is increasingly *de rigeuer*—can take a full week to put together and take down. It's not cheap either, largely because amphitheaters and stadium builders are more concerned with cosmetic matters than practical ones. This makes an already difficult job more difficult than it needs to be. Considering the structural issues associated with some of the larger music venues, it is surprising how stage personnel can make it work. These individuals have to know what they are doing, too, in order to ensure 1) it all comes seamlessly together, and, perhaps more importantly, 2) no one on stage or in the audience gets harmed because something has gone seriously awry.

Conclusion

A considerable body of music has long emanated from Nashville, though its country roots are a driving reason for its Music City moniker. Austin, Texas, as well as any number of other cities across the United States, may rival Nashville in the number of music venues that dot the city. Few rival Nashville as a songwriter's haven—perhaps none if songwriting is narrowed to the country format. This is why so many struggling artist-songwriters gravitate to Nashville. One may be an excellent songwriter, but in order to have your songs heard, Grammy-winning songwriter Kelly Lovelace advised aspiring young songwriters, you gotta be in Nashville. The songwriters in this study, few of whom were native to Nashville, moved to Music City for just that reason.

Nashville is not a magic bullet. Being in Nashville is just the first step in a long arduous process to success . . . or failure. Anecdotal guesstimates from those in the industry suggest that at least 50 percent of the artist-songwriters arriving in Nashville don't have the talent and soon return home. Another 30 percent don't realize the investment that is necessary, and, while there are exceptions, it typically takes five to seven years to build a network that will open publishing doors. That leaves 20 percent[1] who are talented and committed, but in a city where talent abounds, only a fraction of that number will carve out a career in the music industry.

There's a lot of fallout among seasoned songwriters, as well. If these seasoned songwriters don't keep the songs a-coming (even if they don't chart), they are likely to be let go by their publishing house and fade away. Successful seasoned songwriters are at the office by nine and they are there well into the evening hours. Most prefer to work at the publishing house to avoid the at-home temptation to procrastinate. The office also lets them get together with their fellow songwriters with whom they can interact and run ideas, lines, or lyrics by, if they don't actually sit down and co-write.

The process of songwriting requires a lot of hard work. This study refutes the popular notion of "artistic inspiration." Most young songwriters generally take jobs with flexible hours (waiter/waitress, Lyft driver) in order to be able to both pay the bills and continue to develop their talents by playing writers' rounds or co-writing with others. Luck is a factor—being at the right place at the right time—but luck is more likely to happen to those who keep plugging away, and away, and away until they "suddenly" get lucky.

Songwriter demographics are not particularly revealing: there is nothing to distinguish them from others in their cohort who did not pursue a songwriting career or left after a brief period of time in Nashville. Young or seasoned, someone in their families was often musically involved, but few (less than 10 percent) did so professionally. Their family background, then, had little effect on their decision to perform and/or write music. Indeed, many families were skeptical of their child's decision to pursue music professionally, which is why the families often encouraged aspiring artists to finish their education so they would have something to fall back on if things didn't work out. Only two young and two seasoned songwriters in this study did not go to college. Once committed to their musical muse, however, artists' families tended to support their offsprings' choices; some even helped out financially. The only factor separating young from seasoned songwriters is the gender disparity: half of the young songwriters were female, compared to approximately 30 percent of the seasoned songwriters.

Seventy-five percent of those in this study came to Nashville after finishing their education; the other 25 percent worked either as artists or in unrelated professions for a number of years before moving to Nashville to pursue their dream of becoming a songwriter. Those in the latter group tended to adopt a fish-or-cut-bait philosophy. So it was for Drew Kennedy (Y) and John Berry (S), both of whom had successful singing careers in the local community. They knew they had to come to Nashville if they really wanted to be songwriters. People who want to make it as a songwriter gravitate to Nashville because the social environment is so conducive to struggling musicians and neophyte songwriters. Nashville Songwriter Association International (NSAI) is a particularly supportive organization for young songwriters, and many seasoned ones are involved with it in some capacity. Nashville's strength as a songwriter's town exists in the number of songwriter roundtables that give newcomers a chance to display their artistry and connect with other artist-songwriters.

Networking is important in any occupation. It is a form of social capital: the more people you know (and who know you), the better your chances of connecting with someone who might advance your career. Networking is particularly pronounced among Nashville songwriters. Ken Mathiesen at NSAI put it nicely: "Nobody is going to come knocking on your door and say 'Hey, you got some songs?'" Nor can you go knocking on just anyone's door. You have to have connections.

Today, a shrunken musical community makes networking even more critical. Those who have been in the business for some time recall that there were 1,000-plus songwriters making a living in Nashville during the 1990s; today that number is closer to 300. Nashville has experienced tremendous growth since 2000. Still, the shrinking songwriting community makes networking both easier and more critical in advancing one's career. Writers' rounds that take place regularly throughout the city are one way to showcase one's talent and connect with others in the industry. Co-writing is another, increasingly important dimension of networking.

There are two types of co-writes: co-writing with the artist or co-writing with another songwriter. Both have long existed and some of the great songs of the last few decades were penned by professional songwriters: Elvis Presley's "Jailhouse Rock" (written by Jerry Leiber and Mike Stoller), Patsy Cline's "Crazy" (written by Willie Nelson), and George Jones's "He Stopped Loving Her Today" (written by Bobby Braddock and Curly Putman). Today, the artist is more likely to be involved at some level with the writing of a song because it increased the probability that the artist would cut the song. Songwriters do not, however, appreciate an artist tampering with their song. Songs may be tweaked as the song goes into the studio, but tampering with the lyrics is not typically done.

Co-writing is more pronounced among songwriters now. It's common today to write with two other songwriters. The perfect three-way is a songwriter who can build tracks, a lyricist, and a writer who can sing, so that by the end of the day the team has a demo with vocals. The co-writing relationship is not perfectly symmetrical, either. Two songwriters working on a song may not contribute equally: one may write 60 percent of the song, the other 40 percent. At another time, it might be vice-versa. Indeed, one songwriter in this study mentioned that he had no issues with sharing co-writing credit when he was stuck on a song even if the other songwriter only contributed 10 percent, because that 10 percent pulled the song together.

This collaborative aspect permeates the Nashville music community. It is seen here in co-writing with both a peer and across the generations. Young songwriters are understandably pleased to work with, and learn from, a seasoned songwriter, but seasoned songwriters are just as appreciative of the insights their young colleagues provide. Young songwriters keep seasoned songwriters on the cutting edge, something that the seasoned songwriters appreciate because music changes fast. Working with young songwriters keeps seasoned songwriters up to speed. Another collaborative aspect of songwriting is cross-publisher co-writing. This means that the publishing house does not get to keep their 50 percent of the royalties but has to divide it with another publisher. Nevertheless, cross-publishing greatly enhances the chances of a song being cut because instead of one house pitching its three writers to a label, two houses pitch three songwriters to a label.

Even though the three-way songwriter split cuts into the writer's royalties, most songwriters in this study accept that as long as they get paid. Album sales have largely collapsed with the advent of streaming at the outset of the new millennium. Younger songwriters are less troubled by this than seasoned ones, who fondly recall a time when songwriters were adequately compensated for the songs they wrote. Nevertheless, all songwriters (and artists) would like to be paid for the songs that are streamed such as they presently are when the songs are played on the radio. Many streaming services have circumvented royalty payments by arguing that music should be free. NSAI and the three major Professional Rights Organizations (PROs) have been lobbying Congress on behalf of their songwriting members for more stringent regulations that would allow songwriters to receive royalties from the various streaming services. Their effort finally produced results in 2018 with the passage of the Music Modernization Act, which will ensure royalties are generated from the streaming services. The MMA takes effect in January 2021.

ASCAP is perhaps the best-known PRO outside the music industry because it has been in existence for a hundred years. BMI was initially formed because ASCAP did not license many genres outside their Tin Pan Alley members. They each represent about 45 percent of musicians across a wide range of genres. The remaining 10 percent belong largely to SESAC, which, unlike ASCAP and BMI, is an exclusive club: ASCAP and BMI membership is open to anyone who wishes to register, regardless of their songwriting credentials; SESAC is by invitation only. The responsibility of all three PROs is to monitor broadcast and performances of music by their members and to ensure that royalties are appropriately collected and dispensed.

This study found that deciding which of the two dominant PROs to join is done in a very ad hoc way. One-third picked the PRO simply because they had to pick one in order to receive royalties. The other two-thirds picked the one they did either 1) because a songwriter they knew was a member and spoke well of them, or 2) they established a connection with the PRO's representative. The PROs are important to songwriters not just because they collect royalties; they are very proactive in helping their members. They all have some sponsored activities spotlighting their members and offer regular workshops to help their members hone their craft.

Young or seasoned, connecting with a music publisher is key to moving a songwriter's career forward. It may all begin with a song, but the song has to get to someone who, in turn, will produce it for popular consumption. The music publisher stands at this critical gatekeeping juncture. Unlike traditional gatekeepers, however, who simply scan submitted items and pass them on, music publishers actually hire the songwriter and work with them to hone their songs before pitching them to a label executive.

The attraction of a publishing deal is that it provides a draw—an income stream paid by the publisher to the songwriter as an advance against royalties. A draw is attractive because it provides a basic income that allows songwriters to concentrate on their craft. Most seasoned songwriters prefer a modest draw because they don't threaten the company's bottom line if they have a soft year. Publishers recoup their draw and any related expenses when the songwriter's song is recorded.

Contracts are attractive to publishers because they indefinitely own any songs written while under contract. Contracts typically specify that the songwriter writes a certain number of songs during any given year. Eight to ten, 100 percent songs is the norm. This is a modest baseline given that most songwriters write fifty to a hundred songs a year in an attempt to improve the chance of one being recorded. A 100 percent song means the songwriter writes the complete song, so if the songwriter co-writes with one other writer, that counts for only half a contractual song. Contracts tend to run one to two years with a one- to two-year renewable clause. The short contract period is a hedge against a songwriter who fails to produce any recorded songs during the contract period. Generating no income for the publisher would likely mean the songwriter is let go at the end of the contract period. In this case, the publisher does not recoup any expenses since no royalties were generated. This means publishers have to have a very sharp ear, otherwise they can be out a substantial amount of money.

The publishers in this study were mostly in their fifties with twenty to thirty years' experience before moving into publishing. Two-thirds worked in A&R or a related field early in their career; the other third had a career as an artist or studio musician. None entered the music business with the goal of becoming a publisher. For most, it just happened, which is why the section assessing their career trajectory is entitled "a crooked path." It is worth noting that the number of women publishers is fairly small (less than 10 percent), which is perhaps why no female publisher was included in this study. Nevertheless, more women are working today at many of the publishing houses frequented in the course of this study, which suggests that more females may gravitate toward publishing careers in the years to come.

There are two sides to publishing, the administrative and the creative. The administrative is often farmed out to companies, such as ClearBox Rights, that specialize in that aspect of the business. The publishers overwhelmingly saw themselves as creative individuals because they had to spot talented songwriters and help hone their craft. Finding talented songwriters is something that could not be quantified and was likened by at least one publisher to a kind of treasure hunt. Most would say they were looking for the "WOW factor"—that certain something that made them say, "Wow, that songwriter is really good." Identifying the qualities of a potential songwriter is difficult because they are looking for someone ahead of the curve, and while they know where the curve presently is, they have no real idea where the curve will be, yet that is what they are looking for.

The Wow factor is not totally ambiguous, however. There are three things the publishers tended to agree comprised the indefinable Wow factor. First, the publisher is looking for someone to fit with his or her existing writing staff, someone who will complement the existing staff but won't compete with other in-house songwriters and "rock the boat." This leads to the second feature: in order for the publisher and songwriter to connect with one another they need some time to get to know one another and make sure that both can work together. The third factor is particularly important: songwriters need to be open to constructive criticism. This point is just as germane to seasoned songwriters as young ones who may be a bit raw: songwriters need to respect input because they may be too close to the lyrics. Accepting constructive criticism is something all the songwriters in this study were open to; they all recognized the importance of input from other songwriters and their publisher in helping shape their songs for the marketplace. This may be axiomatical, however, since songwriters who are not open to constructive criticism are not likely to last long in the business.

The other major contribution publishers make is getting their songwriters' songs placed. The publisher at small houses may pitch the songs to label executives themselves, but most rely on an in-house pitcher (or plugger), who also largely double as their scout since pitchers tend to be younger, twenty- to thirty-somethings who regularly make the writers' rounds. Most of the publishers still make writers' rounds, but at fifty-something they tend to leave it to their young colleagues.

Pitching is a tough job that is largely unrecognized by those outside the industry. It is wrought with rejections. "I'm told two hundred times a week" that the song doesn't work by label executives, one young pitcher said. It is even more difficult because the executives may dismiss a song after hearing only a few bars or just one or two lines. To make matters worse, the pitcher has to explain to the songwriter—who just wrote the greatest song ever—that the song doesn't "sell"; in this regard, they may have to talk to the songwriter about ways to make the song more marketable. This is why the role of a pitcher is considered to be as creative as writing the song itself; indeed, quite a few publishing companies have broadened the term of plugger to creative director. Young pluggers, which almost all are, also bring a fresh perspective to the table that all the publishers in this study appreciated.

Once a plugged song is placed it enters the production cycle. Recording music didn't start to happen in Nashville until the 1950s and 1960s. It was during this period that studio works moved from two takes "and choose the one with the fewer mistakes"[2] into an art form. The interactive aspect of the studio that emerged during this period would become one of the key dynamics of the Nashville studio system.

The studio promotes deep and personal ties between people, especially when the players have worked together intimately creating music over some years. The famous Nashville Sound (and Number system) is rooted in these early years. The Nashville Sound is more than a melodic technique; it is also characterized by the way musicians in Nashville come together to produce music. The Nashville Sound—then and now—is the improvisation that occurs among musicians working together in a studio. The synergy that takes place in the studio is "as important as the song itself," because, says Ron "Snake" Reynolds, songs can be "made or lost in the recording studio" and some classic recordings happened serendipitously in the studio while musicians improvised with the artist.

Studio work peaked during the 1990s. So many LP albums were being cut that studio musicians were working ten- to twelve-hour days. Then came streaming and EPs that had half or fewer songs on them than LPs. Studio work dropped dramatically. Today demos are largely made by the artist-songwriter on home recording devices. A good-sounding demo can be made this way and many artists and publishers embrace homemade demos because they are more cost efficient than having to go into a studio. Nevertheless, most artists and the major labels still prefer using musicians gathered together in a studio for the final cut. This is no longer necessary, however, and smaller producers, like After Touch Music and DeciBel, have sophisticated state-of-the-art small studios that can produce a quality recording without having all the musicians gathered together.

Home studio technology took a giant leap forward after 2005. Today there are a slew of state-of-the-art electronic programs that allow tech-savvy artists to cut in a drum set or a guitar riff and upload their songs onto one of the streaming platforms. The problem is not the quality of the equipment available to young artists and independent producers today, the problems are

1) the various streaming services are not music companies so the quality of the uploaded material is often poor, even when properly recorded, and 2) there are a lot of artists uploading mediocre songs, and quality songs can get lost in the massive amount of material available. Thus, many artists who begin to garner attention online are quick to accept a production deal by a legitimate company. They know the importance of getting their songs properly distributed and promoted.

The major labels, of course, have a well-established, sophisticated distribution system, which is why a good 10 to 20 percent of the independent producers utilize major labels to distribute their records. The majors charge a percent for distributing independent artists and are happy to oblige since it incurs no real financial outlay on their part. Another 30 to 40 percent eschew traditional distribution channels. These are often artists who are satisfied selling their albums at concerts or home websites. A significant number of these artists are those who parted ways with the major labels and have struck out on their own. The remaining 40 to 60 percent utilize the growing number of small independent distributors who, while often using online platforms, help their artists position their songs to increase their chances of being heard. These small independent producers utilize various promotional mechanisms to help their artists get noticed, which is as important as getting their artists online.

Promotion is a critical component of distribution. Getting the songs out there is relatively easy today; getting them heard is another matter, and where promotion is essential. Even the best artist needs to come to the attention of the public before they can be embraced. Independent distributors promote more modestly than the major labels: one distributor writes and posts press releases for his clients to help them build their fan base; another tries to position his artists online by creating the right playlist "for the right place and the right occasion," similarly increasing the chances of his clients coming to the attention of those interested in the type and style of music his artists are recording. The majors have lagged in this area, relying on more traditional methods of promotion, but they have recently (post-2010) started increasing their online promotional activity. Indeed, all the major and many of the mid- to large-size independents today have an in-house social media department.

The majors have historically relied on promoting their artists and their artists' records via radio airplay. Despite all the changes occurring in record production, this remains essentially unchanged. Just about every person interviewed in the course of this study emphasized radio's preeminent role to make or break a performer, especially in country music. That's because, one label executive said, that while social media may help draw a few hundred, even a few thousand people to an artist's concert, the artist needs radio to get them to 10,000- or 20,000-seat venues.[3] It remains to be seen whether radio will continue with the younger generation, but it appears that radio will remain vibrant for country music in the foreseeable future.

Social media isn't sufficient to connect to radio executives. It may make executives aware of this or that artist or of a new song coming out, but personal relations are necessary to "connect" with the radio executives, who are taking a chance on new artists and want to get to know him or her. To accomplish this, label promoters get in their car, often with the artist(s) in tow, and go station to station. It is grueling, time-consuming work, but absolutely essential if the label wants to expose their artist(s) to major markets. Mid-sized labels do this the same as the majors, the only difference being that independent label promoters cover a wider territory and, once a connection is made, the promoter is likely to stay with the radio executive even when they move outside their geographical territory. Promoting is not just sales, either; it is also creative since promoters, being in the local radio market, are always on the lookout for new talent.

A key aspect of social media and promotions is to make people aware of the artist and their songs. As an artist gains a following, he or she generally seeks someone to manage their career. Artist managers, unlike managers in the corporate sphere, are very private individuals. Modest as they may be, they are very assertive on their client's behalf.

More than any other musical profession examined in this study, artist managers tend to stumble into their vocation. Becoming an artist manager is, as one manager put it, an "accidental profession." Their entrance into management notwithstanding, managers have two things in common. One is "babysitting," which is the artist manager's forte. Artists have creative temperaments, and it is the manager's job to ensure whatever is interfering with their ability to perform is smoothed over. Every manager in this study knew exactly what I meant when I asked them if they ever had to babysit their clients, and many gave examples of how they had to do just that at some point with at least some of their clients. The other dimension of management is corporate relations. This is a relatively new aspect of management and is increasingly important in 1) generating an income for the artist and 2) maintaining the artist's name recognition in the public sphere.

There are two types of corporate relations. One is advertisement generated by tour sponsors. Previously eschewed as "selling out," sponsorship in the age of 360 deals is becoming more and more important in generating an income. A national sponsor can ensure heavy promotion for the artists and their concerts, but even a local sponsor for a small tour can help offset concert costs and bolster the bottom line.

The other revenue stream is linking the artist with a product. The artist is promoting a brand, but he or she is also staying in the public limelight, and staying in the limelight helps generate name recognition that can translate into concert sales. The artist manager is primarily responsible for establishing these types of corporate relations. In doing so, they bolster their income—which is based on a percent of what the artist makes—but they are also bolstering their artist's income, which is their primary responsibility.

While radio play can make or break them, today an artist's primary revenue stream comes from concerts. In the past, concerts were important because they helped promote record sales, which was where the artist made their money. Record sales are now a fraction of what they once were, so artists rely on concerts to generate an income. Some artist managers handle booking, but this tends to occur with young, yet-to-be-known artists who appear on small, local stages. As the artist gains name recognition and starts to perform at larger 2,000-plus seat venues, booking at the regional and national level becomes more time consuming and beyond the pale of many artist managers. The artist manager brings in a booking agent. The booking agent's job is to match the artist with the right venue and to do so in a way that utilizes the artist's time to their best advantage.

The booking agents interviewed for this study underscore both the stress and complexities of booking, which are not widely recognized outside the music business. Artist managers clearly appreciate the critical role booking agents play. It is something anyone might be able to do, one booking agent said, but it consumes a lot of time, and most managers don't have the time to devote to it. The time consumption is such that even agents at the larger agencies tend to handle only a handful of artists. This study demonstrates how agents deal with different musical genres within their respective markets.

One of the big changes in the industry is the shift toward consolidation—economy of scale gives the major agencies a lot of clout in booking their clients. Some of the smaller agencies have survived this shift because they book in a specialized niche, too small for the major agencies to bother with. This study would suggest, however, that the smaller agencies are fading fast.

Now that the song has been selected, recorded, and a concert booked, the artist has one last step to take: that is, onto the stage. This is not a simple task where one "just" sings their songs. Concert goers expect a *show,* and artists want to please their fans with a memorable one. To this end, a growing rehearsal industry has arisen to help the artist make sure that their sound comes seamlessly together. These facilities range in size from small on-site rooms for bands that will be performing at local venues, to larger rehearsal spaces for artists who are reaching a regional or national audience. Locally geared bands who play regularly may only need a few hours to hone their material; bands reaching a larger audience may need weeks, even months, to get things right.

Rehearsal facilities do more than just provide a room to practice in; they try to accommodate the artists' needs. This might include anything from providing lockers to store their gear, or on-site manufacturers that can provide anything from cartage services to designing PA systems. Some, like Soundcheck, may even have a gym on site to allow band members to break up their long rehearsal day.

A key reason for these rehearsal facilities is that staging a show today is more complex than ever, so the lights and video feeds integral to large venues can be intercut to perfection. A few decades ago, staging a show was as simple as building a stage and, if possible, adding some lighting to help enhance the performance. Since then, both the stage and the lighting have become more complex. Indeed, lighting has become a special subset within the staging industry and has given rise to any number of companies that specialize in this aspect of the show.

Today, staging requires more than getting the right lights to enhance the performance and setting up feeds into the video screens; it requires getting all the apparatus into place. This is no easy task, given that most concert facilities are not built to structurally support the paraphernalia needed for a contemporary concert. Newer facilities are designed to enhance the audience experience often without taking into account easy access for riggers to work. This makes the job of setting up the sophisticated and often cumbersome equipment more difficult than it need be.

The audience, and even some artists, take the stage sets (and the stagehands) as a given until something goes wrong and the show is ruined. Given all that could go wrong, it is surprising how seldom this actually happens. Those working in this area of the music business take pride in seeing that it doesn't. It is their contribution to making the music happen.

Appendix

One hundred and ten individuals involved in the music industry participated in this study. Ninety are listed if the seven asterisked ones are not recounted—the asterisked denotes individuals who shed substantive light on more than one area; for example, Robert Ellis Orrall discusses his early career as a songwriter, though he is presently the head of an independent label. In addition to those listed, eight others were interviewed but did not wish to be "on the record." Another twelve contributed significant information though they were not formally interviewed; for example; I talked at some length with John Berry's manager, Brian Smith, about his career while waiting for Mr. Berry who was tied up in a meeting across town. The organizational affiliation indicated was the one held at the time of the initial interview in 2016–2017.

Songwriters

Marc Beeson (Seasoned)
John Berry (S)
Thornton Cline (S)
Jaida Dreyer (Young)
Drew Kennedy (S)
Calista Garcia (Y)
Amy Gerhartz (Y)
Benji Harris (Y)
Bonita Hill (S)
Bryan Hill (S)
Mark Irwin (S)
Steve Leslie (S)*
Ken Mathiesen (S)
John Miller (Y)
Jordan Minton (Y)
Robert Ellis Orrall (S)*
Michelle Pereira (Y)
Jennifer Schott (S)
Adam Wood (Y)

Songwriter Association Personnel

Bradley Collins, BMI
Edie Emery, SESAC
Shannon Tipton Hatch, SESAC
Barton Herbison, Nashville Songwriters Association International (NSAI)
John Ozier, Association of Independent Music Publishers (AIMP)*
Shelby Yoder, Nashville Songwriters Association International (NSAI)

Music Publishers

Butch Baker, HoriPro
Barry Coburn, Ten Ten Music Group
Marc Driskill, Sea Gayle Music
Darrell Franklin, 3 Ring Circus Music
Tony Harrell, MV2 Entertainment*
Michael Hollandsworth, Given Music Publishing
Dennis Kurtz, Big Spark Music Group*
Steve Leslie, SNG Music*
Matt Lindsey, Matt Lindsey Music/Big Yellow Dog
Mike Molinar, Big Machine Music
John Ozier, Olé*
Robin Ruddy, Best Built Songs
Bobby Rymer, Writer's Den
Dane Schmidt, Tree Vibez Music
Mike Sebastian, Given Music Publishing
Larry Sheridan, Best Built Songs
Cliff Williamson, Starstruck Entertainment

Publishing Pluggers/Creative Director

Stephanie Cox, Kobalt/Nashville*
Sarah Feldman, Writer's Den
David Harper, musicfromthecloset
Aubrey Schwarz, SNG Music

Music Production

LABEL EXECUTIVES

David Brainard, DeciBel
Stephanie Cox, Kobalt/Nashville*
Shannon Houchins, Average Joes Entertainment
Ed Leonard, Daywind Records
Jon Loba, Broken Bow Records
Robert Ellis Orrall, Infinity Cat*
Roger Ryan, After Touch Music

RECORD DISTRIBUTORS

Steve Norris, MondoTunes/Los Angeles
Emmanuel Zunz, ONErpm/Nashville

STUDIO MUSICIANS

Sharon Corbitt-House, All Good Factory*
Tony Harrell, MV2*
David Pomeroy, Nashville Musicians Union
Ron "Snake" Reynolds, sound engineer

RECORD PROMOTIONS

Lee Adams, Broken Bow Records
Kellie Longworth, Cold River Records

Artist Managers

Sharon Corbitt-House, All Good Factory*
David Corlew, Charlie Daniels Band/Blue Hat Records
John Dorris, Hallmark Entertainment
Ross duPre, 333 Entertainment
Fletcher Foster, Iconic Entertainment Group
Eric Griffin, Brand X
Scott Gunter, Durango Artist Management
Rusty Harmon, Harmon Management Music Group

Greg Hill, Hill Entertainment Group
Dennis Kurtz, Big Spark Music Group*
Stephen Linn, AmpliFLY Entertainment
Danny Nozell, CTK Entertainment
Norm Parenteau, Slipshod Management
Mitchell Solarek, Maximum Artist Management
Preston "Shoes" Sullivan, Global Eyes Entertainment
Josh Terry, Workshop Management
Samantha Thornton, G Major Management

Booking Agents/Promotions

David Galea, United Talent/New York
Liz Gregory, Liz Gregory Talent
Ed Harper, The Harper Agency
Steve Lassiter, APA/Nashville
Lance Roberts, United Talent/Nashville
Keith Richards, Brave World Artist Agency
Dan Steinberg, Emporium Presents
Buck Williams, Progressive Global Agency

Related Industry Personnel

John Barker, ClearBox Rights
Marghie Evans, Do Write Music
Carolyn Brackett, National Trust for Historic Preservation
Kelly Stephenson Farris, Farris, Self & Moore
Denise Garcia, mother of songwriter Calista Garcia (Y)
Ben Jumper, Soundcheck
Jeff Jackson, Crew One
Tony Morrelas, Average Joes Entertainment
Jackie Patillo, Gospel Music Association
Catherine Stein, Farris, Self & Moore
W. Tim Walker, Nashville Metropolitan Historic Zoning Commission

Notes

PREFACE

1. Keith McKay Evans. "One More Drinkin' Song': A Longitudinal Content Analysis of Country Music Lyrics between the Years 1994 and 2013." Ph.D. Dissertation, Brigham Young University, 2014. Andrea Millwood Hargrave and Sonia M. Livingstone. *Harm and Offence in Media Content: A Review of the Evidence.* Bristol: Intellect Books, 2009. Silvia Knobloch-Westerwick, Paige Musto, and Katherine Shaw. "Rebellion in the Top Music Charts: Defiant Messages in Rap, Hip-Hop and Rock Music 1993 and 2003." *Journal of Media Psychology* 20.1 (2008): 15–23. Sarah Diamond, Rey Bermudez, and Jean Schensul. "What's the Rap About Ecstasy? Popular Music Lyrics and Drug Trends Among American Youth." *Journal of Adolescent Research* 21.3 (2006): 269–298. John Markert. "Sing a Song of Drug Use-Abuse: Four Decades of Drug Lyrics in Popular Music–From the Sixties through the Nineties." *Sociological inquiry* 71.2 (2001): 194–220.

2. Ronald Weitzer and Charis E. Kubrin. "Misogyny in Rap Music: A Content Analysis of Prevalence and Meanings." *Men and Masculinities* 12.1 (2009): 3–29. Travis L Dixon, Yuanyuan Zhang, and Kate Conrad. "Self-esteem, Misogyny and Afrocentricity: An Examination of the Relationship Between Rap Music Consumption and African American Perceptions." *Group Processes & Intergroup Relations* 12.3 (2009): 345–360. Terri M. Adams and Douglas B. Fuller. "The Words Have Changed But the Ideology Remains the Same: Misogynistic Lyrics in Rap Music." *Journal of Black Studies* 36.6 (2006): 938–957. Edward G. Armstrong, "Gangsta Misogyny: A Content Analysis of the Portrayals of Violence Against Women in Rap Music, 1987–1993." *Journal of Criminal Justice and Popular Culture* 8.2 (2001): 96–126.

3. Nicolai Graakjaer. *Analyzing Music in Advertising: Television Commercials and Consumer Choice.* Vol. 20. New York: Routledge, 2015. Mark Alpert, Judy Alpert, and Elliot N. Maltz. "Purchase Occasion Influence on the Role of Music in Advertising." *Journal of Business Research* 58.3 (2005): 369–376.

4. Zach Whalen. "Case Study: Film Music Vs. Video-Game Music: The Case of Silent Hill." *Music, Sound and Multimedia: From the Live to the Virtual* (2007): 68–81. Sylvie Hébert, et al. "Physiological Stress Response to Video-Game Playing: The Contribution of Built-in Music." *Life Sciences* 76.20 (2005): 2371–2380.

5. Bethany Klein. *As Heard on TV: Popular Music in Advertising.* Burlington, VT: Ashgate Publishing, 2013. Simon Frith, "Look! Hear! The Uneasy Relationship of Music and Television." *Popular Music* 21.03 (2002): 277–290.

6. Kevin Donnelly (Ed.). *Film Music: Critical Approaches.* Edinburgh: Edinburg University Press, 2001.

7. The popular press is replete with commentary on the performance of popular artists. Scholarly presses likewise touch on these artists but are just as likely to assess how the structure of the industry may promote or inhibit innovations in music form. In the former category, see José I Prieto-Arranz. "The Semiotics of Performance and Success in Madonna."

The Journal of Popular Culture 45.1 (2012): 173–196. Mark Watts. "Electrifying Fragments: Madonna and Postmodern Performance." *New Theatre Quarterly* 12.46 (1996): 99–107. In the latter category, see Brian Hracs and Deborah Leslie, "Aesthetic Labour in Creative Industries: The Case of Independent Musicians in Toronto Canada." *Area* 46.1 (2014): 66–73. Matthew Wheelock Stahl. "A Moment Like This: American Idol and Narratives of Meritocracy." Pp. 212–234 in C. J. Washburne and M. Demo (Eds.), *Bad Music: The Music We Love to Hate.* London: Routledge, 2004.

8. Sean Wilentz, *360 Sound: The Columbia Records Story*. San Francisco: Chronicle Books, 2012. Gary Marmorstein, *The Label: The Story of Columbia Records*. New York: Thunder's Mouth Press, 2007. Warren Zane, *Revolutions in Sound: Warner Bros. Records, The First Fifty Years*. San Francisco: Chronicle Books, 2008. Fred Goodman, *Fortune's Fool: Edgar Bronfman, Jr., Warner Music, and an Industry in Crisis*. New York: Simon & Schuster, 2010. Brian Southall, *The Rise & Fall of EMI Record*. London: Omnibus Press, 2012.

9. Clive Davis with Anthony DeCurtis, *The Soundtrack of My Life*. New York: Simon & Schuster, 2013; Clive Davis, *Clive: Inside the Record Business*. New York: William Morrow, 1975. See also Seymour Stein with Gareth Murphy, *Siren Song: My Life in Music*. New York: St. Martin's Press, 2018. Berry Gordy, *To Be Loved: The Music, The Magic, The Memories of Motown*. New York: Grand Central Publishing, 1994.

10. The best of the wide variety of insights into how records are produced is by Michael Jarrett who interviewed a host of well-known recording artists and producers. The interviews, instructive as they are, only comprise two to three paragraphs and thus provide no substantive details about the recording process or how production is critically linked to other aspects of the industry. Michael Jarrett, *Producing Country: The Inside Story of the Great Recordings*. Middletown, CT: Wesleyan University Press, 2014.

11. Colin Escott, *Good Rockin' Tonight: Sun Records and the Birth of Rock 'N Roll*. New York: St. Martin's Press, 1991. Rock Hall with Terry Pace, *My Journey from Shame to Fame*. Monterey, CA: Heritage Builders Publishing, 2015.

12. Bobby Braddock, *A Life on Nashville's Music Row*. Nashville: Vanderbilt University Press-Country Music Foundation Press, 2015.

13. Zollo and Cline and Carpenter both go into some depth about the songwriting process. Most critiques, like Brown's and Horstman's, focus on a specific hit song, but even then don't provide more than a paragraph or two that detail the process of writing the song being discussed. Paul Zollo, *Songwriters on Songwriting*, 4th Expanded Edition. Boston: DeCapo Press, 2003; see also Paul Zollo, *More Songwriters on Songwriting*. Boston, DeCapo Press, 2016. Thornton Cline and Lacie Carpenter, *Profile of a Hit Songwriter*. Anaheim Hills, CA: CENTERSTREAM Publishing, 2019. Dorothy Horstman, *Sing Your Heart Out, Country Boy*. New York: Dutton, 1975. Jake Brown, *Nashville Songwriter: The Inside Stories Behind Country Music's Greatest Hits*. Dallas, TX: BenBella Books, 2014.

14. The titles of the articles alone in *SOS* (November 2015) suggest their esoteric leaning: "NI iMaschine 2 intros 3D Touch Support," "Giorgio Moroder Soundpack for MiniNova Launched," and "iZotope Ozone 7 Out nNw."

15. Nashville includes Nashville-Davidson County along with Murfreesboro and Franklin, TN; New York includes the Metropolitan New York area, plus Newark and Jersey City, NJ; Los Angeles also encompasses Long Beach and Anaheim, CA. Barnes Reports. *U. S. Industry and Market Outlook, Music Publishing Industry: 2017*.

16. John Bowe, Marisa Bowe and Sabin Streeter (eds), *Gig: Americans Talk About Their Jobs*. New York: Three Rivers Press, 2001.

17. John Lomax III. *Nashville: Music City USA*. New York: Harry N. Abrams, Inc., 1985: 7

18. Ibid., p. 8

19. Tony Harrell's experience as a studio musician is touched on in Chapter 3.

20. A snowball sample is when one starts with a handful of people and these individuals introduce the investigator to other members in the industry who they work with. This is a relatively easy method to gain access in Nashville since practically everyone knows someone in the music business. My sample started, then, with two people who I knew (David Corlew and Ron "Snake" Reynolds) and built from there.

21. Intimate is a key word. Individuals who only had passing contact with others outside their area of expertise did not have sufficient knowledge to elaborate upon decision-making in those areas, whereas "intimates" suggest the person had spent considerable time interacting with those outside their own area and thus were able to comment on aspects of those areas.

22. Dan Cornfield, *Beyond the Beat: Musicians Building Community in Nashville*. Princeton: Princeton University Press, 2015. Brian Hracs and Deborah Leslie, "Aesthetic Labour in Creative Industries: The Case of Independent Musicians in Toronto Canada." *Area* 46.1 (2014): 66–73. Gregory Kordsmeier. "State of the Art: Boundary Work in Stage Management and Its Aesthetic Consequences." Presented at the American Sociological Annual Conference, 2009. Mako Fitts. "'Drop It Like It's Hot': Culture Industry Laborers and Their Perspectives on Rap Music Video Production." *Meridians: Feminism, Race, Transnationalism* 8.1 (2008): 211–235. See also John Markert, *Publishing Romance: The History of an Industry, 1940s to the Present*. Jefferson, N.C.: McFarland, 2016.

CHAPTER 1

1. Interview with Shelby Yoder, Director of Professional Membership and Events, Nashville Songwriters Association International.

2. Cindy Watts. "Walk This Way." *The Tennessean*, 20 July 2016: 1A, 6A

3. Monte Dutton, *True to the Roots: Americana Music Revealed*. Lincoln: University of Nebraska Press, 2006.

4. Kelley Lovelace. *If You've Got a Dream, I've Got a Plan: How to Get Your Song Heard by Music Industry Professionals*. Nashville: Rutledge Hill Press, 2002: 27–34.

5. Cover songs are those that were written by other than the performer.

6. Two excellent reviews of the creativity literature are relied upon in this brief section. Michael D. Mumford, "Where Have We Been, Where Are We Going? Taking Stock in Creativity Research." *Creativity Research Journal*, Vol. 15, Nos. 2 & 3 (2003): 107–120. Phillip McIntyre, "Rethinking the Creative Process: The Systems Model of Creativity Applied to Popular Songwriting." *Journal of Music, Technology and Education*, Vol. 4, No. 2 (2011): 77–90

7. George Becker. *The Mad Genius Controversy: A Study in the Sociology of Deviance*. Oxford, Sage: 1978.

8. The foregrounding of cities as cultural centers is specifically addressed by Patrick Cohendet, David Grandadam, and Laurent Simon in "Economics and the Ecology of Creativity: Evidence from the Popular Music Industry." *International Review of Applied Economics*, Vol. 23, No. 6 (November 2000): 709–722.

9. Pierre-Michel Menger, "Artistic Labor Markets and Careers." *Annual Review of Sociology* Vol. 25 (1999): 549.

10. Colt Ford's career path is sketched in Chapter 3.

11. Bart Herbison with NSAI interviews seasoned songwriters regularly and these interviews are published by Dave Paulson weekly in the Sunday edition of *The Tennessean*. This alone constitutes a large body of songwriter information: the interview typically relates to their career and one (or more) of their hit songs.

12. Mark Guarino, "Where Have Country Women Gone?" *The Guardian*, 4 Aug. 2016. Elias Leight, "What Happened to Women in Country? An Investigation Using Year-End Billboard Charts." *New York Magazine*, 8 June 2015.

13. Emily Yahr, "Nashville's Newest Female Artists Are Challenging the 'bro'-Dominated Country Music World. *The Washington Post*, 28 April 2016.www.washingtonpost.com /entertainment. Cindy Watts, "'Girl' Power on the Rise for [2019] CMA Awards," *The Tennessean*, 29 August 2019: A1. Kristin M. Hall, "Women Push for Equality, and Quality, in Country Music." *San Diego Tribune*, 11 August 2015. https://www.sandiegouniontribune .com/sdut-women-push-for-equality-and-quality-in-country-2015aug11-story.html.

14. Artist-songwriter Ben Folds takes up to one-third (100 pages) of his autobiography to drive home how his parents and teachers helped shape his youthful artistic aspirations. Ben Folds, *A Dream About Lightning Bugs: A Life of Music and Cheap Lessons*. New York: Ballantine Books, 2019.

15. It is worth a small aside to note, since this chapter is about songwriters, that the Diffie song was co-written by Paul Nelson and Dave Gibson.

16. Both Trisha Yearwood and Alan Jackson were discovered (landed a contract) at Douglas Corner. Other luminaries whose careers were launched at Douglas Corner include Blake Shelton, Marc Collie, The Kentucky Headhunters, Hunter Hayes, and Michael Tyler, among others. Email communication with management at Douglas Corner. Douglas Corner closed in 2020, another small club casualty of the coronavirus.

17. The Christian dimension was never showy—even among Christian songwriters, publishers, and managers—and generally only casually mentioned in the course of our discussion.

18. He actually sang it as a rock 'n' roll song.

19. Nan Lin, "Building a Network Theory of Social Capital." *Connections*, Vol. 22, No. 1 (1999): 28–51.

20. More established songwriters are doing house parties today to enhance their income. Hitmaker Wynn Varble does house concerts all over the country. "Some of these people," he says, "have pretty big houses and they'll set up 75–80 chairs and charge people $25 [which goes to the artist]." Lori Hollabaugh, "On the Road: The New Reality for Songwriters." *Music Row Magazine*, January 2018: 38.

21. Two other young artist-songwriters mimic Gerhartz's concern, curiously each lamenting how things will "fall apart" a few years down the road: sixteen-year-old Calesta Garcia gave herself until 25; twenty-eight-year-old Jaida Dreyer gave herself to 35; thirty-five-year-old Gerhartz gave herself to 40–45.

22. Nashville is among the top tiered growth cites in the United States with between 85 to 100 people moving to the area daily. At least some of this growth was spurred by *The New York Times* dubbing Nashville the nation's "it" city in 2013. Meg Garner, "Nashville Jumps Up List of Country's Fastest-Growing Cities." *Nashville Business Journal*, 14 March 2018. Mike Reicher, "Actually, Nashville Did Grow by More Than 100 People a Day Last Year." *The Tennessean*, 12 September 2018: B1. Kim Severson, "Nashville's Latest Big Hit Could Be the City Itself." *The New York Times*, 8 January 2013.

23. The dispersal of publishers and labels beyond Music Row is prompted by zoning restrictions that discourage expansion and the rising cost of property, an offshoot of Nashville's surging population. The changes occurring on Music Row are discussed more fully in the next few chapters. See Regina Cole, "Will Nashville's Runaway Growth Kill Music Row?" *Forbes*, 24 April 2019. Sandy Mazza, "Controversial Development Plan Adopted [for Music Row]." *The Tennessean*, 29 June 2019: A10.

24. Paradoxically, the cost of living may intensify their interconnectivity because for many young people the only way to live in Nashville today is to share living spaces, which one tends to do with people who have similar personalities and interests. See Sandy Mazza, "Musicians Are Being Priced Out of Music City." *The Tennessean*, 10 August 2019: A1

25. It has been suggested, only half humorously, that in lieu of the Parthenon or the honky-tonks on lower Broadway, the Nashville "skyline motif" should have high-rise constructions cranes dotting the landscape.

26. This was the consensus of those seasoned writers who participated in this survey, along with a host of others (managers, publishers, producers) who were interviewed, though some nudged the historic figure upward to the 2,000 mark.

27. Ken Mathiesen (S) at NSAI gave the example from the night before we met about a newly arrived young songwriter who not long after he came to town had someone approached him and said, 'Hey, you give me $3,000 and I will. . . .' You don't *ever* want to do that."

28. Dan Daley, *Nashville's Unwritten Rules: Inside the Business of Country Music*. Woodstock: Overlook Press, 1999: 136.

29. Information pertaining to NSAI in this chapter is based on an interview with Executive Director Bart Herbison unless otherwise cited.

30. A publishing contract would also smooth the way for a renewal of her visa.

31. Ben Folds feels that because artists often have day jobs, the public doesn't consider them serious artists. The goal of his latest book, he says, is to talk to his fellow artists: "I want them to feel like we're all in the same boat. I make stuff, you make stuff." Nate Rau, "Ben Folds Wrote a Book for Artists with Day Jobs." *The Tennessean*, 4 August 2019: C2. See also Ben Folds, *A Dream About Lightning Bug: A Life of Music and Cheap Lessons*. New York: Ballantine, 2019.

32. Ten Ten is discussed in the next chapter on song publishers.

33. Mark Irwin quips, in an interview with Bart Herbison, that one night he was tending bar at the Bluebird while a bunch of songwriters were playing a set and he's the only one there with a number one song. Dave Paulson, "Mark Irwin Wrote a Hit with a Hangover." *The Tennessean*, 26 September 2016: E5.

34. Liz Henger, *The Do's & Don'ts of Music Row*, 2nd edition (September 2012), p. 9.

35. Basic as it was, it was a great training ground because, Hill says, "You got to hear some of the best writers in the company. You got to admire the work of great songwriters. I think I [mostly] learned through osmosis."

36. In 2008, NSAI acquired the Bluebird from founder Amy Kurland.

37. In his book on the music industry, Kelley Lovelace lists a number of venues around town, half of which are a distant memory. It is for this reason that I hesitate to enumerate a list of venues. See Kelley Lovelace, *If You've Got a Dream*, pp. 44–46.

38. It almost didn't happen, either, because Brooks' new (and current) manager, Bob Doyle, was hard pressed to come up with the $35 entrance fee for the Nashville Entertainment Association showcase that night. Dan Daley, *Nashville's Unwritten Rules*, p. 149.

39. Dan Daley, p. 166.

40. Braddock's first song to reach the charts was penned in 1967; he remained active through the 1990s, and even in semi-retirement had two number one hits in the aughts.

41. Bobby Braddock, *A Life on Nashville's Music Row*. Nashville: Country Music Foundation Press/Vanderbilt University Press, 2015.

42. Interview with Bradley Collins with BMI.

43. Ibid.

44. Pierce's version charted in 1959; Tillis charted when he released his own version in 1972.

45. Michael Kosser, *How Nashville Became Music City USA*, Milwaukee, WI: Hal Leonard, 2016: 164.

46. How the publisher is compensated is explored in greater detail in the next chapter, but typically, one-half of the royalties go to the artist and the other half goes to the publisher.

47. See Kathryn Greene, Valerian J. Derlega and Alicia Mathews, "Self-Disclosure in Personal Relationships." Pp. 409–427 in *The Cambridge Handbook of Personal Relationships*, edited by Anita L. Vangelisti and Daniel Perlman. Cambridge: Cambridge University Press, 2006.

48. Charles R. Simpson. *SoHo: The Artist in the City*. Chicago: University of Chicago Press, 1981: 89.

49. Jason Blume. *Six Steps to Songwriting Success*, Revised and Expanded Edition. New York: Billboard Books, 2008: p. 2.

50. In 2018, Collins left BMI to form King Song, a joint venture publishing company with Whiskey Jam and ROAR, because, he says, he "wanted to be closer to the music and artist development." King Song presently (2019) has two artists and one songwriter under contract.

51. Malcolm Gladwell. *Outliers: The Story of Success*. New York: Little, Brown and Co., 2008.

52. Anders Ericsson and Robert Pool. *Peak: Secrets from the New Science of Experience*. New York: Houghton Mifflin Harcourt, 2016. See also Karl Ericsson, Ralf T. Krampe, and Clemens Tesch-Römer, "The Role of Deliberate Practice in the Acquisition of Expert Performance." *Psychological Review*, Vol. 100. No. 3 (1993): 363–406

53. Menger argues that there is an oversupply of individuals pursuing artistic careers. This study would challenge that assumption if one culls out the wanna-bes (50%) and those who move along but get discouraged by the time commitment (30–40%). Pierre-Michel Menger, "Artistic Labor Markets and Careers." *Annual Review of Sociology*, Volume 25 (1999): 541–74.

54. Kelley Lovelace, *If You've Got a Dream, I've Got a Plan*, p. 138.

55. Mark Irwin (S) was the only one who defined himself as "country to the bone."

56. Interview with Byron Hill (S).

57. Nate Rau, "68% of Americans Listened to Christian Music in Past Month." The Tennessean, www.tennessean.com/story/news/2015/06/27/gma-research-shows-popularity-christian-music/29353693/.

58. To put this "small" number into perspective, the Christian market is followed in descending order by Latin music (2.5%), jazz (2.4%), classical (2.4%) and blues (0.9%). Nate Rau, "68% of Americans . . . " See also Ritchie Spence, "Christian Music," *Music Business Journal*, June 2016. www.thembj.org/2016/06/christian-music. The Christian market in Nashville will be developed more fully in subsequent chapters.

59. John Ryan and Richard A. Peterson, "The Product Image: The Fate of Creativity in Country Music Songwriting." P. 13 in *Individuals in Mass Media Organizations: Creativity and Constraint*, edited by James S. Ettema and D. Charles Whitney. Beverly Hills, CA: Sage (1982): 13.

60. S. F. Siman. *Modeling the Success of Country Music Records*. Senior Scholar Thesis, Vanderbilt University, 1976.

61. John Ryan and Richard A. Peterson, "The Product Image," p. 17.

62. I would also suggest that the songwriters in the 1970s, when the Ryan and Peterson study was done, had a high degree of control over their product and it is not simply a matter of changing aesthetics, since, as the authors themselves point out, few artists (10%) were involved in the actual writing of the song at that time.

63. Interview with Mark Irwin.

64. Ibid. The studio musician and how home recordings have impacted the industry are dealt with in Chapter 3.

65. This is the conclusion reached by Mumford in his survey of the creative literature. Michael D. Mumford, "Where Have We Been, Where Are We Going? Taking Stock in Creativity Research," *Creativity Research Journal*, Vol. 15, Nos. 2 & 3 (2003): 110

66. Morgan K. Ward, Joseph K. Goodman and Julie R. Irwin, "The Same Old Song: The Power of Familiarity in Music Choice." *Mark Lett*, Vol. 25 (2014): 1–11.

67. Robert B. Zajoncrt B. "Attitudinal Effects of Mere Exposure." *Journal of Personality and Social Psychology*, Vol. 9, No. 2 (1968): 1–27

68. Derek Thompson, "The Four Letters to Selling Just About Anything: What Makes Things Cool?" *The Atlantic*, January/February 2017: 68–71. See also Derek Thompson. *Hit Makers: The Science of Popularity in the Age of Distraction*. New York: Penguin Press, 2017.

69. John Ryan and Richard A. Peterson, "The Product Image," p. 25.

70. Interview with Marc Beeson.

71. "The market is more limited now," says Benita Hill. Bryan Hill mimics the concern of many in the business: "There aren't as many [record] outlets now, so it doesn't pay like it did."

72. Song royalties are first used to pay back the publisher for any advance draw, after which any income for the song goes 50 percent to the writer and 50 percent to the publisher; a staff songwriter who gets a third of the writer's share has to split his or her share with the publisher. These arrangements are dealt with in greater detail in the next chapter on music publishers.

73. Daniel Deahl, "The Music Modernization Act Has Been Signed into Law." *The Verge*, 11 October 2018. www.theverge.com/2018/10/11/17963804/music-modernizationact-mma-copyright-law-bill-labels-congress.

74. The other major issue the MMA addresses is to allow legacy songwriters (those who wrote songs before 1972) to be compensated for their musical contribution.

75. Nate Rau, "Publishers, Songwriters Unveil Bid to Run Music Licensing." *The Tennessean*, 6 February 2019: A11. See also Jordan Bromley, "The Music Modernization Act: What Is It & Why Does It Matter." *Billboard Magazine*, 23 February 2018. www.billboard.com/articles/business/8216857/music-modernization-act-what-is-it-why-does-it-matter-jordan-bromley.

76. Nate Rau, "Streaming Research Sparks Music Row Buzz." *The Tennessean*, 22 October 2017: D1–2.

77. The Music Modernization Act created a new licensing group that will identify and pay copyright holders the royalties they are owed when their music is played on a streaming service. In 2019, the U. S. Copyright Office selected the Music Licensing Collective—comprised primarily of NSAI songwriters—to begin collecting royalties from streaming services on January 1, 2021. Nate Rau, "Nashville-backed Group to Run Digital Licensing Collective." *The Tennessean*, 9 July 2019: A8, 12.

78. There are two other, smaller relatively new PROs. SoundExchange was formed as part of the Recording Industry Association of America in 2000 and spun-off as a separate entity in 2003. Global Rights Music (GRM) was founded in 2013 by industry veteran Irving Azoff as

an alternative to the traditional performance rights model. One PRO executive interviewed in the course of this study estimates that jointly these two PROs comprise between 1 to 2 percent of the market.

79. The distinction may be getting less pronounced. In 2017, ASCAP and BMI announced the creation of a new comprehensive music works database. More than one PRO source suggests this may be a step to the merger of ASCAP and BMI. A merger would be attractive to licensees because they could pay one source rather than two, though it would be likely, since each has a distinct following, that they would retain their individual identities. See "ASCAP and BMI Announce Creation of a New Comprehensive Musical Works Database to Increase Ownership Transparency in Performing Rights Licensing," 26 July 2017. www.ascap.com/press/2017/07–26-ascap-bmi-database;" www.bmi.com/news/entry/bmi-ascap-announce-creation-of-new-music-works-database.

80. Nate Rau, "BMI Wins Legal Battle with DOJ." *The Tennessean*, 20 December 2017: A10. The initial issue is nicely summarized in an article by Jon Healey, "Justice Department Rocks Music Industry with ASCAP-BMI Decision." *L.A. Times* (4 August 2016). www.latimes.com/opinion/opinion-la/la-ed-ascap-bmi-justice-department-20160804-snap-story.

81. Nate Rau, "Amazon Incentives Run Afoul of Royalty Tiff." *The Tennessean*, 16 March 2019: A8–9.

82. Article 1, Section 8, Clause 8 of The United States Constitutions reads that it is the role of the federal government "To promote the Progress of Science and useful Arts, by securing for limited Times to Authors and Inventors the exclusive Right to their respective Writings and Discoveries." At SESAC offices in Nashville, the Constitutional provision greets one in the entrance hallway. According to "How Songwriters Get Paid," on NSAI's website, the royalty rate is set by a Copyright Royalty Board made up of three judges who meet every five years to set rates. The original mechanical royalty was established in 1909 and set at 2 cents; today, the rate hovers around 10.5 cents (typically split with co-writers and publishers).

83. Nate Rau, "ASCAP Sent Out $1B in Royalties." *The Tennessean*, 20 April 2018: 10A.

84. I am making the active-passive distinction to circumvent those "passive" songwriters who are simply registered with ASCAP or BMI and are halfheartedly pursuing a career.

CHAPTER 2

1. Lewis Coser. "Publishers as Gatekeepers of Ideas." *The Annals of the American Association of Political and Social Sciences*, Vol. 421 (1975): 14–22; R. Simon and J. Fyfe. *Editors as Gatekeepers: Getting Published in the Social Sciences*. Lanham, Maryland: Rowman & Littlefield, 1992. John Markert, "The Publishing Decision: Managerial Policy and Its Effect on Editorial Decision-Making." *Book Research Quarterly*, Vol. 3 (Summer 1987): 33–59; see also *Publishing Romance: The History of an Industry, 1940s to the Present*. Jefferson, N.C. McFarland, 2016.

2. Jeremy L. Smith. *Thomas East and Music Publishing in Renaissance England*. Oxford: Oxford University Press, 2003. Rebecca Herissone. "Playford, Purcell, and the Functions of Music Publishing in Restoration England." *Journal of the American Musicological Society*, Vol. 32, No. 2 (2010): 243–290. Agostine Zecca Laterza, "Manuscript Music Published in Naples, 1780–1820. *Fontes Artis Musciae*, Vol. 59, No. 2 (April-June 2012): 145–158. Anita Breckbill, "Music Publishing by Subscription in 1820s France: A Preliminary Study. *Notes*, Vol. 69, No. 3 (March 2013): 453–471. Asta, Zivile Casalite Bielinskiene and Julija Paliukenaite. "Music Publication in Lithuania After 1990: A Typological Analysis." *Fontes Artis Musicae*, Vol. 62, No. 2 (April-June 2015: 110–117).

3. Nashville includes Nashville-Davidson County along with Murfreesboro and Franklin, TN; New York includes the Metropolitan New York area, plus Newark and Jersey City, NJ; Los Angeles also encompasses Long Beach and Anaheim, CA.

4. Barnes Reports. *U. S. Industry and Market Outlook, Music Publishing Industry: 2017.* www.barnesreports/com/us-industry-market-outlook. Other data about the Big Three in this section is based on this report (more detailed statistics assessing the Big Three can be found in Chapter 3).

5. Arnold Broido. "Music Publisher." *Music Educators Journal*, Vol. 63, No. 7. (Mar. 1977): 111–112.

6. Joseph Taubman. "The Role of the Conglomerates in the American Entertainment Industry." *The University of Toronto Law Journal*, 30: 2 (Spring 1970): 236–247.

7. Even when they have the space for their writers, Marc Driskill at Sea Gayle Music laments the lack of parking availability, which is due in no small part to nearby Vanderbilt students and staff parking along Music Row because it is proximate to the campus but has unrestricted parking, unlike the metered streets proximate to the university.

8. Nate Rau. "Rockers Unveil Music Row T-shirt." *The Tennessean*, 6 June 2016: A7.

9. Publishers are quick to make a distinction between a songwriter with a track record and one with a *current* track record. A seasoned songwriter whose catalogue is dated is unlikely to get a draw because they are not writing for the current market, an issue that was addressed in the last chapter. More than one publisher mentioned songwriters of some repute that they know who are now in their 60s and cannot get a contract because their writing is still rooted to an earlier point in time.

10. Interview with Darrell Franklin.

11. Co-publishing is different than sub-publishing, which is arranging the sale of songs outside the United States and its territories.

12. Interview with John Barker at ClearBox.

13. Some sources suggest this rate is set by Congress under the Constitution. They are referring to the license between the product company and the publisher. The 9.1 cent rate is "willing seller, willing buyer," says John Barker at ClearBox. "It is the agreed upon rate the industry abides by."

14. Performance, mechanical, and synchronization are the three primary revenue streams for publishers and record companies. Synchronization revenue, according to the Global Music Report (2018) is minimal and since 2010 accounts for less than 2 percent ($300M) of all music revenue. There are two other revenue sources: print (e.g., sheet music) and grand or dramatic rights (e.g., Broadway shows or parks, such as Disney or Six Flags that license songs they perform on stage). See IFPI (International Federation of the Phonographic Industry), *Global Music Report 2018: State of the Industry*. www.ifpi.org/news/IFPI-GLOBAL-MUSIC-REPORT-2019.

15. Interview with Barry Coburn.

16. Publishers and songwriters are, of course, open to allowing an existing piece to be used by a television or film producer if the placement is acceptable.

17. Once a song has been released, anyone can subsequently produce the song, in which case both the songwriter and publisher receive mechanical and/or performance royalties.

18. A songwriter may average 50 or more songs a year with only one or two connecting, so the chance of resurrecting a song in the catalogue is extraordinarily problematic considering the number of new songs that are being written every year.

19. Information regarding John Chisum and Royalty Exchange, including any quotes in

this section, are based on Nate Rau's story in *The Tennessean*, "Investors are Increasingly Buying into Music Copyrights," 15 December 2017: 1A, 12A

20. Rau reports that Royalty Exchange has generated over $11 million from some 200 auctions in less than two years (2016–2017). Royalty Exchange makes its profit, as most auction companies do, by taking 15 percent of the sale price.

21. Judy Harris of Judy Harris Music and Melanie Smith Howard, who owns both Melanie Howard Music and Child Bride Music, are but two well-regarded contemporary female music publishers in Nashville.

22. "There were a few [instructors] who really knew the music business but most just had book knowledge and were way behind [the times]." It should be kept in mind that Franklin is referring to the very early stages of the music program.

23. Dick James was the original publisher of the Beatles, Elton John, and Gerry and the Pacemakers, among others.

24. "Rick did Aretha Franklin, Mac Davis, the Osmonds; you name them, he did them," Hollandsworth quips.

25. Arista and Jive Records, two cornerstones of Zomba, were sold to BMG in 2003: BMG, in turn, became part of Sony in 2008.

26. Brentwood is in Williamson County, just across the line from Nashville-Davidson.

27. At Zomba, he connected producer Matt Lange with Shania Twain. The resulting albums during that period, *The Woman in Me* and *Come on Over*, went on to sell more than 60 million copies.

28. The deep pocket partner, Anderson Merchandising, which was a dominant player in the distribution of books, magazine and newspapers, and had a CD distribution agreement with Walmart, was hit by the digital revolution and the subsequent decreased sale of books, magazines, and newspapers, as well as the downswing in CD purchases, and was, therefore, forced to liquidate, and that included the sale of Full Circle. The rapidity of the sale did not give Hollandsworth the opportunity to put a financial deal together with another partner.

29. At the time I interviewed Steve Leslie (2017) at recently launched SNG Music, SNG had just hired Sebastian as a consultant, Leslie having a relatively modest background in some of the dynamics of publishing.

30. Some of the issues that prompted Mike Sebastian's departure from Given would resurface with Hollandsworth and result in his departure from Given in late 2019.

31. Almo/Irving was founded in 1962 by Herb Albert and Jerry Moss—the name was taken from the first two letters of each man's last name. Almo subsequently became Rondor Music and in 2000 Rondor was bought by Universal. A key reason for the acquisition by Universal was that Rondor controlled a substantial catalogue of songs, including some by the Beach Boys, Al Green, and The Carpenters.

32. In late 2018, Rymer lost his financial backer—he was indicted by the federal government for issues surrounding some of his more questionable investments. All accounts that the backer was involved with were frozen (placed in receivership) for the next 4–6 months. Some of Rymer's established songwriters remained because they had an income stream, but the younger ones, such as Sara Feldman (creative director/plugger) and Drew Kennedy (songwriter), parted ways because they had bills to pay and could not wait until the financial issue was resolved. Rymer was able to acquire full ownership of Writer's Den in late 2019.

33. She has since started Eleven Eleven.

34. See the discussion of multitasking later in this chapter.

35. Harrell's experiences as a studio musician will be traced more fully in the next chapter.

36. Baker estimates that HoriPro is about 5 percent of the overall business for the Japanese firm of the same name.

37. HoriPro was acquired by MOJO Music & Media in early 2019. Baker, who is now senior vice president at MOJO Music, says, MOJO "needed what we had and [they had] what we needed—strong in synch." Email communication with Butch Baker. See also "MOJO Music Acquires HoriPro Entertainment Group." Jessica Nicholson, *Music Row Magazine*, 20 March 2019.

38. They have numerous real estate properties they own and manage which "is really our stability." Much of the property is tangentially related to the music business.

39. The half-dozen or so publishers with whom I had follow-up clarifying interviews while I was writing this chapter generally conceded that my estimates are reasonable.

40. Business managers are typically accountants who also address these aspects with individual artists or publishing companies. These firms are specifically geared to understanding aspects of the music industry that are beyond the pale for traditional accounting firms which allow them to make financial projections based on air time and performance revenue.

41. Contracts were discussed with at least 50 percent of the publishers, and they were in general agreement that while there is a general contractual format, no two contracts were exactly the same and each had to be negotiated in its own right.

42. Interview with Butch Baker at HoriPro.

43. The hooky chorus is something that is a real selling point. Randy Goodman, CEO of Sony Nashville, says that what convinced him to sign newcomer Maren Morris was "she breaks into this verse [on "Sugar'], this sing-songy, hip-hop thing, and then it breaks into that incredible hooky chorus. I was like, 'What is this?' It was the freshest thing I'd heard." Nate Rau, "Breakout Success: Sony Nashville 'Changes the Story Line.'" *The Tennessean*, 17 July 2016: A1. See also Eric T. Parker, "Maren Morris: Breakthrough Artist of the Year ." *Music Row Magazine*, June/July 2016: 22.

44. A number of songwriters and music publishers who have been associated with the majors likened the majors to banks because they have deep pockets and rush to duplicate whatever hit is currently in vogue. The problem with that, Barry Coburn at Ten Ten says, is that "the flavor of the month this year is not likely to be the flavor of the month next year."

45. Interview with Butch Baker.

46. The traditional means, which still exists, is to be referred by another songwriter or by one of the personnel at a PRO. Artist-writer rounds have existed since at least the 1980s when the Bluebird was founded but are much more numerous today.

47. This is the general assessment of these shows by publishers and tends to reflect the analysis of these shows in the scholarly and popular presses. Amanda Scheiner McClain. *American Ideal: How American Idol Constructs Celebrity, Collective Identity, and American Discourses*. Lanham, MD: Lexington, 2011. Su Holmes. "Reality Goes Pop!" Reality TV, Popular Music, and Narratives of Stardom in Pop Idol." *Television & New Media* 5.2 (2004): 147–172. Bill Kevensey, "TV Singing Show Fails to Create Stars." *USA Today*, 14 Jan. 2014.

48. Interview with Bobby Rymer.

49. Interview with Darrell Franklin

50. Interview with Butch Baker

51. "People in the U.K," Hollandsworth says in an aside, "still think country music is Jim Reeves; they're so far behind. What they think is country music is 20 years out of date."

52. Interview with Mike Molinar.

53. Extended play means that it is longer (extended) than a single, but it is roughly half the length of a long playing (LP) album or CD.

54. Interview with Michael Hollandsworth.

55. Jed Hilly, executive director of the Americana Music Association, would disagree with my linking Americana to country, even though a substantial number of award nominees would be identified by listeners of music as being country musicians. To be fair, Americana goes beyond (classic) country and embraces both bluegrass and folk music. Hilly says that Americana music is not "trying to write a No. 1 hit for commercial radio; [the Americana artists] are trying to tell a story through music in the best way they can. It has nothing to do with country. It has everything to do with art, and the art of making music." Most of the songwriters and music publishers in this study would say that you can make a commercial song and still "try to tell a story through music in the best way they can" and that they struggle to make music an art. See Nate Rau, "Hilly Talks State of Americana." *The Tennessean*, 13 September 2015: D1–2

56. Interview with Aubrey Schwartz.

57. The quality of computer-generated sound when contrasted to that which is made in the studio is addressed in Chapter 3. While the ability of computers to rival the sound produced in the studio is debatable, there is no doubt that computer-generated music makes a decent, cost-feasible demonstration cut.

58. The role of the internet in attracting the attention of label executives is developed more fully in the next chapter.

59. Interview with Marc Driskill.

60. Schwartz credits Dan Keen at Belmont for teaching her about publishing: "He made me fall in love [with that side of the business]."

61. Interview with Sarah Feldman.

62. Interview with Bobby Rymer.

63. The critical input Maxwell Perkins provided in shaping the novels of Fitzgerald, which basically made *The Great Gatsby* a classic, and in making sense of Wolfe's meandering prose is aptly described by A. S. Berg, in *Maxwell Perkins: Editor of Genius*. New York: Washington Square Press, 1978.

CHAPTER 3

1. Artists selling their product directly makes up the balance. Mark Mulligan, "2018 Global Label Market Share," 13 March 2019. www.mediaresearch.com/blog/2018-global-label-market-share. . . . See also "2018 Global Label Market Share." 13 March 2019. www.musicindustryblog.wordpress.com/tag/record-label-market-share.

2. See also Bill Lamb, "Top Three Major Pop Record Labels," 18 May 2019. www.liveabout.com/top-major-pop-record-labels.

3. Sean Wilentz, *360 Sound: The Columbia Records Story*. San Francisco: Chronicle Books, 2012. Gary Marmorstein, *The Label: The Story of Columbia Records*. New York: Thunder's Mouth Press, 2007.

4. Warren Zane, *Revolutions in Sound: Warner Bros. Records, The First Fifty Years*. San Francisco: Chronicle Books, 2008

5. Brian Southall, *The Rise & Fall of EMI Records*. London: Omnibus Press, 2012.

6. Some industry statistics put Sony ahead of the independents but always before Warner. Though hard numbers are proprietary and hard to evaluate, this order still gives the independents a sizable stake in the market.

7. Paul Resnikoff, "Two Thirds of All Music Sold Comes from Just Three Companies." *Digital Music News*, 3 August 2016. www.digitalmusicnews.com/2016/08/03/two-thirds-music-sales-comes-from . . .). See also IFPI (International Federation of the Phonographic Industry), *Global Music Report 2018: State of the Industry*. www.ifpi.org/news/IFPI-GLOBAL-MUSIC-REPORT-2019

8. Richard Smirke, "Indie Label Earnings Climb to $6.9 Billion as Market Share Grows to Nearly 40 Percent." *Billboard Magazine*, 4 December 2018. www.digitalmusicnews.com/2016/08/03/two-thirds-music-sales-come-three-major-labels/. Worldwide Independent Market Report (WIN), *The Global Economic & Cultural Contribution of Independent Music, 2015*: 14.www/infoformusic.org/filesWINTEL%25202015 Daniel Sanchez, "Indie Labels Now Account for 39.9% of the Global Recorded Music Market." *Digital Music News*, 4 December 2018. www.digitalmusicnews.com/2018/12/04/win-indie-labels-artist-2017-report.

9. Ray Stevens interviewed Don Schlitz, who wrote "The Gambler," on his weekly PBS show, *CabRay*. Schlitz commented that when he came to Nashville in 1973 he didn't know you could make money writing songs, to which host Stevens quipped that "You'd probably agree with me, but we'd pay someone to do this if we had to." Ray Stevens, *CabRay* (Cabaret Ray), Season 1 Episode 2, recorded 28 January 2017 at WNPT2 studios in Nashville.

10. Presley's contract was sold to RCA for $35,000 in 1955 to help Sun deal with some financial difficulties.

11. Rap had been around for some years but can be said to have earned its "tag" when the Sugarhill Gang released "Rapper's Delight" in 1979. In 1989, rap would be recognized as a legitimate musical genre when the Grammy Awards included it as a separate musical category.

12. Interview with Robert Ellis Orrall. Orrall, who now runs Infinity Cat, discussed later in the chapter, wrote with Swift on some of the songs that appeared on her first album.

13. The label would become one of the big-little successes in Nashville, in no small part because of Taylor Swift, whose first album for Big Machine sold eight million copies. Interview with Robert Ellis Orrall.

14. Rick Kenney and Randy McNulty penned *Little Labels—Big Sound: Small Record Companies and the Rise of American Music*. Bloomington: Indiana University Press, 1999.

15. John Cook with Mac McCaugham and Laura Balance, *Our Noise: The Story of Merge Records, the Indie Label That Got Big and Stayed Small*. Chapel Hill, NC: Algonquin Books, 2009.

16. Sherod Robertson, "BMG Acquires Nashville-Based BBR Music Group." *Music Row Magazine*, 30 January 2017. www.musicrow.com/2017/01/breaking-news-bmg-acquires-nashville-based-bbr-music-group. Marc Schneider and Ed Christman, "BMG Acquires Nashville Indie BBR Music Group, Home of Broken Bow Records and Jason Aldean." *Billboard*, 30 January 2017. www.billboard.com/articles/business/7670055/bmg-acquires-bbr-music-group-broken-bow-nashville-indie.

17. The sale was reportedly for $300M. See Andrew Flanagan, "Taylor Swift's Former Label Big Machine Is Sold, Rankling The Star." WUWM 89.7 Milwaukee, 1 July 2019. www.wuwm.com/post/taylor-swifts-former . . . , 15 July 2019. Joe Coscarelli, "Taylor Swift on Scooter Braun Buying Her Old Label: 'My Worse Case Scenario.'" *The New York Times*, 30 June 2019. www.nytimes.com/2019/06/30/arts/music/taylor-swift-music-scooter-braun.

18. Nate Rau, "Young Movement." *The Tennessean*, 8 February 2018: 1A, 5A.

19. Morris, like Chris Stapleton, was well known among songwriters and independent music publishers in Nashville long before Sony recognized her talent. At indie publisher Big Yellow Dog, Morris wrote "Last Turn Home," which Tim McGraw cut on *Sundown Heaven Town* (2014), and "Second Wind," which Kelly Clarkson sang on *Piece by Piece* (2015).

20. "The Masters of Music Row." *Billboard*, 6 August 2016: 60–69.

21. Quoted by Tariq Muhammad in "The Real Lowdown on Labels." *Black Enterprise*, 26:5 (Dec. 1995): 76

22. The importance of independent labels in cultivating creative talent and "feeding" the majors is well established in the literature. See Martin Talbot, "The Fragile State of Independents: Worrying Signs from Indie Label Sector is Bad News for the Entire Music Industry. "*Music Week*, 24 April 2004: 14. Theo Papadopoulos, "Are Music Recording Contracts Equitable? An Economic Analysis of the Practice of Recoupment." *MEIEA Journal* 4:1 (2004): 83–104.

23. James E. Hearn, "The Representation of Major and Independent Record Labels in *Billboard* Magazine." MEIEA Journal, Vol. 9, No. 1 (2009): 113–125. See also Steve Jones, "Music That Moves: Popular Music, Distribution and Network Technologies." *Cultural Studies*, Vol. 16, No. 2 (2002): 219.

24. Cherie Hu, "The Record Labels of the Future Are Already Here." *Forbes*, 15 Oct. 2016. www.forbes.com/sites/cheriehu/2016/10/15/the-record-labels-of-the-future-are-already-here.

25. A similar situation occurred in the book publishing industry. Mainstream publishers were beginning to look at e-book publishing but when the dot.com bubble burst in 2000, they abandoned it. The low cost of entry allowed many self-published authors who the mainstream houses had shut out to start companies and stream books. They gained a strong foothold during the aughts before mainstream houses started to realize just how lucrative e-books were and began to (re)enter the market circa 2010. John Markert, *Publishing Romance: The History of the Industry, 1940s to the Present*. Jefferson, NC: McFarland, 2016.

26. "Strength of Independents: Economy Not All Bad for Indie Labels as They Weather the Fading Fads." *Billboard*, 3 May 2003: 15.

27. Quoted by Waller, "Strength of Independents . . . ," p. 15. Cited in James E. Hearn, "The Representation of Major and Independent Record Labels. . . ," p. 115.

28. Cherie Hu, "The Record Labels of the Future . . . "

29. Erin M. Jacobson, "360 Deals and the California Talent Agencies Act." *The Entertainment and Sports Lawyer* 29:3 (Fall 2011): 9–15.

30. Swift left Big Machine when her contract expired in late 2018. Thirty days after she become a free agent, she signed with Republic Records, a division of Universal Music Group (UMG). Swift no doubt was attracted to UMG because she would maintain control of any master recordings she made with Republic, something she did not have with Big Machine: BM maintains control of the six albums she made with them. Melinda Newman, "Taylor Swift Leaves Big Machine, Signs Deal with Universal Music Group. *Billboard*, 19 November 2018. www.billboard.com/news.

31. Sherod Robertson, "BMG Acquires Nashville-Based BBR Music Group." See also Marc Schneider and Ed Christman, "BMG Acquires Nashville Indie BBR Music Group . . . "

32. Adams is now senior vice president of promotions. Her input regarding her job is discussed later in this chapter.

33. The Koinonia Coffeehouse opened across the street from Belmont Church in 1973.

Its critical role in promoting contemporary Christian music was recognized with a historical marker in 2019. Amy Grant and Michael W. Smith spoke at the commemorative ceremony. Dave Paulson, "Nashville Recognizes Christian Music with Historical Marker." *The Tennessean*, 27 July 2019: A2.

34. Word was founded in Waco, Texas, in 1951. It was purchased by the Nashville-based Christian book publisher Thomas Nelson in 1992 after which its headquarters relocated to Nashville.

35. Daywind has four studio packages. The package selected determines the number of songs recorded, CDs burned, and musicians provided (one soloist or a complete ensemble).

36. Spencer Ritchie, "Christian Music." *Music Business Journal*, June 2016. www.thembj.org/2016/06/christian-music.

37. The 2014 tour surpassed the attendance of Bruce Springsteen tour and Beyonce's. Spencer Richie, "Christian Music."

38. National sales figures are provided by the Gospel Music Association. Nate Rau, "Best-Selling Christian Artists in 2014." *The Tennessean* 27 June 2015: B2. See also Brandon Gaille, "Christian Music Industry Statistics and Trends," 25 May 2017. www.brandongalla.com/11-christian-music-industry-statistics-and-trends.

39. Nate, Rau, "Best-Selling Christian . . . "

40. Interview with Jackie Patillo.

41. Spencer Ritchie, "Christian Music."

42. A wonderful sixty-minute film gives the history of Jack Clement and the array of musicians that hung out at his place; it also nicely captures the home-studio flavor of his residence-office. See *Shakespeare Was a Big George Jones Fan: Cowboy Jack Clements's Home Movies* (2004). The video is available at a very modest streaming price on Amazon.

43. In 2016, Infinity Cat sold its office building in the rustic Wedgewood/Houston warehouse neighborhood. Orrall couldn't help but succumb to the price escalation, so took the money and moved his business across town.

44. Steve Haruch, "JEFF the [*sic*] Brotherhood, Infinity Cat Recordings and a Decade-Long Ride from the Indie Trenches to the Majors (and Back)." *Nashville Scene*, July 12, 2012: 37.

45. A concept album typically revolves around a central narrative theme.

46. Berry Hill is off the main 8th Avenue South corridor leading out of downtown Nashville. The area has long been zoned to attract small businesses: see Buzz Cason's documentary "Berry Hill: From Creative Workshop and Beyond" (2018), which is about Cason's legendary production studio, Creative Workshop, established in Berry Hill in 1970. More recently Berry Hill has seen both 3 Ring Circus and HoriPro (see Chapter 2) relocate to the area; Berry Hill also houses Blackbird, owned by Martina and John McBride. Also located on "Music Hill" in Berry Hill are Berry Hill Studio, Pentavarit's five-studio recording complex, and Beaird, voted the best recording studio in Nashville by *Music Row Magazine*. More recently (2018), Universal purchased the eight-building House of Blues complex on burgeoning Music Hill.

47. Take 6 was formed in 1980. They have ten Grammys across a range of categories and ten Dove Awards.

48. The first was with CeCe Winans for George Bush.

49. The song was co-written with Curtis Wright.

50. Ale Degado was a Belmont intern at Infinity Cat. After graduating she fournd a job elsewhere in the music industry, but returned to Infinity Cat within sixty days because she "just loved working here." She is their voice on Twitter and other social media platforms.

51. John Lomax III. *Nashville: Music City USA*. New York: Harry N. Abrams, 1985: 146.

52. Ibid.

53. Tully Potter, "Recording and Strings: Sounds of the Century." *The Strad*, May 2015: 33.

54. Ibid.

55. Information about the Bradleys and their studios is based on Michael Kosser's book, unless otherwise cited. Michael Kosser, *How Nashville Became Music City USA: 50 Years of Music Row*. Milwaukee, WI: Hal Leonard, 2006: 12–26.

56. The studio was sold to Columbia Records in 1962.

57. It still bled, says Ron "Snake" Reynolds, who worked in Studio B, "but we tried to limit the amount to some degree." Interview with Ron "Snake" Reynolds.

58. Michael Kosser, *How Nashville Became Music City USA*: 40. Subsequent quotes in this section are from this source unless otherwise specified.

59. Steven Parker and Robert Davis, "More than Microphoning: Capturing the Role of the Recording Engineer from the 1980s to the 1990s." *Popular Music History*, Vol. 81, No. 46 (2013): 46–67.

60. Volkmann's contribution was discussed in an interview with Sharon Corbitt-House, a former studio manager on Music Row and now the artist manager for Ben Folds.

61. Steven Parker and Robert Davis, "More than Microphoning . . . ," p. 49.

62. Ibid. See also Susan Schmidt Horning, "Engineering the Performance: Recording Engineers, Tacit Knowledge and the Art of Controlling Sound." *Social Studies of Science*, Vol. 34. No. 5 (2004): 703–731.

63. This was remarked on by any number of individuals interviewed in the course of this study, including some who have studio experience in Los Angeles or New York. See also endnote 71.

64. Interview with Sharon Corbitt-House.

65. Interview with Ron "Snake" Reynolds.

66. Amandine Pras, Caroline Vance, and Catherine Guastavino, "Record Producers' Best Practices For Artistic Direction—From Light Coaching to Deeper Collaboration with Musicians." *Journal of New Music Research*, Vo. 2, No. 4 (2013): 381–295.

67. Ibid., 385.

68. Ibid., p. 390.

69. Matthews was first tenor for the Jordanaires from 1953 to 2000. He died in 2003. See "The Official Website of the Legendary Jordanaires, at www.jordanaires.net.

70. Email communication with Brian Kilian, Professor of Music at Cumberland University in Lebanon, TN.

71. The studio system is key to Nashville's musical heritage. Bob Dylan, for example, came to Nashville in 1966 (after an unfruitful number of months in the New York studio) and in short order made his iconic *Blonde on Blonde* folk-rock album using some of Nashville's top session musicians. Daryl Sanders, *That Thin, Wild Mercury Sound: Dylan, Nashville and the Making of "Blonde on Blonde."* Chicago: Chicago Review Press, 2018.

72. Interview with Dave Pomeroy.

73. L. B. Rogers and Eric T. Parker, "2018 Top 10 Albums: All-Star Musician Awards." *Music Row Magazine*, June-July 2018:32ff. See also *Billboard*, Year-End Charts 2018. www.billboard.com/charts/year-end/2018.

74. Interview with Dave Pomeroy.

75. Interview with Tony Harrell.

76. Interview with Aubrey Schwartz.

77. Interview with Sharon Corbitt-House.

78. Gerhartz's career is discussed in Chapter 1.

79. Most large metropolitan areas typically have one or more independent record stores that specialize in vinyl records and often have an array of self-produced albums by local artists. There are three large independent record shops in Nashville: Grimey's New and Pre-Loved Music, The Groove, and Phonoluxe.

80. Interview with Cliff Williamson.

81. Adam Patrick Bell, "Trial-by-Fire: A Case Study of the Musician-Engineer Hybrid Role in the Home Studio." *Journal of Music, Technology & Education*, Vol. 7, No. 3 (2014): 295–312.

82. Blair Jackson, "Producer/Engineer/Musician Bryan Bell: Making a Laptop/Studio Hybrid Work." *Mix* (June 2014): 48–51, 80.

83. Ibid.

84. Sara Jones, "Master Class: Hearing is Believing." *Electronic Musician* (January 2015): 66–70. www.musician.com.

85. Ibid.

86. In September 2008, Napster was purchased by Best Buy and merged with Rhapsody. In 2016, Rhapsody was rechristened Napster.

87. See Tom McCourt and Patrick Burkart, "When Creators, Corporations and Consumers Collide: Napster and the Development of On-Line Music Distribution." *Media, Culture & Society*, Vol 25 (2003): 333–350.

88. Patrik Wikstrõm, "The Music Industry in an Age of Digital Distribution." Pp. 1–24 in Manuel Castells, David, Gelmter, Juan Vazquez, and Evgeny Morozov (eds.), *Change: 19 Key Essays on How the Internet is Changing Our Lives.* Madrid: Turner House Publications, 2014. www.bbvaopenmind.com/en/article/the-music-industry-in-an-age-of-digital-distribution.

89. Gary Sinclair and Todd Green, "Download or Stream? Steal or Buy? Developing a Typology of Today's Music Consumer." *Journal of Consumer Behavior*, Vol. 15 (2016): 13.

90. Ibid., p. 8.

91. Patrik Wikstrõm, "The Music Industry in an Age of Digital Distribution," p. 3.

92. Ibid.

93. Gary Sinclair and Todd Green, "Download or Stream? . . . ," p. 9.

94. Dan Rys, "Four Takeaways From the RIAA's 2018 Year-end Report." *Billboard Magazine*, 28 February 2019. www.billboard.com/business.

95. Jessica Nicholson, "The Playlist Professionals." *Music Row Magazine* (February/March) 2018:14. See also Dan Rys, "Four Takeaways . . . "

96. Interview with Emmanuel Zunz, a Nashville-based independent distributor.

97. Helienne Lindvall, "Behind the Music: The Real Reason Why the Major Labels Love Spotify." *The Guardian* 17 August 2009. www.theguardian.com/music/musicblog/2009/1ug/17/major-labels-spotify.

98. Interview by Jessica Nicholson, "The Playlist Professionals," p. 15.

99. Ibid, p. 15.

100. Ibid., p. 15.

101. B. Weijters, F. Goedertier, and S. Verstreken, "Online Music Consumption in Today's Technological Context: Putting the Influence of Ethics in Perspective." *Journal of Business Ethics*, Vol. 124 (2014): 537–550.

102. Gary Sinclair and Todd Green, "Download or Stream?"

103. Sinclair and Green's study is particularly illuminating because they break illegal

streaming into more finite categories then the one monolithic "pirating" that is typical in the literature. The only (minor) drawback to their study is that they make no estimates into how small/large each of the four categories may be.

104. B. Weijters, F. Goedertier, and S. Verstreken, "Online Music Consumption . . . "

105. Big and Rich released four albums with Warner between 2004 and 2012 before parting company. Their 2014 and 2017 albums debuted on their own label, Big and Rich Records. See Cindy Watts, "Big Risk, Big Success." *The Tennessean*, 19 January 2016: A1, 12.

106. Scotty McCreery was released by Universal Music Group despite having sold nearly 3 million albums and had two Top 10 singles to his credit before he was let go. An *American Idol* favorite, he had a strong fan base that kept him in the limelight until he eventually signed with Triple Tigers Records (Sony). Cindy Watts, "Betting His Career on [his song] 'Five More Minutes.'" *The Tennessean*, 20 March 2018: A1ff.

107. Interview with Steve Norris.

108. Zunz estimates that the monitoring process keeps 97 percent or more of the infringed material from being aired. Nevertheless, Zunz pointed out in our interview, 2 or 3 percent is still fraud.

109. Zunz started his distribution company in Brazil in 2010. ONErpm was an outgrowth of Verge Records, which was launched by Zunz in 2005 to provide music from impoverished neighborhoods to yield profit to invest back into the communities in need.

110. Phil Guerini with Radio Disney says this is why Radio Disney debuted the streaming station Radio Disney Country in 2016. Sarah Skates, "We're All Ears: Phil Guerini Talks Radio Disney Country." *Music Row*, Vol. 37, No. 1 (February/March 2017): 8–12.

111. Nate Rau, "UMG Exec: Country Radio Still Strong. " *The Tennessean*, 11 February 2016: A1

112. Nate Rau, "UMG Exec," A11.

113. See also Nate Rau, "Country Radio's Staying Power." *The Tennessean*, 20 February 2017: A11.

114. Interview with Lee Adams.

115. One can fill a stadium without radio, and while there are exceptions that do in country music, they are more likely to come from outside country. For example, alt-pop singer Halsey's [Ashlely Nicolette Frangipane] seven million digital fans helped her sell out Madison Square Gardens nine months in advance, less than three weeks after tickets went on sale in the fall of 2015. See Patrick Ryan, "Artists Turn Social Networking Into Album, Ticket Sales." *The Tennessean*, 27 August 2016: B1.

116. Nate Rau, "Streaming Research Sparks Music Row Buzz." *The Tennessean*, 22 October 2017: D1–2. See also Jim Wright, "In a Streaming World, One of the Industry's Most Traditionally Dominant Genres Struggles to Keep Up." *Billboard Magazine*, 2 September 2017. In 2018, streaming of country increased but the numbers don't line up with the headline since "country moved in the same direction as the total industry, but not as dramatically": 50.88 billion streams compared to overall music industry's 901 billiion. See Tom Roland, "Country Music Consumption Up in 2018 as Shift to Streaming Continues." Billboard Magazine, 15 January 2019. www.billboard.com/articles/columns/country/8493656/country-music-consumption-2018-nielsen-streaming.

117. A generation spans 20 years and is typically broken into two ten-year cohorts (e.g., 1946–1965); Markert argues that those at one end of a cohort (1946–1955) have different tastes than those at the other end of the cohort (1956–1965). Coincidentally, Markert uses musical tastes to differentiate the various groups. John Markert, "Demographics of Age: Gen-

erational and Cohort Confusion." *Journal of Current Issues and Research in Advertising,* Volume XXVI, No. 2 (Fall 2004): 11–26.

118. Nate Rau, "UMG Exec," A1, 11.

119. Patrick Ryan, "Artists Turn Social Networking Into Album, Ticket Sales." *The Tennessean,* 27 August 2016: B1.

120. Interview with Cliff Williamson, COO at Starstruck.

121. Jessica Nicholson, "Cold River Records to Close." *Music Row Magazine,* September 17, 2019. Nicholson reports the president, Pete O'Heeron, also owns a biologics company and decided to concentrate more on the medical business.

122. Interview with Kellie Longworth at Cold River. Longworth quickly found a parallel positon (Pormotions Manager) at Reviver Music when Cold River ceased operating.

123. Adams doesn't like to use the term "secondary" markets because, she says, all markets are important, even though *Music Row Magazine* (February/March 2017) ran a full issue devoted to secondary radio stations and their importance.

124. Interview with Lee Adams.

125. Alex Kobrick, "Country Radio in Retrospect." *Music Row Magazine* (February/March) 2018: 20–22.

126. It seems the practice of payola continues today, even if it doesn't get the exposure the payola "scandal" of the late-1950s did. See Douglas Wolk, "The Other Foot: The FCC Sweeps Eliot Spitzer's Payola Findings Under the Rug." *The Village Voice,* 22 August 2005; see also "Sing a Song of Spitzer: Sony BMG Admits to Paying Radio Stations to Play Its Artists." *The Economist,* 28 July 2005. www.Economist.com/node/4234148.

127. It is almost axiomatic that the larger the company becomes the more bureaucratic layers are necessary to see that the organization runs smoothly. Both the big-little and mid-sized labels have a bureaucracy; they differ only in the number of layers they have. The key distinction between them and the majors is that the majors are tied to a bureaucratic structure beyond their immediate confines (e.g., corporate "headquarters" is located elsewhere and thus any decisions have to be cleared by others outside the immediate knowledge nexus).

128. In 2017, Sony merged RED (Relativity Entertainment Distribution) with its other free-standing independent distributor, The Orchard. See "Sony Red's Distribution Operation Folded into the Orchard in Worldwide Consolidation." *MusicBusiness Worldwide,* 5 June 2017. www.musicbusinessworldwide.com/sony-reds-distribution-operation."

129. Alec Ellin, "The Future of Record Labels, Part 2: Who Needs a Label Anyway?" *Laylo - Medium,* 16 February 2016. www.medium.com/laylo/the-future-of-record-labels-part2–34216c582a9.

130. Sherod Robertson, "Pandora's CEO Tim Westergren." *Music Row Magazine* (February/March 2017), p. 18.

131. Alex Kobrick, "Country Radio in Retrospect," p. 20.

CHAPTER 4

1. I am referring here to "legitimate" artist management texts. There are those online texts that often come with (expensive) supplemental material (seminars) that are immodestly priced and offer a quick guide to getting rich by managing artists. Neophytes should be wary of material that 1) is offered primarily via online sales and not from a legitimate publisher, 2) seems reasonably priced but includes all kinds of supplemental material that add extensively to the initial cost, and 3) makes grandiose claims to managerial fame and fortune.

2. Interview with Greg Hill of Hill Entertainment.

3. "Time" was one of the four top twenty hits on their debut album, *Cracked Rear View* (1994).

4. Average Joes is discussed at some length in Chapter 3.

5. The artist roster on the Harmon Management website shows different artists at the time of the interview in 2016 versus 2018.

6. AC music is fairly all-inclusive pop, rock format. It is easier to categorize by those genres that it does not encompass: hip-hop, dance, teen, and hard rock. AC radio targets the 25–44 age groups.

7. Projects are not branding, which many management companies are involved with. Branding is when a company's name is featured prominently at concerts. Branding is dealt with later in the section on management.

8. The job was actually in Mt. Juliet, a then-small community just across the Davidson County line in Wilson County.

9. Mercury Records used all the musicians they showcased.

10. Songwriting credit is shared by Dylan and Secor. Just about all the producers in town passed on it when they were pitched the song.

11. Interview with Josh Terry at Workshop Management.

12. In all my communiqués with Nozell or a member of his staff, he was simply referred to as Danny. His website has a strong presence but one would be hard pressed to find his name. I found his surname on *Music Row Magazine*, a professional publication for those in the trade. Nozell reflects the tendency of artist managers to promote their artists, not themselves.

13. Their hesitancy about Parton's ability to sell-out stadiums is not without merit. By Nozell's own admission, prior to signing with CTK, Parton had never headlined as an arena act. Country acts, such as Dolly Parton, Loretta Lynn, Brenda Lee, and George Jones, despite their name recognition, historically played relatively small venues. It has only been in the last decade that country newcomers, such as Luke Bryan, headline arenas.

14. Corlew was born in Mt. Juliet, where he still lives; Dorris was born in White House, where he, too, still lives. Both Mt. Juliet and White House are just outside Nashville-Davidson county.

15. The author was one of those young men. He finished high school, however, but only because he couldn't join the military at 17 without his father's permission. So, he (begrudgingly) finished high school and the next day was on a train to Great Lakes, IL (Navy boot camp).

16. Daniels, say Corlew, "loves being on the road. He loves being in a different town every night. The intrigue of the road; somewhat of a gypsy life."

17. Cash's song, written and sung in 1974, deals with patriotic issues surrounding the Vietnam War. Fast-forward nearly a half-century: Daniels's version addresses patriotism in post-9/11 America.

18. Corlew created a documentary called "The Journey Home: A Soldier's Story" that airs occasionally on GAC and is the companion DVD to "Charlie Daniels Band: Live in Iraq." Beverly Keel, "Corlew Shares Soldiers' Stories." *The Tennessean*, 7 July 2015: A1, 8.

19. Daniels has strong appeal among conservative males between 45 and 65 years of age, who, Corlew says, are those still trying to figure out what it means to be an American in post-9/11 America.

20. Daniels was inducted into the Country Music Hall of Fame in 2016.

21. One of Corlew's many "sidelines" is producing documentaries. He is recounting what Scruggs told him in a documentary he did.

22. When Daniels made his foray into country music at the outset of the 1980s, the music industry in Nashville was moving away from classic country and into country-pop.

23. Butch Baker's career is discussed in Chapter 2.

24. The Whites are comprised of a father and his two daughters, one of whom, Sharon White, is married to Ricky Skaggs.

25. Dorris, being old-school, says he never requires "papers." He feels a handshake is quite sufficient, since both are only as good as the person behind it. His attorneys don't agree with him.

26. "Nickels and Dimes and Love" appeared on Montgomery's debut album *Life's a Dance* (Atlantic, 1992). It was certified a triple platinum recording by the RIAA.

27. Dorris mentions this only because it is public knowledge. The Kentucky officer who pulled Montgomery over was fired after posting a picture of himself on Facebook posing beside the car wearing Montgomery's hat.

28. Dorris lived in Nashville for most of his career, but returned to the family farm in White House a few years ago.

29. In 2017, Dorris forged an alliance with Mike Kraski to form New Vision Artist Management. He still runs Hallmark, however.

30. Health issues prompted Simmons to retire in 2016.

31. Yee yee is an excited exclamation by country folk—hunters and fishermen, in particular

32. Eric T. Praker, "The Fuel Behind Granger Smith's 7 Million-Strong Lifestyle Brand." *Music Row Magazine*, (February-March) 2019: 18–21.

33. Quotes in this section are largely unattributed because the subject is somewhat sensitive.

34. Label executives are likely to be more sensitive to the creative musings of their superstars since their bruised egos could substantively affect the bottom line. They are less likely to be overly concerned with day-to-day matters of others on their roster, mainly because they are legitimately pressed to deal with more weighty (corporate) matters.

35. Cindy Watts, "Betting His Career on '5 More Minutes.'" *The Tennessean*, 20 March 2018: A1, 14.

36. McCreery established a managerial relationship with Scott Stem not long after his break with Universal Music Group and the two worked to extricate him from a record deal that was tied to his win on *American Idol* and helped get him back the rights of some of the songs he wrote under UMG. Cindy Watts, "Betting His Career . . ."

37. Jessica Nicholson, "The Road to Recovery." *Music Row Magazine*, January 2019: 34.

38. Counselors are called porters at Porter's Call.

39. Jessica Nicholson, "The Road to Recovery," p. 35.

40. Corlew says that Daniels "never embraced alcohol, but he did [personally chew] tobacco and we did sponsorships with tobacco."

41. Interview with Danny Nozell at CTK Management.

42. Bill C. Malone, *Country Music, U.S.A.* Austin, TX: 1968: 212–14.

43. Ibid.

44. The larger talent agencies are multi-dimensional and represent a wide diversity of artists (actors, producers, writers) across a range of media (television, books, video games). This study is only interested in the aspect of the company that deals with musicians.

45. Interview with Keith Richards.

46. Interview with Josh Terry.

47. This number is based on those agencies listed in *Music Row Magazine*'s special edition, "Artist Roster: The 2017 Report." August/September, 2017: 36–40.

48. Garth Cartwright, *More Miles Than Money: Journeys Through American Music*. London: Serpent's Tail, 2009: 218–19.

49. The Bridgestone Arena hosts the Predators hockey team [17,000 seats]. Concert seating is slightly higher because floor space can be utilized. An end stage performance seats 18,500; a center stage performance (surround seating) can hold 20,000.

50. Interview with Steve Lassiter.

51. Ibid.

52. Daniels is not handled by UTA.

53. Ska is a Caribbean-inspired music genre that mingles calypso with American jazz and rhythm and blues. Some ska music embraces the harder edges of punk rock, which makes the two styles mix well.

54. Richards specified William Morris in our interview.

55. Tennessee has a sales tax but no income tax. The state is phasing out the Hall Tax on dividends (6%), which should make it even more attractive to stock-owning management-level personnel.

56. Si Kahn, *How People Get Power: Organizing Oppressed Communities for Action*. New York: McGraw-Hill, 1970.

57. The Philips Arena is now State Farm Arena. It is home to the Atlanta Hawks (basketball) and the Thrasher's (hockey). The arena can seats between 17,000 (hockey) and 19,000 (basketball) people.

58. The different types of Christian music are discussed in Chapter 3. In summary form, southern gospel is more traditional Christian music with four-part harmony; contemporary Christian is more like today's pop music with a Christian theme.

59. Ed Harper's brother Jeff has been involved with the company for twenty-some years. His other brother, Clay, was initially involved with the company but has since moved on to other ventures.

60. She admires Garth Brooks because he dresses with some style, connects with his audience, and puts on "one hell of a show."

61. Dan Machalski, "13 Things You Didn't Know About Las Vegas Showgirls" *Thrilllist*, July 1, 2015. www.thrilllist.com/entertainment/las-vegas/behind-the-scenes-with-las-vegas-showgirls.

62. Jessica Nicholson, *Inside the Spectacle." Music Row Magazine*, January 2018: 75

63. Ibid.

64. Chris Lisle is owner of Nashville-based Chris Lisle Lighting Design.

65. Jessica Nicholson, "Setting the Stage: Illuminating Superstars and Newcomers." *Music Row Magazine*, January 2017: 24–25.

66. Jessica Nicholson, "Carrie Underwood Shares the Storytelling Tour with Nashville." *Music Row Magazine*, September 2016.

67. Jessica Nicholson., "Setting the Stage. . . ," pp 24–25.

68. Sara Skates, "Tri Star's Touring Division: Guiding Artists Through Budgets and Creativity." *Music Row Magazine*, January 2017: 20–21.

69. Jessica Nicholson, "Setting the Stage: Illuminating Superstars and Newcomers." *Music Row Magazine*, January 2017: 24–25.

70. Jessica Nicholson, "Life Between the White Lines, Tour Management with Chris Littleton." *Music Row Magazine*, January 2018: 28–31.

71. Premier Global has been in business for 30-plus years but its focus was primarily on providing stage lighting. It has only recently expanded by adding rehearsal facilities.

72. Fort Knox Studios is based in Chicago where it has a 120,000-square-foot rehearsal and production facility. The Nashville launch facility has 70,000 square feet; the planned 80,000-square-foot second phase will cater to music, film, and video production. Nate Rau, "Donelson to Get Band Rehearsal Facility in '17." *The Tennessean*, December 16, 2016.

73. There is a 360-degree layout of all the studios on Soundcheck's website: www.soundchecknashville.com.

74. All 250 lockers are rented and there is an extensive waiting list for any that might become available.

75. Nozell's career is sketched more fully earlier in this chapter.

76. His wife, Katie, is co-owner and controller of Soundcheck. His three children, Kindal (marketing), Case (rental manger), and Britten (office manager) are all involved with Soundcheck.

77. Scott Scovill of Moo TV reminisces that in the early days (circa 1990) "video was new and everyone was hiring his or her brother who went to film school . . ." When he first broached the idea of starting Moo TV with Lee Griffin in 1993, his subsequent partner rejected the idea but then had a change of heart: Griffin told Scovill that "I think you are inventing an industry and there is a need for it." Jessica Nicholson, "A New Dimension: Moo TV Owner Scott Scovill's Rise to the Top." *Music Row Magazine*, January 2017: 2930.

78. Friedman found that, on the average, 60 percent of employers in the solar power industry could not find qualified technicians in fields that parallel that in staging, such as project foremen and electricians. Mullally and Frize found a similar percentage of employers in the medical field could not find qualified technicians. Barry Freidman, "PV Installation Labor Market Analysis and PV JEDI Tool Developments." Presentation, World Renewable Energy Forum, Denver, CO (16 May 2012). S. Mullaly and M. Frize, "Survey of Clinical Engineering Effectiveness in Developing World Hospitals: Equipment Resources, Procurement and Donations." *Engineering in Medicine and Biology Society* (2008): 4499–4502.

79. Tour manager Chris Littleton recalls that a massive tour in the 1980s would take one to three trucks, whereas today eighteen or twenty trucks are necessary. Jessica Nicholson, "Life Between the White Lines." *Music Row Magazine*, January 2018: 28.

80. Municipal Auditorium was the first public assembly facility in the Mid-South with air conditioning. Seating capacity is 9,700 "in the round." The acoustics are terrible.

81. A fall arrest system (harness) is a form of protection that OSHA requires for workers on construction sites who are exposed to vertical drops of 6 feet or more.

82. The major labels tend to have more people in development because they are looking for "fresh faces" and attempting to launch careers. Their deeper pockets allow them to spend more time developing artists they have signed who are yet unknown, but even then they typically want the artist to have a track record.

CONCLUSION

1. Numerous industry sources felt this is too high and that it is closer to 10 percent.

2. Tully Potter, "Recording and Strings: Sounds of the Century." *The Strad*, May 2015: 33.

3. Interview with Lee Adams, senior vice president of promotions at Broken Bow Records.

Index